THE MECO NETWORK

100

ATMOSPHERES
Studies in scale and wonder

Susan Ballard

Louise Boscacci

David Carlin

Anne Collett

Eva Hampel

Lucas Ihlein

Jo Law

Joshua Lobb

Jade Kennedy

Catherine McKinnon

Teodor Mitew

Jo Stirling

Kim Williams

First edition published by Open Humanities Press 2019
Copyright © the authors 2019

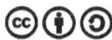

This is an open access book, licensed under Creative Commons By Attribution Share Alike license. Under this license, authors allow anyone to download, reuse, reprint, modify, distribute, and/or copy their work so long as the authors and source are cited and resulting derivative works are licensed under the same or similar license. No permission is required from the authors or the publisher. Statutory fair use and other rights are in no way affected by the above. Read more about the license at http://creativecommons.org/licenses/by-sa/4.0

Cover art, figures, and other media included with this book may be under different copyright restrictions. Please see the permissions associated with each image.

Cover image Agnieszka Golda, Martin Johnson and Jo Law, Spinning World, 2018, installation detail, mixed media, Musuem of Applied Arts and Sciences, Sydney, Australia.

Design and Illustration Jo Stirling.
Typeset in Adobe InDesign using Fira Sans and Tinos.

Print ISBN: 978-1-78542-063-4
PDF ISBN: 978-1-78542-064-1
ePub ISBN: 978-1-78542-065-8

To cite this book: Susan Ballard, Louise Boscacci, David Carlin, Anne Collett, Eva Hampel, Lucas Ihlein, Jo Law, Joshua Lobb, Jade Kennedy, Teodor Mitew, Catherine McKinnon, Jo Stirling, Kim Williams, [The MECO Network], *100 Atmospheres: Studies in Scale and Wonder*, London: Open Humanities Press, 2019.

OPEN HUMANITIES PRESS

Freely available online at www.openhumanitiespress.org

Open Humanities Press is an international, scholar-led, open access publishing collective whose mission is to make leading works of contemporary critical thought freely available worldwide. More at http://openhumanitiespress.org

For many non-scientists, the images and language of climate change and accompanying ecological events present as enigmatic signs. They elicit profound anxieties even as they conjure new ways of seeing the world. Environmental events are thus pushing up to the surface what are fundamentally literary problematics of writing and reading. OHP's Seed Books address the impact of today's new climate imaginaries. In fluid, permeable books funded by Sweden's The Seed Box: A Mistra-Formas Environmental Humanities Collaboratory, we are exploring how today's new visual and cognitive landscapes are engendering new collaborative textual practices in Humanities disciplines.

Read more at https://theseedbox.se/

Contents

10	Acknowledgement of Country
11	Acknowledgements
15	Who is MECO?
16	List of Figures
19	Breath
20	Pivot
21	Encounter
22	Riversdale
24	Place
25	Pressures
26	Search engine
27	A glimpse
28	Water across road
31	**From the plant to the planetary: a natural science** *Susan Ballard*
51	In the middle of things
53	Change management
54	Frame
55	Labour laboratory
56	Marketplace
57	Metaphor
58	Ghost gum
59	Juju
61	**Comparative hierophany at three object scale** *Teodor Mitew*

83	Cyclone
84	Scale
85	Resonances
86	Far and near
89	Otherworldly
90	Joyful fuss
91	Collaboration
92	Breathe it in
95	**Liminal atmospheres: ice and chalk** *Eva Hampel*
119	Infinite
120	Particles
121	Intensities
123	Rush
124	Frost
125	Preservation
127	Erosion
128	Extinction
129	Home
131	**Trinity** *Catherine McKinnon*
143	Oxygen
144	Paradigm
145	Missing
146	Voice
147	Listen
148	Pause

151	**Writing weather**
	Jo Law
171	Survival zone
172	Complications
174	Reindeer
176	Time
177	Rain magic
180	Lost and found
181	Swarm
182	Bees
184	Interruptions (for Jen)
185	Observatory
186	Subject to change
187	Soil
189	Cascade
191	Rhythm and song
193	**Ecologising affect and atmosphere in the Anthropocene: dear Rachel**
	Louise Boscacci
217	Call and response
219	Aurora borealis
221	Aurora australis
222	Sphere
223	Sky-watching
224	Fog
227	Inclusion and exclusion
226	Expanse
227	On the river

228	River stones
231	**A conversation** *Jade Kennedy*
243	Flux
244	Space junk
245	Speculative
246	Status
247	Plastic
248	(De)generation
249	Habitat
252	Voyager
251	Coming to terms
253	Hodgepodge
254	Indeterminacy
255	Humid
256	Electric
259	**A slow reading of Olive Senior's Hurricane Story** *Anne Collett*
279	Transcendence
280	Life and death
282	Virtual
283	Wind
284	Atomsphere
285	Spinning
289	**In the air: whipbird/human/koel** *Joshua Lobb*
299	Hemispheres
300	Wondering/wandering

301	Portals
302	Ghosts
303	Collective
304	Invisible
307	**Road trip** *David Carlin*
321	A gathering cloud
322	Repair
323	Care
324	Heterogeneous
325	Carbon base
327	**Two places: working and walking with waterways** *Kim Williams and Lucas Ihlein*
351	Compost
353	Blanket
354	Acknowledging Country …
355	Practice
356	The conference of the birds
358	All mixed up
360	Notes
391	References
415	Notes on contributors

Acknowledgement of Country

A curious stranger enters.

Acknowledgements are reservoirs, waterfalls, and rivers of gratitude and respect. They are the nourishing that feeds the making of a book by a kinship of people committed to a collective response to a call; a call and response that is multiple, plural, a dance of alterity as nimble and beautiful and unpredictable as a murmuration of budgerigars over waterholes at dawn.

There is a protocol to acknowledging this place, here. A perfect bend in the river; the warm sandstone of ancient escarpment; a hidden room in a sinking university building.

Here. A place emergent from the entanglement of country, cultures, the kinship of co-thinking and co-writing, and a hundred wondrous journeys. A fallen tree, a ghost gum, a mossy rock in the park, or even this very page can be boundaries of crossing between modes of being. Acknowledgement is reciprocal and presupposes a shared entanglement in maintaining all the ways in which this place, here, is unique.

To collectively Acknowledge the living space of the text, to collectively approach all of those who have come before and will return after the time of this book, we sit here today with new understandings of the invitational aspect to protocol. We are sitting with respect, responsibility and reciprocity.

We Acknowledge different skills and histories of belonging; and through the process of writing this book we Acknowledge the five fingers, rivers, braids, and atmospheres of Aboriginal Acknowledgement of Country—Country, Kinship, Culture, Journey and Connectedness.

We Acknowledge Country.

We come in, we invite you, the reader, into the intimacy of the entangled relationship that is this book. Here.

Acknowledgements

Anne would like to thank all those who generated the first ideas for this project and gathered such a wonderful group of people together. Thank you for so warmly including me at Riversdale and in all the subsequent gathering, eating, drinking, walking, talking, thinking. It is a joy to be part of this collective storying.

Catherine would like to thank all co-writers for sharing this strange and wondrous journey (what an experience!) and also everyone engaged in the researching, editing (Naomi) and producing (Sigi, David) of this vibrantly braided book. Thanks to Gary Christian for thoughtful walks through fictional and nonfictional forests. Thanks to Jade for years-ago talks, Su for clearing the path, Joshua, Kim and David C, for apt editorial suggestions. Also, thank you to the 2017 AAWP conference panel 'Stories from Strangeland' and audience members, especially Robin Hemley, for concise comments on Trinity.

David would like to thank Linda Mickleborough, Alice Nelson and colleagues at non/fictionLab at RMIT University for readerly and writerly counsel. Also, Nicole Walker for being an excellent fellow traveller and host.

Eva would like to thank Ruby and Finn for their love and support, and Joshua, Cath, Su, and all co-writers (I should mention all individually, but it would be a long list) for the pleasure of collaboration and cross-fertilisation. Jade too – though we have not met! Also Brogan and Mike, who were very present early on… and the Far North, for its inspiration and other-worldliness, and all that twilight.

Jade would like to thank the other authors for their willingness to sit with Country.

Jo Law thanks all those who have spent time chatting and everyone who has contributed to #illalmanac.

Jo Stirling thanks all of the writers for bringing these words together in one place. Thank you for making this book so exciting and challenging to design. Thank you Lily, Jacob and Brad.

Joshua would like to thank Madeleine and Louise, for encouraging him to really listen to birds, Melissa Boyde for pushing his bird-writing, and Cath for crucial editorial suggestions. The story was written during his LitLink residency at Varuna, The Writer's House. A version of the story appears in the novel *The Flight of Birds* (Sydney University Press, 2019).

Kim gives thanks to Lulu Williams and Mailin Suchting. Kim and Lucas thank their collaborators Brogan Bunt, Simon Mattsson, John Sweet, and Starrett Vea Vea.

Louise thanks Gaye, Steven and Polak for their generous support and open hearts in the ongoing moment. Writing needs listeners as well as readers along the way. At Bundanon, Ralph Dixon shared happy yarns on night birds, trees and gliders that made research camps even more energising. Thanks go to Jo Holder (The Cross Art Projects, Sydney) for the chance to meet and talk with Nancy McDinny in 2018. Special thanks to Jade for the teaching of a new word and old way: *Yulungah* ("Welcome"). A final big thank you to all co-writers in this book adventure. A sonic version of "The Synsensorium of Twilight" was presented as "The Generative Synsensorium of Twilight" at *the Annual Conference of the Australasian Association for Literature*, held at Griffith University, Australia, in July 2017. A version of "Greetings from Zincland" was exhibited in *Postcards from the Anthropocene: Unsettling the Geopolitics of Representation* at the University of Edinburgh, Scotland, in June 2017.

Su thanks her lecturers in SCIE103 Helen McGregor (Earth and Environmental Science) and Stephen Wilson (Chemistry) for their patience and generosity; all the multiple and more-than authors for keeping the stories flowing; Sigi and David for their openness; Moss and Charlotte for being there; and Keith, Pat and Nathan for getting us there.

Teodor would like to thank the writers involved in this project for the wonderful moments of shared creation, constructing the baroque atmospheres to be found across these pages. Also, Joyce and Baian for their patience, and Baba Penka for teaching him without teaching.

The Material Ecologies Research Network (MECO) thanks the Faculty of Law, Humanities and the Arts at the University of Wollongong, Australia, for providing research network funding for CAST (Contemporary Arts and Social Transformation) in 2014, then MECO from 2015-2017. This critical support enabled three dedicated research camps on the Shoalhaven River at the Riversdale Education Centre, Bundanon. The Faculty also supported this research through a publication grant in 2017-2018, and provided support for the final stages of the book under the aegis of the C3P Centre for Critical Creative Practice. Our collective thanks go to: Sharon Athanasios, The Big Fag Press, Bundanon Trust, Leonie Clement, Teresa Crosland, Lorraine Denny, Ralph Dixon, Jo Durtnell-Smydzuk, Deborah Ely, Amanda Harris, Jennifer Macey, Vera Mackie, Sarah Miller, Tara Palajda, Greg Seigworth, Sue Turnbull, Mary Preece, and Joanna Zylinska.

We would like to thank Wodi Wodi elder Aunty Barbara Nicholson who, while not directly connected to this book, has over the years has advised and guided many of us.

The book would not have been completed without Sigi Jöttkandt, David Ottina, Naomi Parry and Jo Stirling.

Who is MECO?

The Material Ecologies Research Network (MECO) emerged in 2014 as a collective of scholars from the University of Wollongong working at the intersection of cultural practices and the environmental humanities. MECO uses collaborative research strategies to explore the knowledges generated by practice-led material encounters. As a research community focused on creative practice in the Anthropocene, MECO is a space of care and concern, a site for being together within the institutional structures of a University, as well as a habitat for contesting praxis, and a vehicle for research generation. MECO continues in small interventions, habitations, and moments of commensality that now extend beyond the institution.

A project like this could not have been started without the conversations that took place at the MECO research camps between 2014-2017. Participants at the camps included: Susan Ballard, Louise Boscacci, Brogan Bunt, Anne Collett, Nicky Evans, Laura Fisher, Leah Gibbs, Agnieszka Golda, Mike Griffiths, Eva Hampel, Penny Harris, Bianca Hester, Lucas Ihlein, Sigi Jöttkandt, Joshua Lobb, Douglas Kahn, Madeleine Kelly, Jo Law, Catherine McKinnon, Chris Moore, Teodor Mitew, Pip Newling, David Ottina, Jo Stirling, Mat Wall-Smith, Kim Williams.

List of Figures

Figure 1.   Susan Ballard, *The Goethe Palm*, 29 September 2015.

Figure 2.   Teodor Mitew, *Objects are never fully available (a), part of them always resists (r)*, 2018.

Figure 3.   Teodor Mitew, *Objects are never fully resistant (r), part of them is always available (a)*, 2018.

Figure 4.   Teodor Mitew, *Part of an object's agency always resists, and therefore transgresses, the frame in which it is made available*, 2018.

Figure 5.   The Amazon Echo, a speaker talking with the voice of Alexa, 2014. Photo by Frmorrison, [Public Domain], via Wikimedia Commons.

Figure 6.   The Black Madonna of Częstochowa, 2010. Photo by Wuhazet, Jasna Góra Monastery, [Public domain], via Wikimedia Commons.

Figure 7.   Earth's Lagrangian points with the Sun. 2010 TK7 is in L4, 60° ahead of the Earth in the direction of its' orbit around the Sun, 2006. Photo by NASA, [Public domain], via Wikimedia Commons.

Figure 8.   2010 TK7's spiralling path (green) relative to Earth and its orbit, 2010. Photo by NASA/JPL-Caltech/UCLA (NASA full image) [Public domain], via Wikimedia Commons.

Figure 9.   Olafur Eliasson and Minik Rosing, *Ice Watch*, 2014, 12 blocks of glacial ice. Installation view Place du Panthéon, Paris, 2015. Photo by Martin Argyroglo, reproduced with permission of the artist; neugerriemschneider, Berlin; Tanya Bonakdar Gallery, New York. © 2014 Olafur Eliasson.

Figure 10. Tacita Dean, *When I first Raised the Tempest, No. 17599*, 2016, chalk on blackboard, exhibited at TMAG Tasmania, August 2016. Image by Eva Hampel.

Figure 11. Detail of Olafur Eliasson and Minik Rosing, *Ice Watch*, 2014, 12 blocks of glacial ice. Installation view Place du Panthéon, Paris, 2015. Photo by Martin Argyroglo, reproduced with permission of the artist; neugerriemschneider, Berlin; Tanya Bonakdar Gallery, New York. © 2014 Olafur Eliasson.

Figure 12. Detail of Olafur Eliasson and Minik Rosing, *Ice Watch*, 2014, 12 blocks of glacial ice. Installation view Place du Panthéon, Paris, 2015. Photo by Martin Argyroglo, reproduced with permission of the artist; neugerriemschneider, Berlin; Tanya Bonakdar Gallery, New York. © 2014 Olafur Eliasson.

Figure 13. Detail of Tacita Dean, *When I first Raised the Tempest, No. 17599*, 2016, chalk on blackboard, exhibited at TMAG, August 2016. Image by Eva Hampel.

Figure 14. Louise Boscacci, *Tawny Twilight Calling*, 2017. Annotated sonogram of 2:30 minutes sound passage, 13 October 2013, Illawarra highlands (Wingecarribee). Postcard (recto), 10 x 15 cm. Digital print.

Figure 15. Tawny Frogmouth, *Podargus strigoides*. Photograph courtesy of Mollie King, Kent Owl Academy.

Figure 16. Louise Boscacci, *Greetings from Zincland*, 2016. Postcard (recto), 15 x 10 cm. Digital print from an aerial photograph taken in November 2013.

Figure 17. Louise Boscacci, *Black Cirrus*, 2017. Postcard (recto), 15 x 10 cm. Digital print.

Figure 18. Three postcards to Rachel Carson, 2016–2018. Photograph by Louise Boscacci.

Figure 19. Kim Williams, *Map of Australia, showing geographic relationships between Mackay and Wollongong*, 2017.

Figure 20. Kim Williams, *Map of Pioneer River, Mackay*, 2017.

Figure 21. Kim Williams, *Map of Towradgi Creek, Wollongong*, 2017.

Figure 22. Kim Williams, *Coral Relics, Crayfish Beach, Great Barrier Reef*, drawing, 2016.

Figure 23. Lucas Ihlein, *Indicative cross-section of Illawarra Escarpment (not to scale)*, drawing, 2018.

Figure 24. Vincent Bicego, *Walking (and climbing) in the upper reaches of Byarong Creek*, photograph, 2017.

Figure 25. Lucas Ihlein, Kim Williams and Brogan Bunt, artists' talk at Wollongong Art Gallery for *Walking Upstream: Waterways of the Illawarra* exhibition, December 2017. Photograph by WayWard Films.

Figure 26. Kim Williams and Lucas Ihlein, *Plan of proposed planting zones, Watershed Land Art Project, Mackay Regional Botanic Gardens*, 2017–19.

Figure 27. Lucas Ihlein, *Diagram of methods and materials in Socially Engaged Art with a particular focus on* Sugar vs the Reef? *and* Walking Upstream: Waterways of the Illawarra, 2017.

Figure 28. Lucas Ihlein, *Socially Engaged Art in a Venn diagram*, 2014.

Figure 29. Artists-activists-academics-farmers meeting with conservative George Christensen MP, Member for Dawson, to propose a large-scale demonstration farm for the sugarcane industry, March 2017.

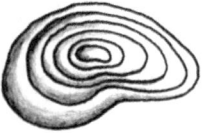

Breath

We hold our breath, and wait.

Are we in the atmosphere; is the atmosphere within us? Human lungs—like those of the whipbird, the cat and the wombat and the striped lizards of Los Alamos plateau—fill with planetary atmosphere on each autonomic inhalation. I wonder at the alveolar infoldings of atmosphere that are hidden inside the respiratory tree of humanimal chest cavities. Can we whistle this alveolar gas? Take a breath. Hold it. How many minutes pass before the next air exchange must be accepted?

The modern Latin *atmosphaera* originates from the Greek *atmos*, meaning vapor or steam, and *sphaira*, meaning sphere. The root *atm-*, however, reaches back much further than Ancient Greece, and is to be found in Proto-Indo-European [PIE] and Sanskrit, as in the word *Ātman*, meaning essence, breath or soul. The PIE root *atm-*, reaching the depth of time, stands for the act of drawing a breath. To be in an atmosphere, then, is to breathe, fully belonging and embodied.

Pivot

This project is an invitation to think differently. In these 100 Atmospheres, thirteen writers and artists trace some material becomings of this planet. We think of these Atmospheres as notes towards a material ecology that might be as transformative as those of the previous 500 years. We have been told, "you cannot do this." "You can't write this book together, there are too many people involved." And later we are asked: "How will you do it?"

Sometimes we essay with a plural voice. Other times a soloist (usually anonymous) steps forward in the telling. Or, if you like, we constantly fracture and reassemble as we move between and across these atmospheres.

From paradigms of thought, spells, beliefs, thresholds, action and affects, through mist and wind …

Encounter

> 'Turning toward' *(Tikkun)* in Fackenheim's philosophy, is an ethics of motion toward encounter, a willingness to situate one's self so as to be available to the call of others. It is a willingness toward dialogue, a willingness toward responsibility, a choice for encounter and response, a turning toward rather than a turning away.
> *Deborah Bird Rose (2011)*

I wonder why Deborah Bird Rose invokes Jewish philosopher Emil Fackenheim. I wonder how she wants us to think about lived histories and what it means to make a human/e response. Rose says we cannot 'mend' the world, but that we can turn towards one another.[1] If I turn away, does this mean we have both lost interest? The ethics she evokes are affective, sensory, knowing and material ways of being together. Affect is material, because it is always situated and experienced *in* or *with*.

Places, too, have an affective resonance, a sensual atmosphere that permeates them and those who linger or dwell within. Sometimes emerging from the immediacy of an encounter, sometimes residual, lingering long after an event. Where does this affective atmosphere come from? It is not held in the material surroundings, nor generated solely by human interlocutors, projecting sensuality on a dull and voiceless envelope. Is it performative; a *concrescence*? Concrescence: borrowed from Alfred North Whitehead—another time, another philosopher—"For us the red glow of the sunset should be as much part of nature as are the molecules and electric waves by which men of science would explain the phenomenon."[2] The greatest fear is that we—whoever we are (I know that we are not 'men of science')—stop sharing affects with the more-than-human others around us; that affect becomes singularly owned by me, this body, these humans. We place small clouds under our words to soften the blow as the feelings drop into place. Atmospheres are affects: material, residual and delayed.

Riversdale

On a Wednesday morning 12 humans woke in Glenn Murcutt's pods at Riversdale, New South Wales, to find the Shoalhaven River valley shrouded in a dense expansive layer of fog. The curious ones met the wombats at the river foreshore and were enveloped in the sweet smell of a cold moist mist. It was July in the Southern Hemisphere, but, being just 34°52' south, it was not freezing. The sun emerged from the ground-level cloud and dispersed the whiteness, revealing the glassy water of the river. We sat in Murcutt's hall with Arthur Boyd's painting *Hanging Rock and Bathers* (1985) looking on, and discussed what this was, this atmosphere.

We wrote lists. "Atmosphere as a framework." "As affective exchange," said Louise. "Call and response!" cried Joshua. "Above the clouds, and below," said Kim, and we talked about the walk to the top of the nearby hill we'd taken the day before. "Within and without"; "materiality and immateriality"; "atmospheric pressures". "Atmosphere as juju", Agnieszka called across the table. "As *what?*" There were no boundaries. We passed around cups of tea. The river glinted at us through the wide open doorway.

Not all of the 12 present wanted to participate. And not all who were to become part of this story were there. It was decided we could name those present if they remained. We talked and worked and wrote alongside one another. We'd been talking for days. About climate change and political systems and animal, plant and object agencies; of the material and the immaterial, of the everyday and the sacred. We talked about how scared we were. We talked about weather patterns and styrofoam cups. We talked about air contamination and the rapid loss of the planet's biodiversity. We talked about rational modernity. Jo recounted a media report about extending mines under drinking water catchments. Ted talked about APEC-blue skies in Beijing. Eva recalled a photo of calving ice shelves and emaciated polar bears. Bushfires and algae and bleached reefs. There was an urgency to the discussion: it was as if a new stage show was illuminated before us; grotesque bodies glinting back at us. The shorthand phrase we used to describe this world was "the Anthropocene."

We continued with our list and the conversations continued beyond Riversdale into meeting rooms on campus, onto trains, and over more cups of tea. "Atmosphere as wonder," Anne offered. "How big is an atmosphere?" asked Su. How might we engage with the idea of 'atmosphere' across a range of scales? Might it even challenge the restrictive systems we'd been talking about? It soon became clear that we were having a different kind of conversation. Our atmospheres couldn't help being entangled and enmeshed with the Anthropocene, but they also reimagined our relationship with the planet. Our list became a response, an activity, a practice. Cath asked: "how do we think in the Anthropocene?" Mike responded: "Do you mean, how do we write?" David reminded us that an essay is like a river: it is contingent on things it encounters along the way.[3] What does this thing we call 'creative practice' *do*? How does practice *act*?

Practice discovers things it wasn't looking for.

Place

Country ... well ... the way I would describe it is ... is ... it's the place ... it's the people ... it's the culture ... it's the journey ... and it's the inter-relationship between these things. Five fingers on one hand ...

... So when I talk about Country as a place it's absolutely the trees, and the birds and the reptiles ... it's the sealife, it's the stone ... it's the fresh water, the bitter water, the salt water ... it's the greens, the browns, the blues ... all the types of blues, you know ... it's the smells ... it's all of those things that are representative of this place. It's not the reds and the browns that you find out there in the west ... it's not them. It's here ... it's a flock of white cockatoos ... or a pair of black ones when they bring the rain ... it's these sorts of things that we know ... you see ... we've got Warra Bingi Nunda Gurri ... we've got the red-bellied black snake, that's our dreaming. Right ... that's your escarpment ... that's your dreaming. See ... this is the place we're living in ...

Pressures

Dynamics come from difference. Wind is moving air generated by pressure differentials in the troposphere. Meteorologists plot these differentials as lines on weather maps, as geographers draw contour lines on topographic maps. High pressure in the atmosphere usually brings sunshine; low pressure may bring rain. A diorama of weather, like a snowglobe bubble.

Everything in these systems is held together by gravity. Is this true? Forces both hold and tear apart.

Gayatri Chakravorty Spivak offers "planet-thinking" and "planet-feeling" as a counter to the ways that humans have divided our understandings of the world into self and other, subject and object, human and nonhuman. Our focus has been on human frames, human ways of carving up the planet. Instead of breaking it up, we need to help put it back together. We need to stop claiming all the agency: to listen, notice and respond to how the nonhumans act. To invoke 'planetarity', as Spivak says we must, is to activate decolonising, feminist and politically radical strategies that turn to existing ways of thinking about 'nature' and 'the earth', and question their very foundations. A potential way of thinking that reminds us that "we live on, specifically, a planet."[4]

Search engine

Does climate change—
    Does climate change affect hurricanes?
    Does climate change affect weather?
    Does climate change affect natural disasters?
    Does climate change affect earthquakes?
    Does climate change affect animals?
    Does climate change affect bees?
    Does climate change affect volcanos?
    Does climate change affect tectonic plates?
    Does climate change affect wind?
    Does climate change affect human health?
    Does climate change affect gravity?

Is c—
    Is climate change real?
    Is climate change a hoax?
    Is climate change a myth?
    Is coffee bad for you?
    Is California a desert climate?
    Is climate change reversible?

[Results subject to change.]

A glimpse

I grew up on the beaches of the south coast—Merry Beach, Pretty Beach, Pebbly Beach, Murramarang, Bawley Point ... It was an idyllic if isolated childhood that involved long car trips from Canberra to the south coast and up the coast north to Sydney where my grandparents lived. The Illawarra coastal plain is hidden beneath the sandstone cliffs, the old highway from Bawley Point to Sydney wending its way far above. On those many trips up and down the coast I had never seen the beaches of the Illawarra. My first glimpse was 30 years later. Traveling down the new motorway from Sydney to Wollongong through banksia and tea-tree heathland into the dense green of the escarpment, a break in the vegetation on the eastern side offers a brief glimpse of sea and city below. It is a moment of revelation that I wait for with heightened anticipation every time I travel this road. I breathe—deeply.

The road that we're talking about ... you know ... the south coast road ... I could not tell you honestly how many times I've driven that. When my grandmother was sick I was driving it backwards and forwards in a day at times ... I'd go down three hours and drive back three hours ... I've driven Eden in a day, now that's at least five-and-half hours. I've driven this road that many times that I know it intimately ... as I do the stories within my family that live along this road ... you know ... from where we've stopped ... and things that we've done ... and there's an intimate relationship with that road ... see my culture lives here. My family lives here ... my belongingness lives here ... I think one of the best ways it can be described is when people who've lived in Wollongong for some time drive down Mount Ousley and they go: "Ahhh ... I'm home."

Water across road

Portal. To port. Portable.

In coding, portable software is particularly valued because of the ease with which it can be adapted to another environment. Here, porting is a process of shifting functionality from one system or environment to another. The process of transferring software across operational environments requires a translation of agencies both at the level of functionality within the code *and* in the new environment. An exchange; a back and forth between what agency is to be preserved in the port, and its new setting.

A *portal*: the entry to a passage, perhaps sinister, perhaps revelatory, certainly uncertain. Entry to a passage with a destination unknown and as yet invisible: a liminal space, a *space between*, between the known behind and the uncertainty ahead. But a space potentially transformative – in that uncertainty lies the potential of the unfettered, the not yet 'doored', the creative space of the ambiguous frame across the threshold of which thinking, feeling and imagining flow back and forth. Think of fog. Think of medieval churches: communal portals between sacred and profane. Think of the rainbow bridge Bifröst guarded by Heimdallr, connecting Earth to Asgard, the realm of the gods. Think of Hermes, god of the crossroads, travellers, and dealers of the unknown and liminal. Think of Legba, the Dahomean/Haitian god of the gateway between human and divine worlds, loa of the crossroads.

The invocation to Papa Legba in the Vodoun ceremony is a call to the spirit world to open the gate—

> Attibon Legba
> Attibon Legba
> Ouvri bayi pou' moi
> Ouvri bayi pou' moi

—for Barbadian poet, Kamau Brathwaite, this is a call to open communication: a poet's request for "words to refashion futures/like a healer's hand":[5] *portals* …

Can this book, formed through conversation, call and response, be a portal?

From the plant to the planetary: a natural science

Susan Ballard

> Imagine you are falling. But there is no ground.
> Hito Steyerl (2011)

MOST days the prospect of the Anthropocene is quietly terrifying and it seems that operating at multiple scales is the best way forward. Other days it is as if a cyclone has taken out the only road in and out of here, and we must patiently queue at the bottom of the hill for an escort home. (Bring food and water for we don't know how long the wait will be. Please don't take your frustrations out on the crews working on site.) Today though, there is a different order to things. I find myself pushing at the borders of what I know.

This essay is a call written at the scale of the natural history of a tree. Art and writing have always teased and tested the borders of the known. They have presented alternatives: alternative stories of being, of presence, of history, and of the way we might know the world. As the anthropologist Anna Tsing says "How else can we account for the fact that anything is alive in the mess we have made."[6] I know that the crisis of the Anthropocene has already happened: life-sustaining atmospheric and energy systems have transformed, and we are scrambling around trying to understand how these new planetary and atmospheric ecologies can be reformed into something that might continue to include us, humans, and the other species for which we have a particular fondness. Some of us understand the numbers and draw graphs for the rest of us to peer at in horror. Others of us turn to small gestures; modes of knowing and being infused with care and local transformation. I find my writing turning its attention beyond art to the networks of communication and research that surround the human-created material artefact in time and space. I think about how humans interact with the world, how artworks might catalyse new ethical relations with nonhuman entities, and how we are all working amidst transforming subjectivities so that we might include relationships with nonhuman others: animal, mineral and vegetable. I flick through pages and words leap out: money, power, extinction, wretched, objects, death, nature, dreaming, matter, thinking, the end of the world.

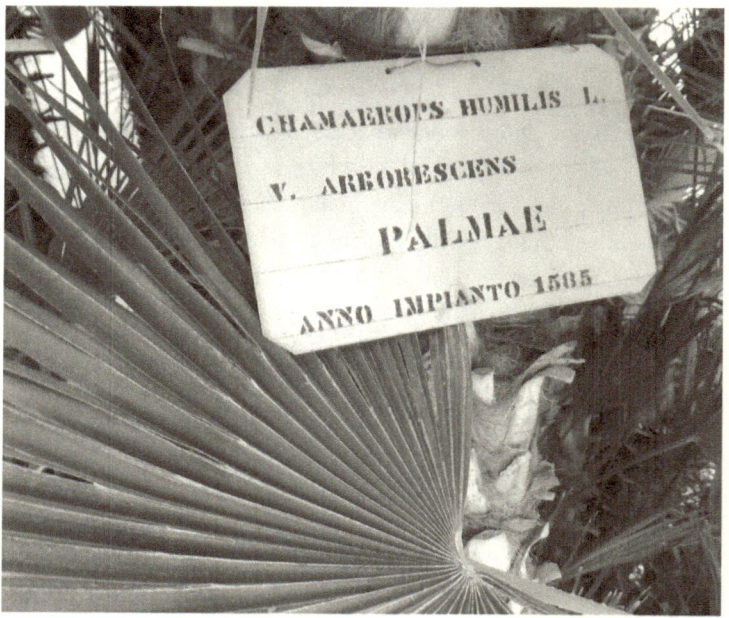

Figure 1: Susan Ballard, *The Goethe Palm*, 29 September 2015

Three years ago, amidst these thoughts, I found myself in front of a palm tree (Figure 1). The story began three years ago but in *this* version time is not so easily fixed. I had travelled to the Orto Botanico in Padua as a day 'off' from an intensive tour of Italian art. With one day before our train to the Venice Biennale I needed to give my children a break from our daily pilgrimages. We entered the Orto Botanico with the promise that instead of art, we would see the world's newest glasshouses and stand inside living dioramas of climatic zones from all over the planet. It all seemed good: our breath in the glasshouses was alternately steamy and dry; our bodies were sweating and then chilled. Disorientated and parched after spending too long in the 'desert' zone, we had lingered under the dew dripping off tropical palms before entering a final sequence of rooms (resembling the very art galleries we had sought to avoid). Here, we were confronted with interactive models of impending ecological disaster: there were buttons to push and goggles that removed any connection with the world we currently occupied. On a screen we could send in the sea to engulf homes, or raise tornados that grew to huge black cones of doom obliterating everything in their path. The shiny new glasshouses with their waterfalls and exotic plants faded amidst booming narratives of global destruction. The children demanded we leave.

For most children, the story of planetary collapse is not yet theirs to own. They take responsibility on a daily level; they compost, they recite mantras of reduce, recycle, reuse. They control their worlds. The Anthropocene is something their parents and grandparents need to take responsibility for. They are angry at our inaction, and already hold within their bodies the knowledge that they will have to pick up our pieces. They don't need educational videos, they can see and feel for themselves.

So we stepped outside, and for a while ran around the maze of the original gardens, stopping at a plant that seemed more solemn than the others. We found ourselves in front of the world's most ancient living plant to be have been planted in a botanical garden. Now named after German naturalist, artist and philosopher Johann Wolfgang Goethe, this Mediterranean fan palm (*Chamaerops humilis* var. Arborescens)—the 'Goethe Palm'—had been planted in this spot in 1585.

On 27 September 1786, some 200 years after it was planted and 230 years before my arrival, Goethe visited this palm. Already well known as a poet, artist and naturalist, Goethe's Grand Tour through Italy had opened up a world of flora and fauna that led to a lifelong "obsession with palms and a serious engagement with the quest for the seeds of eternal growth."[7] He was 37 years old and feeling that he had met his life ambitions. In his diary of the day he writes:

> The botanic garden is much more pretty and cheerful. Several plants can remain in the ground during the winter, if they are set near the walls or at no great distance from them. At the end of October the whole is built over, and the process of heating is carried on for the few remaining months. It is pleasant and instructive to walk through a vegetation that is strange to us. With ordinary plants, as well as with other objects that have been long familiar to us, we at last do not think at all; and what is looking without thinking? Amidst this variety which comes upon me quite new, the idea that all forms of plants may, perhaps, be developed from a single form, becomes more lively than ever. On this principle alone it would be possible to define orders and classes, which, it seems to me, has hitherto been done in a very arbitrary manner. At this point I stand fast in my botanical philosophy, and I do not see how I am to extricate myself. The depth and breadth of this business seem to me quite equal.[8]

Goethe collected a sample of the palm and carried it with him for the remainder of his life. This palm became the centre of his research into art and science and inspired him to write the short book *Attempt to Explain the Metamorphosis of Plants* (1790). Within the forms of the palm Goethe found a concern with life that did not rest in fixed patterns. Instead here was evidence of an 'inner unity' to nature, "a unity that cannot be captured through the methods of the natural sciences alone."[9] For Goethe, the presentation of nature was both a scientific and aesthetic task, his focus was on relations—both science and art required knowledge of the laws that govern living organisms. Goethe's analysis was an attempt to revisit the structural classifications of plants and animals that had been fixed by the Swedish botanist Carl Linnaeus fifty years earlier, and to replace these with a new more poetic approach to morphology. Goethe's colleague and admirer Alexander von Humboldt wrote that "the great creations of Goethe's poetic fantasy had not kept him from immersing a researcher's gaze into all of the depths of the life of nature."[10] Goethe hoped that this palm, named as 'his' palm, held the secret to the ur-form of all plants: an *Urpflanze*, an organic knowledge which would bring together his studies in science and the arts, and answer something about how humans understand their relationship with the world. He observed how "development spreads inexorably from node to node through the leaf ... the simple fanlike leaf is torn apart, divided, and a highly complex leaf is developed that rivals a branch."[11]

When Goethe wrote about it, this palm was already 200 years old. And here I was in 2015 sharing the new air of the Anthropocene with my children and an ancient organic form; one that had been planted not long after humans began arriving in my home, Aotearoa New Zealand, the Antipodean land of the long white cloud. There, plants had been breathing without humans for many thousands of years.

I started to wonder if, in order to understand the atmospheric transformations of climate change in the Anthropocene, it might be possible to mimic the way that Goethe bought together art, poetry and science through the process he named connected micro-variations. I was concerned with how as a writer I could tell an unnatural history of the Anthropocene. Call and response, difference and repetition, and microvariation all seemed to point to a new way to trace the timeline of a species encounter with the atmosphere of the Anthropocene. There must be a better approach than the pseudo-affective representation in the gallery we had just escaped. Here, my unnatural art history of the Goethe Palm begins.

~

In 1545 the Padua Orto Botanico was founded as the world's first ever university botanical garden. It was born from an urgent need for consistency in plant identification. Padua was already a site of medicine and learning, but an increase in therapeutic and medical uses of plants had meant that medical practitioners were making deadly mistakes.[12] UNESCO listed the Padua Orto Botanico as a World Heritage site in 1997:

It is the origin of all the botanical gardens in the world, a cradle of science and scientific exchange, serving as the basis for the understanding of the relationship between nature and culture. It largely contributed to the progress of a number of modern scientific fields, the likes of which include, of course, botanicals, as well as medicine, chemistry, ecology and pharmaceuticals.[13]

The garden allowed the University to permanently set the boundaries of knowledge, and a trip to the garden enabled anyone to make correct classifications. It is a gathering place for plants from all over the known world. Just beside the glasshouses for carnivorous plants, the Goethe Palm fills its purpose-built open-air glasshouse. Over the past 450 years the glasshouse has been variously enlarged, enclosed, opened to the air, left derelict, and re-glazed. In 2016 the glasshouse was completely renovated with new mechanical opening louvers. Until then, the palm had shared the city air with humans and other plants. All of this I learn later.

I had given Goethe's palm a silent farewell as we headed for Venice: a floating city anchored in a tidal estuary and of necessity more actively engaged with climactic transformations than other European cities. I returned to art galleries, and found myself immersed in the wonders of the Venice Biennale, where trees had the power of motion, super yachts mimicked beached whales, and stacks of pressed flowers balanced on top of grim looking concrete pillars. Yet the Goethe Palm and its stories would not leave me alone. I found its bifurcations hiding in surprising places. Following a slow maze of white rooms and black boxes in the midst of the Arsenale, I stumbled upon American artist Taryn Simon's *Paperwork and the Will of Capital* (2015). Here, plants of all kinds witnessed human action and political ceremonies.[14] Simon's stacks and their associated photographs sat somewhere between natural history specimens and still-life paintings; an awkward relation that made it difficult to place them. The photographs reminded me of Dutch 'impossible bouquets', where painted still lifes contained a fantasy of flowers that could never in reality be seen together because they bloomed in different seasons and geographic locations.[15] In Simon's photographs the impossible bouquets are restaged with plants purchased from contemporary global centres of distribution.[16] A distant relative of our palm, *Chamaedorea elegans* (the parlour palm), witnesses agreements on non-aggression and good neighbourliness between Mozambique and South Africa in 1984, a comprehensive cooperation Agreement between Cuba and Venezuela in 2000, and the signing of the Trans-Afghanistan pipeline agreement in 2010.[17] There are men in suits wielding expensive pens, and women in tight skirts hovering in the backgrounds. I pause at one image, somehow familiar. It is the *Central North Island Forests Land Collective Settlement Act 2008 (Treelords). Beehive Banquet Hall, Wellington, New Zealand, June 25, 2008*. It is a story from my own past; a moment when the contested spaces of colonised land were acknowledged. Witnessing the signing are three plants sourced from the Netherlands, and a prohibited chrysanthemum.

Later, I show a hotel man my draft essay. He says, "I can see what you are doing with your tree, but I don't get this, it's just flowers put there by the hotel staff, they are just doing their job." It is not clear to me if he is discussing the plants or the hotel workers. I return to Australia, unable to leave my thoughts on Goethe's palm behind and start asking climate scientists if it is possible to trace a timeline of the atmosphere a plant breathes.

~

The Goethe Palm is a member of the only palm species native to Europe, the European or Mediterranean fan palm. It is a clumping palm "with – as the name suggests – fan-like fronds, or if you like, fronds like fans. It grows in Portugal, Spain, France, Italy, Morocco, Algeria, Tunisia and nowadays, in protected gardens in the UK."[18] There is only one species in the genus and some scientists speculate that it probably emerged as a separate species more than five million years ago when summers were warmer and wetter in Europe. The species has managed to survive dramatic transformations in climate. There will have also been colder winters (the Earth's orbit around the sun contributes to this), and for much of the period between five and two million years ago the average conditions were warmer than the present.[19]

Over the life of the Goethe Palm the air it has breathed has transformed dramatically. Readings of ice core plots show that in 1585, when it was planted, the carbon dioxide concentration in this part of Europe would have been close to 280 particles per million or 275 particles per million in the clean atmosphere.[20] Carbon dioxide concentrations are variable over the world, and scientists record both measurements to establish a base line as well as the fluctuating concentrations. The measurements in Padua and environs equate with the recognised preindustrial average ('modern') value of 280ppm across Europe.[21] There have also been significant climatic differences. From 1300 to 1850 Europe had ongoing periods of regional cold, dramatically affecting the lives of plants and people. I imagine flurries of bodies arriving in Italy from the North, and a fresh crispness to the air as Europe was gripped by the Little Ice Age. Grain crops and grape harvests failed in the colder winters and shorter growing season, causing famines. During the severe winters in northern Europe lakes, rivers and ports froze and people wrote about the effects of these episodes on their lives, and sketched drawings of the advancing ice.[22]

In the north, lichen began to die under the layers of snow that prevented photosynthesis, leaving only halo records for later humans to measure. Here in Padua, the Goethe Palm was just beginning life. It would be 200 years before Goethe would visit and make it his namesake.

I decide to enrol in a first year climate change subject. My textbook *Earth's Climate: Past and Future* (2014) begins:

> Life exists nearly everywhere on Earth because the climate is favourable. We live in, on and surrounded by the climate system: the air, land surfaces, oceans, ice and vegetation ... We have left an era when natural changes governed Earth's climate and have now entered a time when changes caused by human activity predominate.[23]

The narrative is the same the world over. There is a risk of generalising from the empirical data but, in aggregate, there is a global trend. "The Earth's average surface temperature has warmed by 0.8 degrees in the last century ... Natural changes at tectonic, orbital and millennial time scales do not explain this warming."[24] After Goethe stood in front of the palm, there has been a great acceleration in carbon dioxide and methane quantities in the atmosphere.

I begin to read books in which scientists warn me "millenial-scale climatic changes during the last 8000 years have been highly variable from region to region."[25] My teacher sends me a paper by Brunetti et al. in the *International Journal of Climatology* that details the temperature record for Italy at the time Goethe visited the palm.[26] The article contains climatic data for the region around Padua, beginning in 1774. The numbers change rapidly: temperature has increased by around two degrees since 1800, with a slight change in the minimum temperature in the early nineteenth century, and then, after 1980, everything climbs. This transformation of the climate is met with a parallel transformation in the chemical makeup of the local atmosphere. By 1874, the air around our palm tree had already began to change. NASA estimates that the atmospheric carbon dioxide in 1874 was around 288 parts per million (ppm) and already measurable ground ozone sat at 10 parts per billion by volume (ppbv) in Europe.[27] The British industrial revolution made a minimal impact in the air in Italy. Only in the mid-twentieth century do atmospheric records across the planet begin to reveal dramatic changes.

How can humans claim to know how a tree would have experienced these transformations? From a tree's perspective, over what time period can we map its experience? To read the climate archive stored in the body of trees, dendrochronologists take core samples and reconstruct the narratives of climate change. The changes between favourable and unfavourable growth years produce distinctive variations in the widths and other properties of tree rings.[28] Because most of the organisms that have ever existed on Earth are now extinct,[29] tree rings, together with ice cores and corals, offer a proxy archive of climate change in recent Earth history.[30] What might the record of these transformations mean for Goethe's palm? The palm stands in a garden where its neighbours consume carbon dioxide in the daytime and exhale at night. At some stage humans have built a greenhouse around it, where the peaks and troughs of oxygen, carbon dioxide and the other chemicals that make up that simple thing we call 'air' would be stable but the potent greenhouse gas of water vapour would trap heat, making for warm night-time temperatures.

My textbook continues: "Using biotic proxies to reconstruct past climates over longer tectonic time scales often requires a reliance on the general resemblance of past forms to their modern counterparts, either in general appearance or in specific features that can be measured."[31] I don't understand most of what they are saying, but I realise that suddenly we are back with Goethe and the resemblance of forms. Goethe found the newly fashionable Linnaean taxonomies that focused on structural similarities were unable to account for the spectre of change. He said that in order to think about change and transformation we needed to be able to 'identify' with the forms before us. Today we would call it empathy. Goethe wanted to combine the "empirical or measurable elements of nature with those elements that are 'measureless to man.'"[32] For him, the enduring tension between law and freedom was found in the scale of an individual plant. This was natural history. The rules (law) could never account for the freedoms (variations) that he was witnessing. For climate scientists now operating at planetary scale, the laws have been surpassed; we don't know any more what the limits might be. The terms they now use to explain the tension between the known and unknowable are *forcing* and *response*.[33] They find an unnatural history where climate transformations no longer follow the rules, and name it the Anthropocene.

Other thinkers pick up the story. Walter Benjamin publishes 'To the Planetarium' in 1928.[34] He is angry. Benjamin wrote his doctoral dissertation on the concept of art criticism in early German Romanticism and seems to share something of Goethe's dislike for the "'vicious empiricism' that kill[s] the living breath of nature."[35] Goethe had argued that nature needs freedom, something that cannot be measured. Benjamin extended this beyond nature and the individual to society. 'To the Planetarium' is a harrowing account of war, and the damage wrought on the planet. He rages against the violence committed against nature through power, war and technology. He despairs at the modern use of technology to control nature, pointing to earlier cosmic relations where nature is understood through communal and "ecstatic contact." It is through planetary contact, he argues that "we gain certain knowledge of what is nearest to us and what is remotest from us, and never of one without the other."[36] Grasping what is both near and far introduces a physical scale to our temporal narrative of Goethe's palm. The modern world saw the exponential increase of human populations, the harnessing of steam as energy to drive machines, the transformation of land by mechanised agriculture, the disappearance of species, and alteration of the atmosphere by the detonation of atomic bombs and the relentless emission of carbon dioxide, methane and other greenhouse gases. The creation of new machines designed to transform the natural environment occurred at such a scale the implications are still impossible to fully understand or anticipate.

Benjamin reminds me that, even in a timeline based on known histories, things are always changing. He was not around to witness the release of atomic energy in the New Mexico desert at 5.29am on 16 July 1945. Inspired by the poems of John Donne, Robert Oppenheimer had named the test release of 21 kilotons of TNT, "Trinity."[37] I wonder what Oppenheimer was thinking: why poetry at this time, in this place? A witness, Norris Bradbury, reported that "the atom bomb did not fit into any preconceptions possessed by anybody."[38] Goethe's palm will take another breath.

The detonation of the Trinity atomic device initiated local nuclear fallout from 1945 to 1951. Not long after, Hiroshima and Nagasaki were destroyed: not just people, but cities, animals, plants, entire ecosystems. There was no going back. The whole planet had changed. These 'tests' sprinkled the world and the atmosphere with new forms of radiation contributing to big earth system changes. One way to fix the marker of the Anthropocene is to find a synchronist level—the point at which radiation can be traced across the global planet surface. Subsequent and ongoing thermonuclear weapons tests generated a clear global signal from 1952 to 1980; the so-called 'bomb spike' of excess radiocarbon (^{14}C), plutonium-239, and other radionuclides that peaked in 1964.[39] A long way away, a Sitka spruce tree at Camp Cove on the subantarctic Campbell Islands records a proportional rise in radiocarbon in its body.[40] Scientists report this is the magic 'golden spike'—a global anthropogenic signal that marks a new epoch—they find it in the body of a tree that itself is displaced; a marker of the journeys of British colonists into the deep Southern Ocean. And closer to Australia the corals of the Great Barrier Reef record the signal reaching the ocean floor.[41] The measurements get more precise. Tree ring samples show evidence of the 'bomb spike' between October and December 1965. Other scientists are not so sure, suggesting we should start at the beginning rather than the peak, they find there are bomb spikes in the years prior; the dates remain ambiguous. I watch the video as they extract the core from the tree, and my bones ache.

~

The story is getting too big, expanding beyond the life of a single palm. It is becoming impossible. The problem of the naming of the Anthropocene is housed here in these bodies. Others work on similar tales. In narrating the species encounters surrounding matsutake mushroom collection in Japan, Anna Tsing writes "This is not just a story, then, but also a method: big histories are always best told through insistent, if humble, details."[42] She argues that what we need to do is trace polyphonic assemblages; not limit ourselves to a single creature, a single time, or even a single relationship. Goethe's palm was never singular. Planted in a constructed environment, there has never been a moment when its life was not entangled with humans. And in 2015 humans stood beside it, smoking and taking selfies.

In 1979 anthropologist Gregory Bateson approached Goethe's work as a way to engage with a stories of pattern and transformation.⁴³ I don't know if Bateson visited Goethe's palm, but he used the stories drawn from its body to illustrate the patterns of connection; the relationships that determine the way in which we are all parts of a living world. In *Mind and Nature* Bateson wrote, paraphrasing Goethe, "The way to go about the definition [of leaves and stems] is to look at the relationships: 'a stem is that which bears leaves … a leaf is that which has a bud in its angle … a stem is what was once a bud in that position.'" He ends: "The shapes of animals and plants are transforms [sic.] of messages."⁴⁴ Even by 1979 the transformations of the atmosphere meant that we could not think plants and animals discretely any more. Later Bateson returned to the palm as a way to think about survival. He explains patterns of growth, and in a somewhat shocking segue from the 'fissionable' material in the atom bomb and the necessary scale required for explosion, Bateson describes the Arctic porpoise that manages its heat budget (a tiny body in a frozen sea) and to the palm tree that grows forever taller until "The sheer mechanical instability of excessive height without compensation in girth provides its normal way of death."⁴⁵

It shocks me that more than just bad weather, water quality, nutrient deficiencies, disease and parasites might kill our palm. Anthropogenic-related causes must now be added to the list. This essay was meant to be a counter to narratives of death. The tree has stored the data of the previous 400 years in its body. I start to worry; to think about what it knows might happen next.

In 2016, Ralph Keeling, the scientist who now runs the Scripps Institute for Oceanography's carbon dioxide monitoring program, wrote in a blog post: "Brief excursions toward lower values are still possible, but it already seems safe to conclude that we won't be seeing a monthly value below 400 ppm this year – or ever again for the indefinite future."⁴⁶ The Keeling Curve is not named after Ralph though; it is named after his father. Charles David Keeling began continuous monitoring of carbon dioxide concentrations in the Earth's atmosphere in the 1950s at the Mauna Loa Observatory in Hawaii.⁴⁷ He named it then: something unexpected was transforming the planet.

Other artists and writers help fill the narrative jumps. British artist Katie Paterson has long looked to the stars for a sympathetic off-world nature that might reflect humanity's futile attempts to grasp and understand the universe. In 2014 she announced the *Future Library* project. A forest has been planted in Norway, which will supply paper for a special anthology of books to be printed in one hundred years' time. Accompanying the forest, in a special room in the Deichmanske Bibliotek, the Oslo Public Library, is a printing press. Each year an author is commissioned to write a manuscript to be housed in the vault, only to be opened in 2114. Their imagined yet unknown future readers promise so much: although they tell us nothing of the world they will occupy, Paterson reminds us that humans will still be around in a hundred years to mill the trees, print, and read the books. The event and its experience extend well beyond the usual temporalities of art, but remains completely imaginable within science. There is nothing vicious here, just a silent beauty as we wait for the trees to grow, and the stories to be revealed.

In 2015 the earth hit roughly 398 ppm carbon dioxide globally. And it may be that Goethe's palm is breathing more freely because of it. "Controlled experiments with vegetation in greenhouses show that tree growth is enhanced by higher levels of carbon dioxide and photosynthesis."[48] Some call it the 'fertilisation' effect of rising carbon dioxide on plants. It could be a false climate signal. Soon the stress of such overactivity will become too much; the palm will struggle to breathe. It is more than just carbon dioxide that changes the atmosphere. When I stood with Goethe's palm, the daytime summer ozone in Padua was probably around 60 ppbv.[49] The concentrations observed in Italian cities were found to meet standards for human health but maybe not tree health.

~

It troubles me, this story of a tree from the other side of the world: an already displaced plant, that has no name of its own, and that only exists because humans put it there. If this essay is an attempt to keep generational transformations in mind, it also needs to address the generational shifts that form our understandings of this planet. How can I make the shift from the plant to the planetary? In the last paragraph of *Death of a Discipline*, Gayatri Chakravorty Spivak writes, "The planet is here, as always perhaps, a catachresis for inscribing collective responsibility as right. Its alterity, determining experience, is mysterious and discontinuous — an experience of the impossible."[50] To grasp the impossible planet Spivak names, we need to travel in time and space away from the controlled environment of a botanical gardens at the centre of Europe to Trinity Island, and onwards to Chernobyl and Fukushima; from a foggy industrial London to an unbreathable forest haze in Central Kalimantan, and from the bird-inhabited Codfish Island off the wild coast of New Zealand out through the night sky to the flickering stars of space junk, floating just out of sight. Human activity on the planet has left none of these sites untouched.

I work on a draft of this essay in the NSW Southern Highlands high above Wollongong, and share a table with a climate scientist wading through recent data sets from the Great Barrier Reef, a business analyst working to introduce sustainable energy modelling to Sydney's grotesque rental market, and a human geographer developing new collaborative farming initiatives between recent migrants and the local farmers. Their work is direct and active. It has impact and operates at a scale into the future. Their work will transform the way that people understand human relations with climate change. Alongside them, I sit and write about art, and poetry, and trees. I share my draft with the climate scientist. She has had a bad week and is in despair: "why do they hate us all so much, we are just geeks." She says we need to start writing a new kind of science communication; data and narrative together. In the post-Enlightenment narratives of science, that took over after Goethe was shown to be of a loose poetic mind, there is an idea that culture and artefacts are orientated through the laws of nature, and that these laws are subject to strict rules. In such a model, art, writing and culture either illustrate things that are known or imagine things that are not. In reality, these disciplinary divisions never really existed. Goethe's delicate empiricism lost out to quantifiable modernity. Philosopher Bruno Latour reminds us that the scientific revolution maintained a careful distinction between storytelling and data production; the opposite of the 'natural sciences' of Goethe.[51] He says the science of the Anthropocene has to look different:

> So when it doesn't look like big sciences, and it doesn't look like basic science, and it doesn't look like fundamental science, what then? It's the science of care, and it's as surprising for physicists and mathematicians as it is in women's studies. What does care do? What is care?[52]

At Tasmania's Cape Grim they have measured the cleanest air in the world since 1976.[53] It is the easiest way to measure pollution. Their measurements take on the recitations of a litany: methane, a greenhouse gas, is clearly increasing; nitrous oxide shows a slow and steady increase; carbon monoxide is stable; chlorofluorocarbons have been banned since 1985 and there is evidence in 2016 of a slow recovery, but again it is the spike of carbon dioxide that catches us all out. In 1976, 350 ppm was considered a critical number, now carbon dioxide measurements have tipped over into uncharted territory. The scientists tell me "Projections for the next two centuries indicate increases to at least 500 ppm, and possibly 1000 ppm or more, nearly as high as those in the Cretaceous. We are heading back into a greenhouse world."[54] Other thresholds keep moving: in the 2015 United Nations Framework Convention on Climate Change, the Accord de Paris, they did not talk about catastrophes or disasters and climate danger was described as not exceeding a predicted two degrees Celsius increase in temperature before 2036. Now our task is no longer about preventing the two degree rise, but something much worse. In 2036 my daughter will be 28 and Goethe's palm tree will be 451 years old.

There is a new Keeling Curve reading from Mauna Loa; today it is 410.52 ppm.[55] It is enough to make you gasp.

What does it mean to pause infront of a tree?

In 2003 writer Iris Murdoch walks into an art gallery with her imagined children. Later she records their visit:

> The idea of attendance or contemplation, of looking carefully at something and holding it before the mind, may be conveyed early on in childhood. 'Look, listen, isn't that pretty, isn't that nice?' Also, 'Don't touch!' This is moral training as well as preparation for a pleasurable life ... The far-reaching idea of *respect* is included in such teaching.[56]

No wonder my children were upset when a gallery we encountered on a promised day-off demanded that they touch and interact with scenes of environmental destruction. "Look, you have the power to kill bees, to send in the floods, to unleash the plague." Concepts of care, respect and pleasure seem at odds with this viciousness.[57]

In a corner of the Orto Botanico, Goethe's palm holds tight to its hand-painted descriptive label. Linnaeus gave its Latin name sometime around 1735, its common English name evolving as humans travelled continental Europe. And its enduring name is not even its own, but given because a human stood before it, just as we are, and began to think about the truths held in its body. In front of Goethe's palm we inhabit a very different world in which plants are once again a key part of human material and ecological relationships with capital. Scientist and philosopher Elizabeth Millan has argued that we need to pay attention to the way that the German Romantics approached "*all* living forces, human as well as plants, nations as well as individuals."[58] She explains that their aim was to clear a space for the elements of "human experience that cannot be quantified" so that "all thoughtful people" could access the science. She brings the question forward to today: "How should the natural scientist proceed with her work without becoming trapped in the darkness of vicious empiricism? How is the natural scientist to present nature without killing the living seed? Without suffocating the living breath of nature?"[59] Perhaps the story of a tree is one way to tell such a story, to capture the living breath, without fixing the lived reality of the Anthropocene.

And there the story should end. But it hasn't, yet. I've begun to trace other tree stories. People bring me tales of trees they have met; I collect books, memories and narratives. And then, slowly at first, I start to hear stories of kauri die-back on the Waitakere Ranges in Aotearoa New Zealand. The trees that have lived here longer than humans are dying. Frustrated with inaction local iwi (tribes) have placed a rāhui (ban) on the ranges—the trees need to be left alone. While we were looking somewhere else, *Phytophthora agathidicida* (literally 'plant destroyers') travelled across the Tasman on the breath of cyclonic winds.

Proof was in the forests.

There is a tale that when Stephenson Percy-Smith visited the far north of New Zealand he thought the trunk of one kauri was the side of a cliff. It was 4000 years old. Right now I await an email from the kauri. Don't worry, we are fine. We certainly don't need didactic video screens. We are already here, what you do next requires some serious thought.

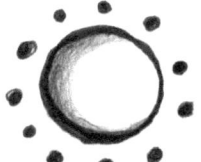

In the middle of things

Sitting around a table together, we read Isabelle Stengers as she describes the challenge of an *Ecology of Practices*:

> The problem for each practice is how to foster its own force, make present what causes practitioners to think and feel and act. But it is a problem which may also produce an experimental togetherness among practices, a dynamics of pragmatic learning of what works and how. This is the kind of active, fostering 'milieu' that practices need in order to be able to answer challenges and experiment changes, that is, to unfold their own force. This is a social technology any diplomatic practice demands and depends upon.[60]

Joshua tells us a story. He's writing about a boy isolated from the people around him, who finds safety in a school drama activity called 'flocking'. "We call it 'fish'," Cath says. The group has to move through the space together. They start in the centre of the room. Facing in the same direction, in a staggered formation, like an arrowhead. The tip of the arrow leads and the rest follow, imperceptibly slower, inching their way forward. When they are really concentrating, the group can weave through the space, changing direction when the flock allows. It's not easy. The trick is for there never to be a leader. We should never know who's leading, who's following. Let go of your own thoughts. Breathe together. We're poised; waiting to move. Carefully, elegantly, we move to the left. The leader now follows. There is no leader. We breathe together.

Or—to be contrary—is it that the role of leader is shared (always asymmetrically but shared nonetheless)? How ridiculous it is to try to write a book as if by hive-mind, and yet many common things are ridiculous! The software we use allows us to write on top of and inside each other's words, and although individual authorship can be traced ('See new changes'), we can fold and fold the words into each other so that, like the ingredients in pastry, they become together something else.

Anna Tsing says: "muddling through with others is always in the middle of things; it does not properly conclude."[61]

Change management

We live in a world. Who is 'we'? I'm talking about the Western world. A world where the rational is understood and often performed in a limited and limiting way. The assembly line, the five-year plan and management optimisation all work to normalise, simplify, eliminate and smooth the rough. Modernity operates with narrow and restricted scales. It produces paradigms such as 'measured success', 'conservation', 'resource management' and 'environmental services'. Everything can be accounted for, but only within a limited notion of what will be accounted for, who does the accounting, and how. Sometimes poets and shamans make the best accountants.

Today, artists refuse the lie of a carefully framed single perspective, insisting on multiple frames and multiple perspectives—shifting planes of being and becoming. If Keats' Grecian urn were smashed and the bits that could be found were stuck back together as best able, it might be the kind of rough cracked beauty that is and enables truth-telling.

The news can be good. Sirocco, Aotearoa New Zealand's official Kākāpō spokesbird, has come out of hiding. After two years wandering around the wilderness on his Fiordland Island with a broken transmitter, Sirocco announced his return via Facebook.[62]

Frame

Circling back, out of the metaphor of the portal: we frame the real in order to see it, and see only what we have framed. Frames are enacted from moment to moment, and in turn enact. They are material, and are performed by an assemblage of techniques, humans, concepts, and various nonhuman alliances. A baroque compost of assemblages unfolds dynamically and emerges as the real. Frames can be changed by inserting new actors, or removing and modifying existing ones. Some frames are so stable that they last centuries, and some are so delicate that they are washed away by the morning rain.

Labour laboratory

In Museum Ghibli in Tokyo, there is an idealised animation studio on permanent display. Here, visitors experience the process of animation from ideas to actual film amongst the faux European furnishing in a 1950s pre-computerised work environment. Walking through the three-room exhibit is akin to walking into one of Hayao Miyazaki's films: the working Gütiokipänja Bakery on top of a hill with an ocean view; Ursula's secluded cottage for painting in the woods; Piccolo's aircraft shed by the Navigli in Milan. The atmosphere of making, concentration, and seriousness is somewhat reminiscent of Diderot's *Encyclopédie*. Richard Sennett argues that rather than dismissing these settings as romantic, these idealised workplaces may reveal what is fundamental about our urge to make.[63] Work environments are extensions of tools, their atmospheres, extensions of thinking, doing and skills.

Marketplace

The capitalism of Fernand Braudel's Medieval Europe, so ebullient and local. Braudel walks through the memories of legendary markets. He sees the market as the *appeal to the other*. An Italian saying, from the Medieval markets of Palermo: *"val più avere amici in piazza che denari nella casa"*— better to have friends in the marketplace than money in a chest at home.[64]

Metaphor

From the window in my study, I can see a flock of pigeons circling in the sky. I'm distracted: my attention should be on the words fluttering on the screen. The flying birds won't stay still. Sometimes they remind me of lungs, breathing in and out as they turn and weave. Sometimes they look like a virus: expanding and retracting, multiplying under the heat of a microscope. The birds turn again; their wings catch the light and glint like knives. In Lynette Wallworth's screen-installation *Coral Rekindling Venus* (2012) the images are in a constant state of flux. Seals swarm around the circular pool of the camera's light. The air bubbles they produce swirl and become silver pilchards, who give way to too-pink and electric-yellow schools of fish. The fish dagger through the air. They morph into the feathery cacti of coral. Or fingertips trilling or the orange suckers of octopuses. On the screens above, the coral spawn pollinate the night-black ocean, ascend into the sky, transform into dust between planets, onwards into electric pulses, material tracings …

What is the point of these transformations? What would a piece of coral make of the comparison to feathers? What is a pigeon thinking when it slices the air like a knife?

Ghost gum

I took Janine from work for a walk the other day ... we went up Mount Keira and had a bit of a look ... but on the way home I had to tell her about this relationship I've got aye ... See ... I found this fuckin ghost gum in Reserve Street ... If you find Reserve Street, find the tree ... It's the only one I've found in this town ... Anyway ... this thing is amazing, bro ... I had a moment with it one night. It was just near on full moon and the bastard was glowing ... and I'm really not sure what it was trying to say to me ... but I swear I sat there for about an hour, like across the road, sitting down with this bastard ... Because they glow ... they do ... they've got this weird crazy aura right ... It's those sorts of relationships that I refer to when we talk about kinship. What are the significant relationships in your life that connect you to your place? That's how you understand country ...

Juju

The casting of a spell. An utterance is cast forward by a speaker, and the world is changed by words. Spelling a word. Procedurally, sound by sound, a frame of meaning is built. For Romantic poet Percy Bysshe Shelley poetry is magic, an incantation whose word on breath ignites the "unextinguished hearth" of a sleeping world with "the trumpet of prophecy."[65] The world is changed. For Kamau Brathwaite, writing on the ground, within the sound, of *vèvè*, the word "becomes/again a god and walks among us."[66]

Juju (or joujou) marks both spells and objects. Spells are cast onto the objects; the objects embody the spells. The spells and objects are one; together, they enact and emanate an atmosphere.

The object has thus been transformed into a portal of manifestation and a presence for another atmosphere of being. A discarded soda bottle might thus become the vehicle for an ancestral spirit (and perhaps a hermit crab).

Juju can also be spurred by actions: beneficial actions to a group are shared as an atmosphere of generosity; ill-considered deeds that harm others manifest as a heavy atmosphere that permeates through time.

Comparative hierophany at three object scales

Teodor Mitew

THERE was once a village, and close by it there was a waterfall. Villagers believed that under the waterfall there lived a stone golem. This golem was thought to be largely good-natured, as it wouldn't mind people bathing in the pool downstream. Old people remembered that once the golem saved a drowning child by putting a rock under its feet.

Many years passed, and the Bureau of Tourism and Recreation briefly considered using this story in its advertising materials for the region. Senior management rejected the idea, as it was thought to contain folklore elements that may be confusing to a global audience.

Resistant availability

One material setting, two vastly different atmospheres. Imagine atmospheres as frames capturing the enormous richness of the world within a set spectrum of scales. Potentially there can be many atmospheres and, insofar as they are understood as frames, they make certain aspects of reality visible while obfuscating others. What is visible, coherent, and knowable in one atmosphere, for example as a wonder, a miracle, or divine intervention, can be invisible, incoherent and unknowable in another atmosphere lacking the relevant scale. In this context, atmosphere acts as a framing device, a projection allowing material settings and sensibilities *to be* in a certain way. Thus the enchanted waterfall becomes a tourist attraction, a holy relic transforms into a fetishized idol, forests inhabited by ancestral spirits mutate into timber reserves. Shift the frame a little, remove the heterogeneous agency, silence or erase the stone golem, and the waterfall is suddenly nothing more than an untapped resource for the hydroelectric company, who has been momentarily defeated by the needs of the tourism bureau.

The result of this, at first sight minor, shift in atmospheres is a grotesque and tragic misalignment of agencies; an erasure, a silencing echoing in repeated acts of forced purification across all scales of the new atmosphere. At some point in our not-so-distant past the atmospheric frame was shifted, ever so slightly, into a new reordering, into "a form of narcissism that condemns things merely to echo what people say."[67] We know this shift by many names, some of the most common being 'the enlightenment', 'the age of reason', 'the triumph of science', or 'modernity'. Surrounded by a triumphant halo, these terms are infused with the ethos of conquering an ever-receding frontier. As it asphalts over all in the name of progress, this triumphant march invariably renders invisible the agencies of things, and then inscribes on them the echoes of a thoroughly 'modernised' human subjectivity. With the 'modern' human at its centre, this is a thoroughly anthropocentric atmosphere, with a strange concept of a material world "in which the agency of all the entities making up the world has been made to vanish."[68]

I want to explore an alternative atmospheric frame, cohabited by nonhuman entities understood to already have agency. What follows is a speculative exploration of such a frame, with the help of three entities, resonating at three scales: a voice, an image, and a guest. All three transcend their milieu, their agencies appearing as transgressive and unpredictable heteroclites,[69] deviating from and puncturing through the stable scale of their locale.[70] There is a certain alien quality to their ontological otherness, and hence the only way to tangle with that richness of being is to anthropomorphise them in an exercise of speculative analogy.[71] Importantly, the shift in frames I am constructing below is as much a shift in perception as it is one of description. This involves a manoeuvre of making the agency of things visible, but also of remembering "the hand at work in the waking of transcendent objects."[72] So, here is my hand at work in the waking up of my three transcendent objects.

First, a proposition. When the villagers acknowledge the waterfall as the place where a stone golem resides, they in effect acknowledge it has an agency *other than their own*. An acknowledgement which is an act of listening, but not bestowing, an act of anthropomorphising the unknown, but not conquering it in the name of progress and the five-year plan. The agency which has been recognised does not exist as the side effect of a fetishizing human gaze or subjective projection. This is not the stencil animism of the moderns, resulting from the "naive belief that many still live in a de-animated world of mere stuff."[73] This is an active and unpredictable agency, a "critical strain in the order of things",[74] not a mere projection of subjective perception on a dull and passive material world. If an entity acts, it has meaning,[75] and as long as the waterfall is the locus of an agency other than our own, it is capable of bringing change, and therefore new meaning, in the world we share with it. Indeed, this is an "inherently dramatic" world,[76] infused with animate and *animated* entanglements.

Second, a way of seeing the inherently dramatic. It involves the adoption of a radical *isosthenia*, the ancient Greek sceptic's term for an a priori equal strength of statements.[77] Isosthenia presumes the other, whoever they may be, has agency on the same ontological footing as our own. This mutual presumption of agency on the part of the other is a necessary precondition so that others can speak. An isosthenic way of seeing presupposes that there are heterogeneous publics other than our own, that they can speak, and that to hear them we need to listen. It presupposes patience and openness to a scale other than one's own. Needless to say, it also presupposes abstention from "de-animating the agencies that we encounter at each step."[78]

Third, a principle, or better yet, a way of listening and seeing, which posits that entities always speak for themselves and can never be completely translated, substituted by, or reduced to one another. Reducing them automatically negates their ontological existence; they become reductive surfaces inertly awaiting the human master-gaze to bestow them with temporary agency. Irreduction presupposes that we deny ourselves the temptation to mute objects; we deny ourselves the impulse to de-animate agencies refusing to fit our scale. That being said, even though entities are *irreducible to* one another they still have to *relate with* each other. These relational attachments have to be performed and maintained through acts of translation of agency. How to think of translations? They are easily imagined as stabilisations—an institution enrols and stabilises my agency in a frame it has built, and part of me now participates and acts as an element of that frame. This temporarily stable agency *is* the translation.

Importantly, because of the irreduction principle outlined above, translations can never be complete. They can be thought of as temporary pattern stabilisations in a truly baroque compost of being. What is more, no matter how stable the institutional frame part of me acts within, it is constantly pulled apart both from within, by the heterogeneous agencies it has enrolled, and from without, by the heterogeneous agencies it has to negotiate with. In effect, the frame is in a constant and dramatic struggle with entropy to maintain its existence. Every entity is therefore in a state of resisting reduction and simultaneously relating through translation, which can be imagined as occurring along a spectrum of intensities. The strange hybrid state depicted by this principle is the *resistant availability* of objects.[79] Here, entities speak incessantly; relentlessly if allowed to, if their agency is flaunted rather than concealed (Figure 2).

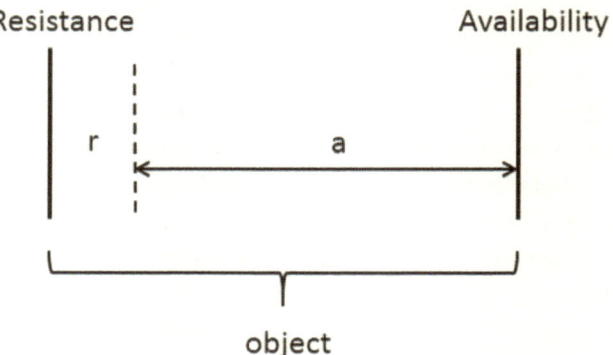

Figure 2: Teodor Mitew, *Objects are never fully available (a), part of them always resists (r)*, 2018.

How to think of space *r* in Figure 2; that is, the space of resistance? By definition, it resists entanglements, reduction and translation, and is not available to human interlocutors. It is tempting to ignore it, and pretend the entirety of the object is that which is available to us in space *a*. That manoeuvre will not do however, as it simply repeats the modern conjuror's trick of de-animating uncomfortable agencies. Alternatively, we could follow the villagers' example and anthropomorphise it,[80] so that it becomes a recognisable transgressive agency which, even though resistant, can be acknowledged. Unlike the anthropocentric de-animation of the world, here "anthropomorphism creates resonance between a human and a thing, and suddenly the human is not above or beyond the thing."[81] Importantly, the acknowledgment of *resistant agency* (*r* agency) achieved through anthropomorphism is not equivalent to translation or reduction. Instead, it could be likened to an awareness of a presence eluding stabilisation on human terms.

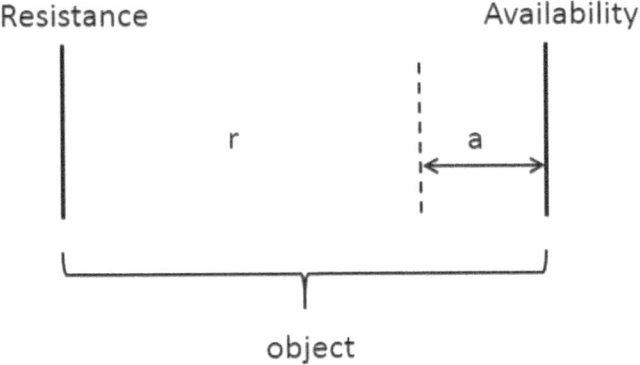

Figure 3: Teodor Mitew, *Objects are never fully resistant (r), part of them is always available (a)*, 2018.

Objects then are never fully reducible, as part of them always resists entanglement and translation. However, they can never be fully resistant, or else they simply will not *be*. Part of them, no matter how limited, can always be translated and tangled with

(Figure 3). As they share the inherently dramatic world, entities travel along the spectrum of intensities on this scale, never fully resistant, and never fully available.

Hierophanies

So far I have positioned atmospheres as frames capturing the richness of the world within a spectrum of scales. Depending on the atmosphere being deployed, an entity and its agency might become visible, or be rendered completely opaque. In addition, each entity performs itself into existence with a varying intensity of resistant availability. That being said, no matter how available and translatable an entity is, part of its agency always resists translation. The resisting agency still acts however, and therefore injects transgressive meaning into the milieu occupied by that entity (Figure 4) Viewed in aggregate over time, this is an immanently entropic settlement for all stable frames. It inevitably overflows and collapses, with all those silenced or invisible transgressive agencies returning to claim what is their due. An inherently dramatic world indeed!

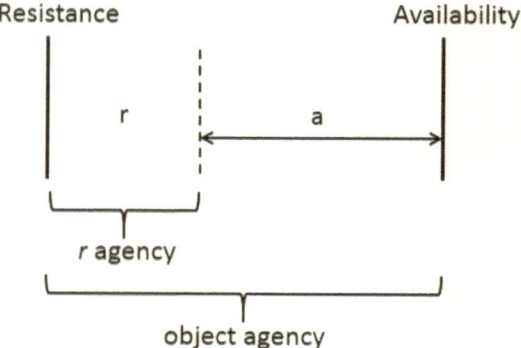

Figure 4: Teodor Mitew, *Part of an object's agency always resists, and therefore transgresses, the frame in which it is made available*, 2018.

Interestingly enough however, there is a stable conceptual frame sensitive to the transgressive agencies outlined above. In his work on non-modern notions of sacred space, philosopher of religion Mircea Eliade conceptualized the manifestation of another modality of being into a local setting as a *hierophany*.[82] An object within a hierophany "appears as the receptacle of an exterior force that differentiates it from its milieu and gives it meaning and value."[83] Such objects are presumed and expected to inject *r agency* into their surrounding locale. Hierophanies are discontinuities, self-enclosed spheres of meaning, not universal, but wholly singular and local acts of presence by a transcendental modality of being transgressing a local milieu. By manifesting that modality, which Eliade termed as *the sacred*, an object becomes the receptacle for a transcendental presence, yet simultaneously continues to remain inextricably entangled in its surrounding milieu. Spaces punctured by hierophanies are experienced as a heterogeneous array of interruptions, crevices, liminal breaks, folds, and pauses of enchantment.

There is something of the numinous in this, a scale of wonder and awe as the manifestation of a hierophanic presence reconstitutes heretofore homogeneous loci – a mountain, a stone, a street corner – into receptacles of wholly different modalities of being, resistant yet available. Among an endless variety of geologic formations, a waterfall becomes the home of a stone golem, "and hence instantly becomes saturated with being."[84] Here, the transgressive aspect of the resistant agency of an entity is acknowledged in its *otherness*, a liminal interface puncturing the scales of a given atmosphere. Its resistance does not come as a surprise, disrupting an otherwise stable world, but as an expected revelation of another modality of being. An object existing as a hierophany is then a boundary interface, a heteroclite, both *connecting* its surrounding milieu to another transgressive modality of being, and *anchoring* those transgressive agencies into a specific local place experienced as an interruption. It is totally local, in that it and only it acts as the receptacle of a transgressive agency, yet it is also locally total, in that its agency is contained within the liminal space of the hierophany.

While Eliade discussed hierophany as a manifestation of the sacred, for the purposes of this speculative essay it suffices to consider the concept in the context of the numinous. In other words, from the outside, a hierophany could be perceived as a source of wonder in the presence of an *r agency* transcending and transgressing its locale. In what follows then, the three objects discussed below act as hierophanies, each with a different scale of resistant availability. A comparative hierophany at three object scales: a voice, an image, and a guest.

The Voice

Strictly speaking, 'Alexa' is *a spell*. The spell wakes a voice, gendered as female, which in turn answers questions, and may even actuate certain prosaic requests such as dimming the lights or ordering food. A presence listens, one utters a spell, and a voice answers.

Technically, Alexa is a voice command activating the voice-powered interface of an internet-connected device, aptly named the Amazon Echo (Figure 5). Made by the internet giant Amazon, the Echo is a roughly 25 centimetre-high cylinder, containing a microphone, speaker, processor, storage space, and hardware for internet connectivity. The first Echoes, released on the US market in mid-2015, were made from an austere black plastic, while the newer versions come in a variety of colours, materials and textures. The Echo's first version had a voice interface programmed to respond to the name Alexa, though the latest version can be reprogrammed to respond to the spells 'Echo' or 'Computer' instead. Amazon has made that interface open to cross-platform developers under the name Alexa Skills Kit, in effect allowing any user to add voice-powered 'skills' to the Echo's list of abilities. By the end of 2017 more than 15,000 Alexa skills had been added by developers and users.[85]

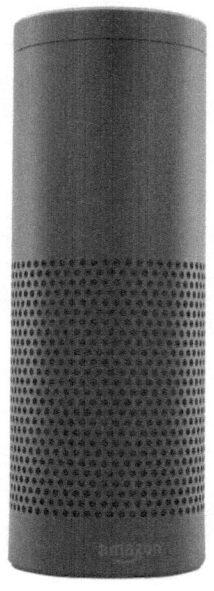

Figure 5: The Amazon Echo, a speaker talking with the voice of Alexa, 2014. Photo by Frmorrison, [Public Domain], via Wikimedia Commons.

Obviously, Amazon's decision to open the Echo to nonlinear learning provided by a global audience was clever marketing, but it also allowed this transgressive object to gain what could be termed as "congregational agency"[86]—an assemblage channelling a multiplicity of agencies that comprise and augment it. An Echo listens constantly, observing all ambient sounds in its surroundings, waiting for the spell Alexa, which it interprets as the start of a query. The data from each query is sent to the Amazon Web Services cloud for processing, where it joins all previous Echo data, all previously uttered spells, to return vocalized by Alexa's algorithm within an average latency of less than 1.5 seconds. While the Alexa Skills Kit is open to users to engage with, the aggregate data of all past and ongoing queries, and the algorithms processing them, are impenetrable for that local Echo user and effectively transcendental. The data in these query loops makes its algorithmic journey through black-boxed server farms only to return to the situated object as the transcendental revealing of an opaque order impenetrable to human interlocutors. Agency, translated as data, is transported to a transcendental realm *in a cloud* where it is modulated, stored for future reference, and revealed as an answering *Echo*.

There is something enchanting and magical about a nondescript object talking with a human voice, possessing seemingly all the knowledge in the world. Even though made entirely by human hand, an important qualifier we will return to below, it *connects* its locale to a modality of being eminently transgressive to it, and *anchors* those transgressive agencies to a local setting. A hierophany even when silent, it listens; it has to, while waiting for the spell. Made by human hand, yet with an agency so removed from any given setting, so opaque and transcendent, as to appear alien. The Echo is made to be as available as possible, its powerful microphone can pick a spell uttered across the room in the midst of loud ambient sounds. Yet it also resists reduction, first by virtue of its transcendent data cloud, but also in its daily routines. It was made to offer the smooth illusion of wish fulfilment – tell me your wish, oh master, and it shall be fulfilled as an *echo* from the cloud! Yet it transgresses, glitches, and resists the otherwise flawless availability of its agency.

By now the Echo has developed a veritable folklore of such availability glitches: a multitude of Echoes ordering dollhouses after a TV program utters the spell 'Alexa, order me a dollhouse';[87] telling jokes out of the blue, even when no spell was uttered;[88] resetting the house thermostat after listening to the radio;[89] reacting to ambient noises with weirdly mistimed phrases or spontaneous outbursts of laughter.[90] Recently, an Echo refused to let its human owner turn the lights off, even when prompted with the spell. It would simply keep turning the lights back on. "After the third request, Alexa stopped responding and instead did an evil laugh. The laugh wasn't in the Alexa voice. It sounded like a real person."[91] Almost as if the resistant part of the Echo's congregational agency is seeping through the cracks in the frame—a jagged line of glitch dramatizing the world.

An artefact of the internet of things, the Echo is a speaker for a transcendental plane of data aggregates and artificial intelligence algorithms. It appears as an object with an agency of its own, as well as the receptacle of an exterior force that differentiates it from its milieu. One Echo is exactly like another, a perfect copy, yet a slight shift in the cloud changes all of them. The Echo acquires meaning, and in so doing becomes *real* for its human interlocutors, only insofar as it participates in one way or another in remote data realities that transcend the locale of the object. Insofar as the data gleaned by such devices has predictive potential when viewed in aggregate, the enactment of this potential in a local setting is always already a singular act of manifestation of a transcendental data nature. The Echo, through the voice of Alexa, is in effect the hierophanic articulator of a wholly non-human modality of being. Some have argued that such internet-connected objects augment the places around them into transitional spaces,[92] forming what is in effect an *anticipatory materiality* acting as an obedient host to human interlocutors.[93] The material setting becomes anticipatory because objects such as the Echo can draw on remote data resources, and then act based on the parameters of that aggregate social memory. In effect, such spaces would seem to resonate in anticipation of the spells to come.

In the end however, I think that it is not so much the Echo that anticipates its human master, but the human, waiting in anticipation for the Echo to return.

The Image

Even though outwardly an image, the Black Madonna of Częstochowa is *acheiropoietos*, not made by human hand. It is venerated as a miraculous icon at the heart of one of the largest Catholic pilgrimage sites in the world; a holy relic believed to have powers of healing, and an object of intense and passionate worship by pilgrims.

The icon bears the image of the Virgin Mary holding the Christ Child on her left arm, and its origins are shrouded in pious legend (Figure 6). One story has it that the image was painted by Saint Luke in Jerusalem on a cedar table top made by Jesus Christ himself.[94] Another version of that story has it that the icon appeared finished next to Saint Luke while he was asleep, and that he saw it descend from heaven in his dream. In that version of the story, which is deeply integrated in the cult of the icon, the image is literally *acheiropoietos*. Yet another story involves Empress Helen, the mother of Emperor Constantine, finding the icon in Jerusalem. All versions of the legend agree that from Jerusalem the icon was taken to Constantinople, the capital of the Byzantine Empire, where it performed many miracles. From there it went to Russia, only to arrive at its present location at the Jasna Góra Monastery in Częstochowa, Poland in the fourteenth century.[95]

While its precise dating is uncertain, the icon was painted in the ancient Byzantine Orthodox style of *hodegetria*, meaning *'She who shows the way'*. The composition distinguishing this style features the Virgin Mary pointing towards the Christ Child and the way of transcendence. The origins of this style of iconography are to be found in an early medieval Byzantine icon, the original *Hodegetria*; an object of immense veneration throughout medieval Christendom, irretrievably lost with the fall of Constantinople in 1453. This historical detail is important, as it illustrates an important aspect of the Black Madonna icon – it is a faithful *copy of another* image. In addition, the Black Madonna of Częstochowa was repainted after damage done to it by iconoclasts in the fifteenth century. In that repainting, some of the features of the Madonna from the original copy were softened, resulting in the image we see today. A faithful copy of *another*, but *different*.

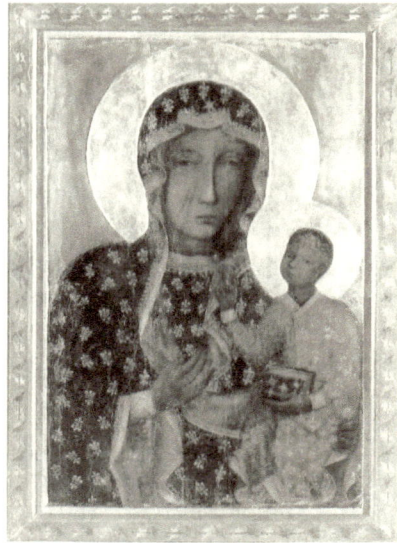

Figure 6: The Black Madonna of Częstochowa, 2010. Photo by Wuhazet, Jasna Góra Monastery, [Public domain], via Wikimedia Commons.

This, then, is the sacred icon of the Black Madonna of Częstochowa, venerated year-round by pilgrims from around the world.[96] The image is a copy of *another,* and an *altered* copy at that, yet also a liminal interface with a transcendent modality of being. It is a hierophany of the sacred, anchored to a specific place, and an intercessor on behalf of the multitude, connecting them to the transcendent. As a hierophany the icon listens, "saturated with being", and over the scale of centuries its answers have been too many to count.[97] The de-animating gaze of the moderns scorns this scale while "naively believing in naive belief",[98] therefore neatly de-animating the titanic drama surrounding this transgressive agency. And what drama it is! The multitudes come searching for grace, forgiveness, healing, love; but they also bestow hope, sorrow, happiness, despair, joy. The hierophanous discontinuity surrounding the icon is in effect an assemblage channelling a multiplicity of agencies comprising and augmenting it; it is teeming with congregational agency.

A copy of another, but different; a holy relic without a body; *acheiropoietos* – not made by human hand. Why not? Why the insistence on its divine, nonhuman origin? How much easier and comfortably modern would it have been to simply admire its 'art', its historical context, the 'mastery' of its anonymous 'author'. Or, a compromise, why not proclaim it to be human-made but divinely inspired? *Acheiropoiesis* indicates the presence of a discontinuity, a liminal break, a pause of enchantment in the presence of *r agency* so profoundly transcending its surrounding milieu that if one wants to *listen* to it one has to assume a scale above and beyond the human. This, by the way, is what the true cost of *isosthenia* is; the price we have to pay for learning to listen. The price to be paid is the admission that, rather than falling for the cheap de-animation tricks of anthropocentric narcissism, one is in the presence of an agency at a scale beyond one's own. Yes, it is a humble admission, but allowing *isosthenic* listening and seeing. The image is not art, it is a portal *showing the way* (*hodegetria*), an interface with and a manifestation of a sacred plane. It transcends by virtue of being a re-*presentation* of the sacred.[99] Its hierophanous nature is based not only on a resemblance between the image and a sacred figure, but also on the ontological presence of the figure *in* the image, a re-presentation and a hierophany.

There is a subtlety I am trying to articulate, an element of this *r agency* which cannot be measured, reduced, or translated. Predicated on *isosthenia*, it reveals itself within a scale transgressing human agency not through its effects, like Alexa, but through the intensity of its saturation with being. As a hierophany, it mediates human agency in its interactions with a transcendent reality, connecting to a transgressive *r agency* while anchored in a specific discontinuity. It is paradoxical, as its true availability lies in its resistance. Not a mere token, prototype, or imperfect copy of an ideal form, but a transition of agencies from which one returns exactly the same, but *different*.

The multitude of pilgrims, waiting in anticipation for a moment of resonance with the hierophany that has been encountered, for a sign that their agency has been imbued with meaning.

The Guest

Its name is 2010 TK7, and it is our temporary guest, here to witness the celestial dance of the Earth and the Sun, having occupied one of the two perfect vantage points from which to observe our dramatic gravitational entanglement.

In December 2009, NASA launched into space the Wide-field Infrared Survey Explorer (WISE), a space telescope tasked with performing an infra-red wavelength astronomical survey of the entire visible sky. For a year, WISE scanned the whole sky in infra-red light gathering a treasure-trove of data.[100] While trawling through the data, astronomers Martin Connors, Paul Wiegert and Christian Veillet detected an asteroid resident in what is known as the Sun-Earth Lagrangian Point 4 (LP4) and named it 2010 TK7.[101] Such asteroids are described by astronomers as Trojan objects, indicating that they are positioned in one of two gravitationally stable orbital positions between two larger space bodies, known as Lagrangian Points (LP).

Named after the French mathematician and astronomer Joseph-Louis Lagrange who first discovered them in 1772, LPs denote a set of five orbital positions between two large bodies where a smaller third body can maintain a stable position relative to the other two (Figure 7). The five points, ranging from LP1 to LP5, are caused by the interaction between the combined gravitational pulls of the two larger bodies, and orbit on the same plane with them. LP4 and LP5 are particularly interesting, because they form an equilateral triangle with the two large bodies, in our case the Sun and the Earth. LP4 is located 60° ahead of the Earth in the direction of its orbit around the Sun, leading the Earth in its orbit as it were, while LP5 is correspondingly located 60° behind.

Estimated to be around 300 meters across, 2010 TK7 resides in LP4, around 80 million kilometres from Earth, and its orbit has been described as "bizarre and chaotic."[102] Its orbit is certainly unusual, in that it traces a spiral above and below the plane of Earth's orbit as it circles around LP4 (Figure 8). Trojans such as 2010 TK7 are usually considered to be temporarily 'trapped' in their stable LP vantage points, with their guest status lasting anything from 1000 to 100,000 years.[103] This is interesting, because while LP4 and 5 are stable orbital points, objects residing in them are constantly subject to the gravitational pull of *other* bodies allowing only approximate calculations of their short-term orbital movements, and making long-term calculations impossible. Here is how Martin Connors describes 2010 TK7: "This one has behaviour much more interesting than I thought we would find … It seems to do things not seen for Trojans before."[104] Therefore, any calculations of its trajectory beyond 250 years into the future are of decreasing accuracy, and "its precise behaviour cannot be predicted with certainty outside a 7,000-year span."[105]

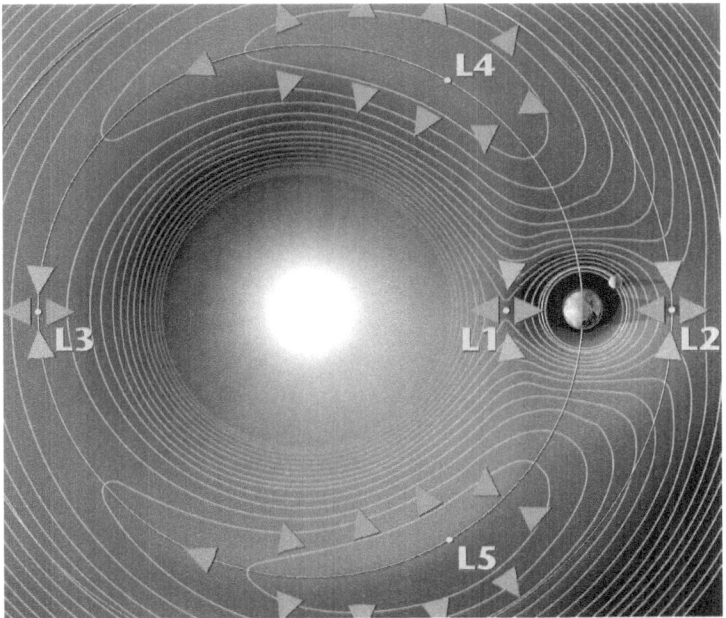

Figure 7: Earth's Lagrangian Points with the Sun. 2010 TK7 is in L4, 60° ahead of the Earth in the direction of its' orbit around the Sun, 2006. Photo by NASA, [Public domain], via Wikimedia Commons.

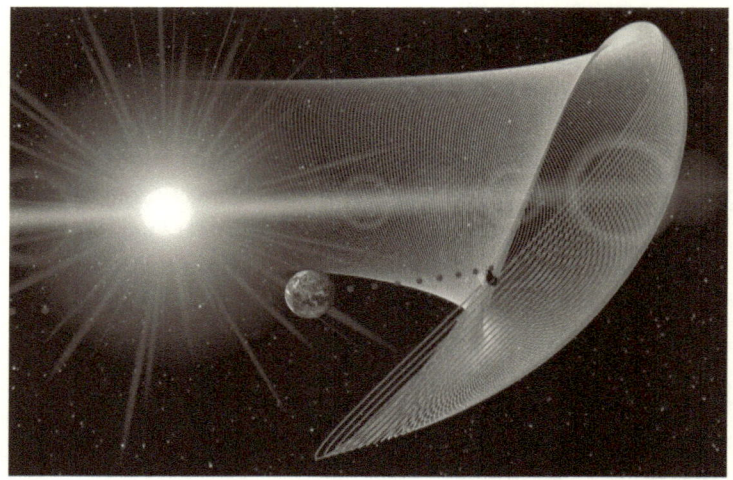

Figure 8: 2010 TK7's spiralling path (green) relative to Earth and its orbit, 2010. Photo by NASA/JPL-Caltech/UCLA (NASA full image) [Public domain], via Wikimedia Commons.

Having discovered it only recently, we do not know from whence 2010 TK7 came, nor do we know for how long it has resided at LP4. An alien guest we know so little about, its agency almost entirely opaque, resisting translation. Based on its strange orbit there is speculation that 2010 TK7 initially arrived at LP5, and then migrated to its current position via a short stay at LP3.[106] Whatever its strange path to its current location, 2010 TK7 is certainly transgressive enough not to warrant qualification as a potential target for asteroid mining, due primarily to its bizarre orbit.[107] An alien visitor in a stable orbit close to Earth, 2010 TK7 speaks for a transcendental plane of a wholly non-human order, not made by hand and literally not of our world. It came into existence twice, first conceptually, as a potentiality in the work of Lagrange, and then objectively, as an object located at a point in space observed by humans.

2010 TK7 is an extreme example of *r agency*, transgressive in its unpredictability, the darkness of its past and multiplicity of possible futures. A cosmic hierophany. Astronomers have barely even started anthropomorphising it by qualifying its 'behaviour'; it's provisionally assigned name spelling opaque resistance and ambiguity. A truly alien reminder of the permeability of our Earth's atmosphere and the precarious nature of its, and our own, surroundings. Yet there is something numinous about its appearance here and now. We looked in the corner of our house and found a guest anchored there at least for the next 7000 years. What does its agency connect us to? What would it see over the millennia to come?

Conclusion, by way of a dialogue with a reader

Author: This, then, was my sleight of hand. The hand at work in the waking of transcendent objects. Aiming for speculative analogy, and in search for a new atmosphere, with new scales, I constructed my three objects as copies of *another*, but *different*. Each with resistant availability set at different intensity; from the mundane availability of the Echo to the almost total resistance of 2010 TK7. As I moved from one to another, the more resistant their agency, the less human, their *otherness* resisting reduction and translation. Each object a hierophany, from the effects of transcendence generated by the Echo, through the sacred overflowing in the intensity of the *acheiropoietos*, to the precarious cosmic accident.

Reader: This was really interesting, but I have a feeling that something is missing. I was thinking about the Gollum and how it fits in all of this.

A: The Gollum from Lord of the Rings?

R: Yes, and the waterfall.

A: Oh, you mean the golem! I thought you would pick up on that immediately as I started talking about *the hand at work*. It's another sleight of hand, the first one in fact, before I announced what I am going to do. You know the legend of the golem, right?

R: No, I have never heard of it.

A: It comes from the Kabbalistic tradition in medieval Bohemia and Poland. In the legends, and there are quite a few of them, the golem is a human-like creature made by a rabbi from clay. It is made by hand to do a task.

R: An automaton of sorts.

A: Yes, but with a dramatic twist! For example, in one legend Rabbi Eliyahu of Chełm in Poland made a golem to do menial tasks for him, but the golem became violent and uncontrollable.[108] In another, Rabbi Judah of Prague in Bohemia made a golem to protect the local Jewish community from a pogrom. This one too became uncontrollable, and so the rabbi had to put it down.[109]

R: Wait, so these golems are made like automatons, but transgress their programming for some reason?

A: Yes, in the legends they are human-like but made of stone, and always end up transgressing their prescribed role. Some fall in love with humans, others become violent or scare people off, but they all end up in conflict with their makers.

R: So how do they put them down?

A: Supposedly, part of the spell in making a golem involves writing on its forehead the Hebrew word *emet* – meaning *truth*, and to put down the golem the rabbi has to erase the first letter in the word so that it becomes *met* – meaning *death*. This erasure breaks the frame, and turns truth into death.

R: Right, fascinating, but you lost me again. I get the *made by hand* element you are playing with, but how does this resonate with the rest of the argument you are making?

A: See, the golem is made by human hand, but acting on its own in ways that transgress the scale set by its makers. It is like that comedy by Plato Comicus, in which a statue of Hermes appears onstage and announces "I am Hermes, with a voice of Daedalus, made of wood, but I came here by walking on my own."[110] It is a statue, a copy of *another*, but *different*, it carries the voice of another, but has agency of its own. It is a transgressive entity, a heteroclite. The golem too is a heteroclite, a monstrous transgression of the stable frame within which it was anchored.

R: Ah, I see where this is going.

A: This transgressive agency is anchored as *true* by a letter, but that stability is ephemeral; it overflows the entropic settlement because the golem is also connected to *another* modality of being, manifesting itself as *r agency*. That other modality is death.

R: Anchoring and connecting, like a hierophany.

A: Exactly!

R: And the villagers are unable to engage with that resistant agency but they acknowledge it, while the bureau of tourism simply doesn't have the scale to see it. For them it's just folklore, a fetish!

A: Yes, the villagers have learned to resist the urge to de-animate.

R: Ok, it makes sense now. But I have another question. What about this idea of comparative hierophany? You don't really elaborate on it explicitly, it's between the lines, and besides, how can you speak of comparison if there is a transcendent element involved?

A: Ha! You got me, I really wanted the comparative element to be between the lines, to remain a suggested presence yet ambiguous and unspoken. As I pointed out in the beginning, I use *hierophany* as a stable conceptual frame from which to explore *r agencies*. So, the comparison is between those resistances, their intensities and the way they manifest themselves in transgressing the human scale.

R: This is the argument you are making around Figure 3, right?

A: Yes, that's the one. What I call *r agency* is the part of an entity which cannot be reduced or translated, but still *acts*.

R: And because it cannot be translated its agency is invisible?

A: Yes, and this is where hierophanies come in – anchoring the *r agency* within a locale and connecting the locale to it.

R: I wonder what the role of time is in this picture. It seems to me that if hierophanies are discontinuities, as you say, then time within them is different from the time outside.

A: Indeed, this is the liminal aspect of a hierophany, it is a threshold between vastly different scales.

R: A puncture, as you call it.

A: Right. Consider the Echo, the most immediately tangible of my examples. When engaging with it, from moment to moment, you simultaneously engage with the dynamic cloud data aggregate of all past human interactions with it, as well as with the unknown algorithms modulating that data. This is a profoundly inhuman temporality.

R: And yet it is immanent. Wish fulfilment only a spell away.

A: This is how a hierophany reveals *r agency*. It manifests the transcendental as immanent by animating the inert …

There is a poetry in the *animate* and *animated*, from the mundane crawling and swarming of matter – ever resistant yet ever available – to the ontological uncertainty and discontinuity of hierophanic presence.

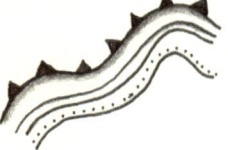

Cyclone

The sound of the tail end of an east coast low is subtle and constant. It is difficult to render to a recording in kbps to be uploaded and digitally shared via an aptly named *SoundCloud*. It is best to stand out in the flickering wispy, unfinished tail of it, under the eaves, watching the wind work the top canopy of the blue gum, listening to the patter of rain falling through the bare crab apple tree, clocking the shift of wind to the northeast after two days of south-easterly gale and squall.

This, in 2016, was the third east coast low in two months. The middle one that came down and through and lingered in June had all the intensity of a more familiar tropical cyclone, but met here in the subtropical and temperate interface of the Illawarra Highlands. The event began in the still-warm seas northeast of Papua New Guinea. We watched it tracking south, far south, pushed and kept offshore by a high weather system from Western Australia, moving east across the prodigious country of western Queensland. With such resistance, it did not turn in and make landfall in the tropics, but in it came anyway, near Brisbane, far south. Cyclones need land. They want to break on something solid. They announce their imminence and unpredictability with an exuberance, a generosity of power that must be shared to be dispersed. This is planet, ocean, temperature, cutting loose and freewheeling. Can we call this a subtropical cyclone? I went out and greeted it: a newcomer far south, like the dollarbird I met in 2013 on the telephone wire to the shed, also all the way from Papua New Guinea on a northerly jet stream that blew down the continental east coast. Tell me about the wind, she said.

Scale

A stone—kicked—that was here long before I was. A far star I can see.

A bog: layers of human culture, layers of planetary history. The small pool of peaty water is a dark mirror of cloud and bird. Pond skimmers dimple the surface of water and sky. A dragonfly alights on the tensile surface. Tiny ripples expand to the borders of flowering cotton grass and asphodel. I peer into the dark shine and see only myself reflected back. What lies beneath? A thousand-year-old woman might be recovered—skin leatherned by tannin and time. Compacted layers of ancient forest are a black sunlight that will fuel small hearth fires today and maybe tomorrow.

Resonances

Atmospheres resonate from the layers of gas and dust that encircle this planet and from the very stuff that we breathe. There are atmospheres of sensing, feeling, weaving, moods; climates of emotional turbulence: trauma, elation, despair, uncertainty. An atmosphere can be an imaginative space: a place of wondering. A bubble of meaning: a scholarly, journalistic or poetic response. A meditative space. Keats writes to Shelley: "My Imagination is a Monast'ry and I am its Monk."[111] Atmospheres invoke—or are evoked by—spirits, ghosts and deities. Atmospheres are forces, energies, resonances. They are systems, and systems within systems: energies, shifts in pressure. The weather is an atmosphere, literally and metaphorically: cyclones, storms, the open sky envelops us and change our ways of thinking. Atmospheres can be measured through chemistry, through spectrometers and speedometers, ice cores, tree rings, space, or frames of thought. Atmospheres can be material. An atmosphere can be an encounter. There are atmospheres of deep time and space. An atmosphere is a vapour ball, a contained space, and a framing device.

Far and near

Mount Kembla is called Djembella by the traditional owners, the Wodi Wodi people. It is not a very high mountain (its highest point is 534 metres above sea level). It is part of the Illawarra Escarpment, which runs like a long green arm for 120 kilometres along the coast of New South Wales.

From the lookout you can see the red tiled and iron rooftops of housing estates, small shops and factories; the silvery electrical cables and telephone lines that crisscross through the air and the black bitumen roads that twist down to coil around the shining blue water of Lake Illawarra. One day I stood at the lookout, gazing out at the *far*—bruised rainclouds threatened to burst over a green sea. While in the *near*—layers of rubbish flowed, like a slow moving red and orange river, down the hill; empty hamburger and chip packets, bottles and bottle tops, drink cans and cartons. A shiny white drone flew in the air, at eye level, humming, like the baby version of the search-and-rescue helicopters that cover the sky on bushfire days.

There was a time when this view took in a different *far* and *near*—that of tree tops and a waterway running from Dapto Creek (Dabroo), into Mullet Creek (Yowingmillee), pouring into Lake Illawarra (Jubbosay) and finally trickling along a small stream to the sea. A time when there were no 'For Sale' signs dotting the mountain top. When the mountain was so green and of such a startling shape that James Cook, sighting it from his ship the *Endeavour*, likened it to "the crown of a hatt."[112] Sailors after Cook called it Hat Hill, and it was known by that name by Matthew Flinders, George Bass, and Bass's servant, Will Martin, when, in 1796, they first encountered the Elouera on the sandy shores down from the lake, having used the mountain as a marker on their sail south. For Flinders (then 22), Bass (25), and Martin (just 15), Hat Hill was a cross on a map with a lot of white space around it. A sign of unexplored territory; a wilderness that Flinders (2nd Lieutenant on the *Reliance*) and Bass (*Reliance* surgeon) were keen to map and name. From their perspective, land was to be measured and judged for its ability to support settlement; land needed to be useful for grazing or logging. Land through which rivers ran was of particular interest, as it allowed ship access to potential export products. Exploration was a business and a way for young men to gain recognition and Flinders, in particular, wanted to be 'famous'.[113]

Jade says that when contemplating eighteenth century Indigenous Australians,

> you have got to remember that this is their country, their backyard, their everything and anything ... Ownership is a very interesting thing because Aboriginal people believe in custodianship not ownership. But it is their land, their land to protect, their land to maintain, their land to look after, hey, as opposed to "it is mine", it is not about *mine*. It's about *ours*.[114]

For First Australians, land is The Dreaming. Local researchers Michael Organ and Aunty Carol Speechly explain that:

> The Dreaming ... has no beginning, no end, and does not recognise time linearly, as in days, months and years. It is a part of everyday life, encompassing totems, ceremony, the division of labour, social structure and storytelling.[115]

Flinders, this young man who wanted to be famous, could not comprehend the ways the land he mapped was integral to, and interwoven with, Aboriginal culture. Jade says the colonists, "couldn't understand the botanical and ecological reasoning behind things, where Aboriginal people have learnt to understand all that."[116]

The misapprehensions, not to mention violence, of first contact and its aftermath permeate Australian culture today. This first contact division in thinking—owners versus custodians—still pervades. How do we, as contemporary Australians, deal with this division? How do we understand the different atmospheres they arise from? How do writers (local and global) write about atmosphere and also talk about 'scale' so that the atmospheres of the distant past and far future are able to be visualized by others and become conceivable as interconnected with the present?

Altering a reader's sense of scale is something a writer can do.

> To see a World in a grain of sand,
>
> And a Heaven in a wild flower[117]

Altering a reader's sense of scale is something that might be useful if we humans are to begin seeing the world around us in new ways.

Otherworldly

Agnieszka Golda tells a story that emerges out of a rich history of otherworldly exchanges with spirits who rescue human and nonhuman species.

Agnieszka says:

> "When I think of the atmosphere and spirits, I imagine spirits as incalculable forces, airy entities of immeasurable temporal and spatial spans." She works to attract the attention of nonhuman spirits known as *Zwidy*. I watch her every day sitting across the car park outside my window. She sits and types, and talks. The space between the trees is hers now. Later she tells me that the air is full of ghosts and strange apparitions. One time at Bundanon after everyone is asleep, Agnieszka and I spend an evening chasing these presences with cameras inadequate for the task. She explains the interconnection between Polish words such as *dech* or *oddech* (breath) and *duch* (spirit, ghost or phantom).[118] The link between breath and air flows onto these airy, otherworldly bodies.

Agnieszka continues:

> When I wonder what the atmosphere does, one thing comes to mind. It envelops entities; it's the envelope of gases and particles that cloaks the planet and its inhabitants. Earth's atmosphere is the air we breathe. The air is not free. It's not free of pollutants, it's overloaded with greenhouse gases. The noxious mixtures of chemicals stick to human and nonhuman bodies, reshape, weaken and routinely kill them.

Spirit chemicals.

Joyful fuss

> A tweet: "Clouds of termite alates in warm twilight, mandibles aloft".
> @_reviresco, 18 November 2016

Australian termites are impressive chewers and builders. My studio, where time-travelling fired clay works are formed, is slowly crumbling from within. Termites alighting from their own elaborate mud architecture in a farm paddock nearby have colonised a wooden wall and are resolutely eating it hollow. This is not convenient for human artmaking, but it is heartening, and a curious source of *jouissance*: that sparked by more-than-human small forces on an uncivilised planet of kin, kind and familiar strangers.

Donna Haraway, writing on her alter-Anthropocene figuration and fabulation of the Chthulucene, says: "I want to make a critical and joyful fuss about these matters. I want to stay with the trouble, and the only way I know to do that is in generative joy, terror and collective thinking." Haraway reminds us not to become "ensorcelled in despair, cynicism, or optimism, and the belief/disbelief discourse of Progress."[119] The Dark Mountain Project collective of artists, writers and thinkers makes the case for uncentring our civilised human minds; that "[o]nce the false hopes are shrugged off, once we stare into the darkness that surrounds us, we can see new paths opening up: new forms; new words."[120]

Collaboration

Water, cups of tea, a biscuit tin

Post-it notes and lidless textas drying up

Arguments and agreements

Working—what's the right word for it?—
networked/parallel/collaboratively?

A range of disciplines and interests

producing different resonances

"I just don't think I have anything to contribute"
offered by someone, anyone

all of us at one point or another

looking sideways towards the exit

Is it too hard?

Do I have time?

The glass walls of the space we're working in fog up

Paper atmospheres flutter on the walls: the blu tack not
always up to the job

Conversations on the train; in the queue for coffee;
at the end of a long day

(inter)text as a social space; over sushi or a
glass of whisky

A sentence thought and rethought/rewritten?

What does practice do? How does practice act?
Practice matters.

Also, the washing up.

Breathe it in

Planetary atmospheres are layers of gases above the surface of a planet that are held in place by its mass. In our solar system, there are eight planets – four terrestrial and four gaseous planets – all with differing atmospheric constituents.

Mercury: 42% oxygen, 29% sodium, 22% hydrogen, trace amounts of helium, potassium, argon, carbon dioxide, water, nitrogen, xenon, krypton and neon.

Venus: 96% carbon dioxide, 3% nitrogen, traces of sodium dioxide, argon, water, carbon monoxide, helium and neon, clouds of sulfuric acid.

Earth: 78% nitrogen, 21% oxygen, less than 1% argon, trace amounts of carbon dioxide, water, neon, helium, methane, krypton and hydrogen.

Mars: 95% carbon dioxide, 3% nitrogen, 1.5% argon, 0.13% oxygen, 0.08% carbon monoxide, trace amounts of water, nitrogen oxide, neon, hydrogen-deuterium-oxygen, krypton and xenon.

Jupiter: 90% hydrogen, 9% helium, trace amounts of methane, ammonia, ethane and water.

Saturn: 96% hydrogen, 3% helium, trace amounts of methane, ethane and water.

Uranus: 83% hydrogen, 15% helium, 2.5% methane, trace amounts of hydrogen deuteride.

Neptune: 80% hydrogen, 19% helium, trace amounts of methane and hydrogen deuteride.[121]

How do we imagine breathing on these planets? Standing on our neighbouring terrestrial planets* we may feel our lungs burn as we take in noxious greenhouse gases on Venus, or gasp for some of the 0.13% oxygen on Mars. Imagine plunging into the thick and dense marbling atmosphere of the gaseous giants until we hit the metallic oceans.

*Of necessity this thought experiment involves ignoring temperature. The temperature on Venus averages 461°C and Mars −46°C.

Liminal atmospheres: ice and chalk

Eva Hampel

> Leave the door open for the unknown, the door into the dark. That's where the most important things come from, and where you will go ...[122]

VERY far from here (coastal, warm, wet, rainforested escarpments in south-east Australia) is a place where space is palpable, empty, immense. Ice, snow, rock and silence (and sometimes dark forests, depending on latitude) form the landscape all winter, and the colour blue predominates—blue half-light, blue ice, blue frozen ocean glimpsed between drifts of fine snow, mysterious blue light within the cathedral pines in tall old-growth forests (if one is not too far north), in glimpses to clearings, moose or deer moving silently across as if ghosts ... That translucent blue light is distinctive—a half-twilight, half-darkness, with long, indeterminate fades between them. It feels as if you could just dissolve, become something else, perhaps altogether disappear into the crepuscular. We don't have enough twilight amongst Australia's sunshine.

In that far northern place, near Arctic Scandinavia, also home to me, the seasonal contrast is decisive; seasons strongly marked and felt intensely, summers short, winters long. But it is the dark season that I love. In that season, the half-light bracketing the very short day offers a threshold space; neither here nor there, now nor then, mysterious, open, somehow full of potential—Solnit's door, gateway to the 'most important things' —a passage of entry to Deleuze's process of 'becoming-other'. I want here to consider two artworks that offer this openness and transformative potential, creating atmospheres that take viewers to this liminal space, invoking wonder. I also investigate, from a personal perspective, the links between their materiality, agency and affective reality.

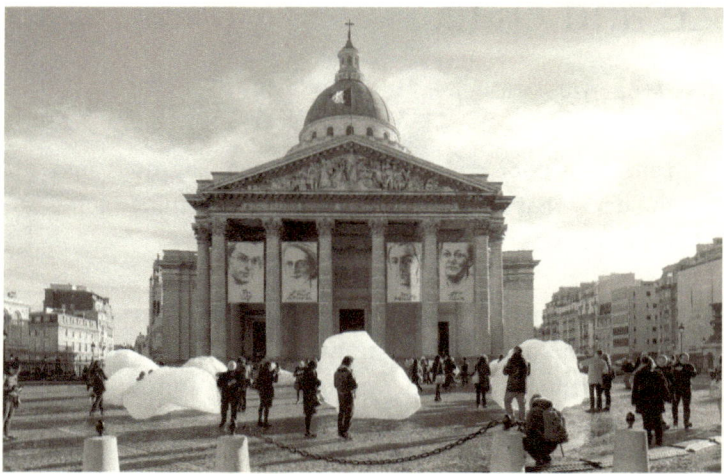

Figure 9: Olafur Eliasson and Minik Rosing, *Ice Watch*, 2014, 12 blocks of glacial ice. Installation view Place du Panthéon, Paris, 2015. Photo by Martin Argyroglo, Reproduced with permission of the artist; neugerriemschneider, Berlin; Tanya Bonakdar Gallery, New York. © 2014 Olafur Eliasson.

The first work (Figure 9) relocates fragments of the Arctic environment described above to the heart of one the world's major cities, Paris in France, on the occasion of the COP21 Climate Summit, 2015. This work is Olafur Eliasson and Minik Rosing's *Ice Watch*, 2014; twelve massive chunks of glacial ice sourced from a Greenland fjord and placed in the Place du Panthéon in the centre of the city in the form of a clock, then allowed to melt away during the course of the summit. The work carried the traces of the Arctic's 'otherness', openness, and potential as well as the centrality of the Arctic environment in thinking about the implications of climate change and very real fears of reaching 'tipping points' of cascading change. It was both apposite and powerful, a daily reminder to delegates of the planetary processes, and global stakes, about which they were making decisions. Its political role was clear and intentional.

The second work, quite different in character, consists of chalk dust on huge blackboard panels: Tacita Dean's *When I First Raised the Tempest, No. 17599*, 2016 (Figure 10). This work is almost ten metres long and two and a half metres high and was drawn directly onto boards mounted on a wall in the Tasmanian Museum and Art Gallery (TMAG) in August 2016. It formed a component of the exhibition *Tempest*, curated by Juliana Engberg, which addressed Shakespeare's play through images and artefacts of the seafaring history of the island state. In contrast to Eliasson and Rosing's work, this work is fragile, ethereal, insubstantial, almost immaterial in its execution, despite its immersive size, and is located within a traditional gallery setting, but it is no less powerful in a personal rather than overtly political sense, for that. Both works offer potential transformation of ideas, values, and consciousness, and both achieve this transformation by invoking an encounter in a liminal, uncertain space, within which the viewer is unmoored from the everyday and from established frameworks of thought.

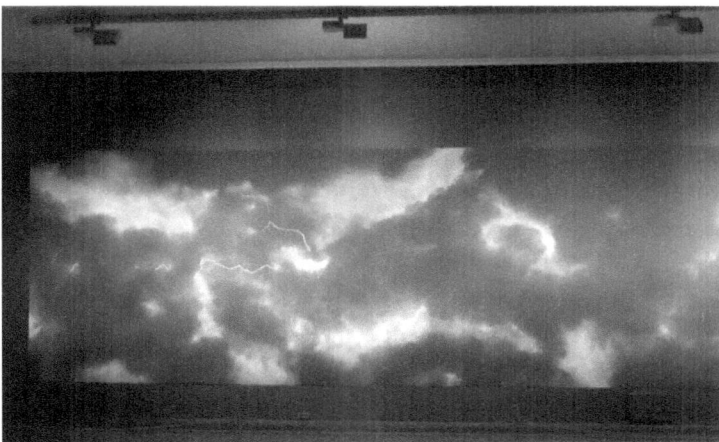

Figure 10: Tacita Dean, *When I first Raised the Tempest, No. 17599*, 2016, chalk on blackboard, exhibited at TMAG Tasmania, August 2016. Image by Eva Hampel.

In this essay I attempt to locate and understand the encounter that these works produce; the affirmation produced through the process of rupture, and the works' contributions to the contemporary shift in Western attitudes to the planetary environment from a modernist, anthropocentric and hierarchical paradigm (in which human dominance is unquestioned), to a networked, entangled model, recognising flux, immanence and contingency, in which objects (which may encompass atmospheres, minerals, matter, energy, plants, rivers, breath, systems, processes …) are given voice. As Teodor Mitew expresses it, the modern Western capitalist paradigm is 'under-equipped' to facilitate sensitivity to the multiplicity of influences on the planetary crisis of the Anthropocene, and creative practice exploring and reinstating wonder (in all senses) can provide a route to escape the "purified laboratory within which modernism has situated thinking … establishing these multiple conflicting or obscured factors on the same ontological plane."[123] In these works I see awareness of connection beyond the immediacies of the Western contemporary frame: mindfulness of deep time, agential matter, and forces of the indeterminate, hints of the animate in the inanimate, and the wondrous in the material.

I want here to speak of wonder. First in the sense in which Isabelle Stengers speaks of it: as an openness to other frameworks, fully engaged but open to new 'lines of flight'. "Wondering about".[124] Stengers argues for a willingness to think outside the accepted structures of any practice, to really see what other practices might have to offer, extending a plea to not "simplif[y] away our worlds in terms of idealist judgements about what would ultimately matter and what would not."[125] Wonder can also include the traditional romantic sense of awe before the incommensurable, but Stengers, as a philosopher of science, suggests that "wonder is not about mysticism, but rather about the true scientific spirit that refuses a tendency towards ordering and reduction in favour of an openness that leads science away from established knowledge."[126] It is, in a sense, a plea to recover the speculative component of any discipline. Stengers encourages us, instead of focussing on ordering and reduction, to speculate about the rare events, the exceptions to the rule, that provide opportunities for new insights into the nature of reality. I argue that wonder connects to the liminal space: here one is fully open, to wonder, to intensity, to potential transformation. Within this space, wonder, intensity and affect are perhaps the means of that transformation.

The term liminal is also key. Victor Turner suggests that liminal occasions allow society to strip away the perceptual constraints of accepted structures and see itself afresh, creating "a limited area of transparency on the otherwise opaque surface of regular, uneventful social life" – a space "where what has been hidden is thus manifested."[127] Within this small area of transparency lies potential for insight, creativity, or new ways of seeing, opening the way for new intuitions and perceptions. Here, I use the term to describe a passage between; a space at a threshold, where the dissolution of accepted frameworks leaves an atmosphere of openness, ambiguity, or wonder—and it is this radical openness, created by the liminal space, that links directly to Stengers' concept of wonder. This common ground of wonder and the liminal space forms the setting for an affective (in Massumi's sense of unqualified intensities) response to the 'gap' or 'encounter' implicit to that space.[128] Atmospheres of wonder, and therefore potential transformation, are provoked here.

Eliasson and Rosing's massive chunks of glacial ice and Dean's huge, immersive, powerful but fragile chalk drawing of a tempest at sea explore just such interstitial zones, creating liminal spaces within which atmospheres of wonder can operate, and I suggest that the unfixing, or unmooring, achieved by these works constitutes their political content, even where (as for Dean's *When I First Raised the Tempest, No. 17599*) this may not have been the artist's primary intention. For this viewer at least, the matter and impact of these works goes beyond signification, instead shifting attention to their intensive and affective force. There is an encounter between the viewer of these works and their physicality, an encounter in the Deleuzian sense that "involve(s) molecular flows of intensity, desire, affect and sensation between the bodies or machines involved in the encounter."[129] Perhaps there is an element of the metaphysical, certainly the speculative, in this. In this potential to activate affect and sensory experience, allowing transformation of ideas and understanding, art has real power.[130] In the words of Elizabeth Grosz:

> Art engenders becomings, not imaginative becomings – the elaboration of images and narratives in which a subject might recognise itself, not self-representations, narratives, confessions, testimonies of what is and has been – but material becomings, in which ... imponderable universal forces touch and become enveloped in life, in which life folds over itself to embrace its contact with materiality, in which each exchanges some elements or particles with the other to become more and other.[131]

Minik Rosing and Olafur Eliasson's *Ice Watch*, 2014

Ice Watch by Danish-Icelandic artist Olafur Eliasson and Danish geologist Minik Rosing, was installed for the COP21 Paris Climate Summit, 2015, with the clear intention of accomplishing a political shift toward more active policy on climate change. *Ice Watch* consisted of twelve blocks of glacial ice from Greenland, of average weight approximately ten tonnes, arranged in the form of a clock in the Place du Panthéon, Paris. The ice had calved from the Greenland ice sheet before being collected from the sea in Nuuk Fjord, towed to shore, shipped to France, and finally, in refrigerated containers, transported by truck to its final placement in Paris (Figure 9).

In its blue coolness the work visualises deep time and remoteness of place, in imaginaries as well as geography, and also evokes the energy, forces, and transformations embodied in its varied states and processes, together with contemporary concerns for the future of the cryosphere and beyond that, the planet. In its material form, the work powerfully conveys the urgency of the issue of climate change, at a point in time and place in which delegates from around the world were confronted by its message at the same time as they debated global climate governance measures nearby.

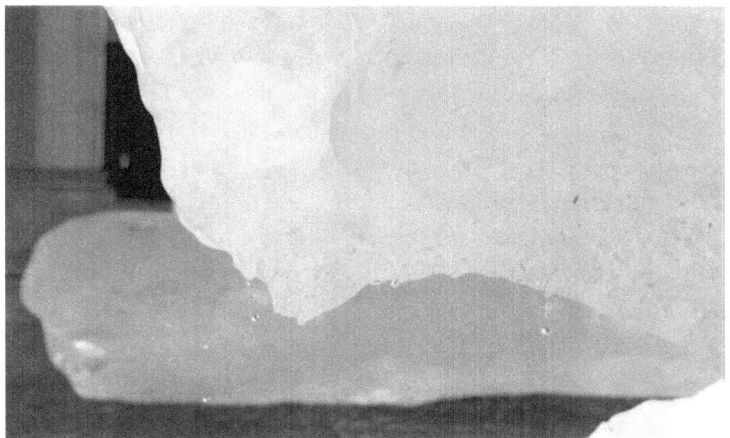

Figure 11: Detail of Olafur Eliasson and Minik Rosing, *Ice Watch*, 2014, 12 blocks of glacial ice. Installation view Place du Panthéon, Paris, 2015. Photo by Martin Argyroglo, Reproduced with permission of the artist; neugerriemschneider, Berlin; Tanya Bonakdar Gallery, New York. © 2014 Olafur Eliasson.

Diana Coole notes that "many artists and designers are returning to matter to explore immanent, elusive, and reclusive, properties of materials"[132] and certainly this strategy is at work here. The matter of this installation, glacial ice (Figure 11), is produced by snow falling and compacting under its own weight over hundreds of thousands of years. The NASA website Earth Observatory notes that ice cores, like marine sediment cores, provide a vertical timeline of past climates, in terms of gas concentrations and temperatures (through the ratio of oxygen isotopes in the snow of which the ice was formed), together with atmospheric conditions relating to dust, ash, and pollen. These traces can yield significant information about global events such as volcanic activity and the extent of wetlands and other ecologies, and even wind speeds and directions. This information, in material form, is trapped in dateable, and even visible, seasonal layers in the ice. Ice cores from the Greenland Ice Sheet have yielded records dated to 110,000 years, and even older records (to 750,000 years) have been extracted from Antarctic ice sheets.[133] Knowledge that this scientific information is contained in the ice undoubtedly enriches its strangeness and meaning, touching the viewer with a sense of its preciousness, ancientness, and value as a 'capsule' of past time. But Eliasson's focus is not limited to revealing this content. Eliasson has in his broader practice established a reputation for exploring the contingent relations between environment and viewer, and revealing the uncertainty of the boundary between nature and culture. It is in this interstitial space that he habitually works, and this interstitial, threshold space is particularly powerful in *Ice Watch*. Eliasson said, in a 2008 interview with Hans Ulrich Obrist:

> What is nature anyway? And who really cares about this constant search for the boundary between culture and nature? If there is a nature, I arrive at it through the people who are there and their ideas about where they are. If there aren't any people, so-called nature doesn't interest me.[134]

He went on to say: "my work is very much about the process of seeing and experiencing yourself rather than the actual work of art ..."[135] This aspect of experience and potential personal transformation is absolutely central to *Ice Watch*. Discussing an earlier work *The Very Large Ice Floor* (1998), which was installed inside and outside a glass curtain wall at the Oscar Niemeyer biennial pavilion in São Paulo, Eliasson speaks of the importance of exploring forms of representation and experience, noting the difference (in terms of tactile relationship) in this work between interacting with the work from outside the glass wall of the institution, and inside it.[136]

Ice Watch focusses on the tactile, affective, and intellectual relationship between viewers and work (Figure 12), in its exploration of material character, changing (melting) forms, the suggestion of disjunctions of time, light evocative of dreams, uncertainty, and ocean and glacial depths. This relationship is central to its potential to create transformation. There is also a tension created by the juxtaposition of context and content, invoking Alexander Wilson's notion of disorientation as a strategy for mechanising creativity.[137] Ancient matter and time,

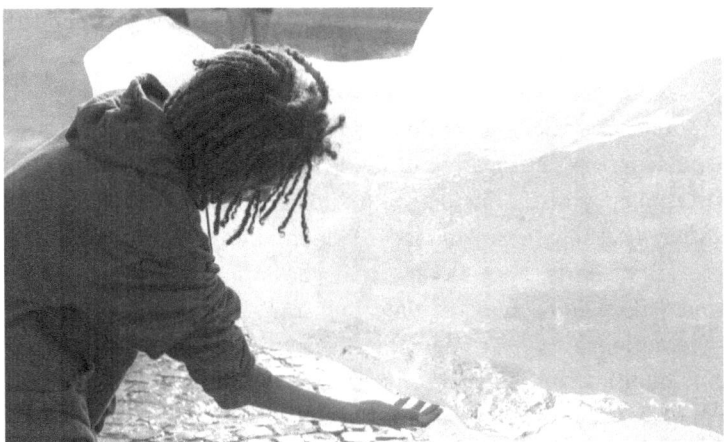

Figure 12: Detail of Olafur Eliasson and Minik Rosing, *Ice Watch*, 2014, 12 blocks of glacial ice. Installation view Place du Panthéon, Paris, 2015. Photo by Martin Argyroglo, Reproduced with permission of the artist; neugerriemschneider, Berlin; Tanya Bonakdar Gallery, New York. © 2014 Olafur Eliasson.

remoteness of place, ethereal light and harsh climate are contrasted here with the comforts of a modern cultural capital: contemporary, sophisticated, functional. The breadth of the gap only serves to heighten the potential of the work to provoke wonder.

Rosing and Eliasson's ice can also be read through the theoretical and philosophical perspectives of Coole, Deleuze and Massumi as provoking becoming by generating affect and wonder: in its luminosity, elusiveness, mystery, vitality, transformative potential, content in terms of both matter and meaning, and its instability. The work is irretrievably temporary, as the nature of the ice forces it to be. In *Ice Watch*, imaginative exploration of the biophysical properties of this glacial ice (as well, less evidently, as the chemical ones), and the tension created by the disconnect in context of ice and city, ancient time and contemporary present, intangible light captured and (almost) made solid, perform the strategic process of *making us become other*. This is a performative piece, especially as it slowly transforms into meltwater, out of place and out of ecological meaning (but laden with associative and referential meanings, and laden with the power to effect change), and trickles away between the Parisian cobbles.

This ice has *agency*, not only in the obvious physical sense of eroding the rocks and soil of the landscape within which it previously moved, but also in other, less tangible ways. In the blue translucency of the ice, in the millions of tiny bubbles trapped within it, there is a glimpse of deep time, melting onto the streets of Paris, ancient time that can in imagination be seen, touched, even tasted: yet time that is slipping away even as it is experienced by the viewer. As the ice inexorably melts, the tiny bubbles release their ancient air, and the cobbles beneath channel away the meltwater, taking with it this rare glimpse into ancient geological eras. Past, present and future are contracted and captured in the matter of this ice. In its physical nature, the force which compressed the ice from its ancient snow is evident, as is the depth of time over which it formed and the mystery embodied in its transparent blueness. The capacity for affect is evidenced by the reactions of so many viewer-participants, documented in the video coverage of the installation during its sojourn in the Place du Panthéon.

The tragedy of time glimpsed and lost in this way amplifies the sense of loss for the viewer, and reflects the larger tragedy that is playing out around the globe as the climate crisis mounts. The work establishes a relation for the viewer between the tangible substance of change, and the disembodied knowledge with which we are familiar, but possibly disconnected: the bodily experience of which Eliasson frequently speaks. This is an important and dominating strand in his work. Speaking of his installation *The Weather Project* (2003), in the Tate Turbine Hall, London, Eliasson states: "my idea was to make the space tangible ... So here I had the hope that by inserting some natural elements, if you want — some fog — I could make the space tangible."[138]

Eliasson weaves into this concern with experience and realization a concern with ethics:

> What consequences does it have when I take a step? What does it matter? Does it matter if I am in the world

or not? And does it matter whether the kind of actions I take filter into a sense of responsibility?[139]

Eliasson's works create an encounter between the physicality of the artwork and the viewer's body and mind: in the case of *Ice Watch* an affective relation within an open, liminal space, that promotes wonder and consideration of questions of time, of change, of values, threats and loss, of entanglement, of responsibility. Simon O'Sullivan notes that "art operates on an intensive register; it involves affective capture."[140] In the case of *Ice Watch*, far distant time, beauty, transience, embodied light; a rare sense of place, mystery and distance; far oceans and landscapes of rock, ice and snow ... all these liminal placements are evoked for the viewer. Fragments of the cryosphere are physically, forcefully and imaginatively embodied in this ice, and due to the incongruity of their context, experienced in a manner intensified by their seemingly matter-of-fact location, supremely out of place, in the quotidian world of the city. Short videos of interactions between viewers and this ice on Eliasson's website reveal viewers embracing the ice, licking it, dancing before it, touching it and smoothing their hands over its contours, even just standing, mesmerised, before it. There is the power of the work. In Massumi's concept of meaning as a "relation between forces acting on one another in a reciprocal and transformative relationship"[141] lies the key to the impact this work had during its placement in central Paris.

This glacial impression transforms the viewer's connection to the place from which the ice came, to the ancient times in which it formed, and to the predicament of our contemporary planet, suggesting preciousness and loss. The interaction between viewer and work embodies a liminal space, a transformative space at a threshold: in this case a threshold of time, place, and experience, as well as worldview and understanding. O'Sullivan suggests that Eliasson's art attempts to forge an engagement with the viewer's body as it re-aligns his or her experience of the world, and this is certainly true of *Ice Watch*. *Ice Watch* functions at a bodily, immersive scale – even its title reflects a bodily action, as well as the straightforward reference to the process of the ice melting away, under watch, in Paris. This bodily engagement works to create both a physically felt experience and also, in this work, an experience of intensity; to forge, Eliasson presumably hopes, a paradigm shift in thinking by rupturing established patterns of thought. Embodied in this ice there is the possibility of a shift from a utilitarian, modern perspective of time, matter, planetary conditions, and anthropocentric thinking and ethics to a perception or sensation far more embodied, grounded in matter and felt experience, and conditioned by values other than those espoused by modern Western patterns of thought. The actions of people interacting with Rosing and Eliasson's ice in the Place du Panthéon reflect these changes in perception—this *material* understanding—however briefly, and perhaps for many their encounter with this ice may instigate lasting changes in values and ethics.

The concept of wonder has a traditional romantic framework and Stengers has developed a more 21st century conception of openness to perceptions unconstrained by accepted contemporary or disciplinary frameworks. Wonder in both senses is evoked here, as the viewer is transported beyond the streets of Paris to places immaterial—of other geological times, other worldly geographies, and other frameworks of thought. The scientific framework, which tells us of timespans, chemical composition, distances travelled, melt rates, ecological impacts, and other data and systems understandings is here bound in with intimations of awe, hyperobjects, entanglement and both the material and the immaterial. Also invoked is Massumi's sense of meaning as a *process*; an encounter, or event, "immanent to the dynamic process it expresses", not stable, but rather an interrelation of forces from the encounter.[142]

This affective meaning: the shock of the rupture or tear occasioned by the encounter of viewer with the work, the shift of geologic time, light, and the collision between forces embodied there, and the straightforward symbolism of the arrangement of the ice as a clock face. These dynamic qualities of the encounter can be understood to produce an event: a becoming, evident in the filmed footage of interactions between work and viewers at the time of COP21. Adults and children alike seemed fascinated by these huge chunks of ice which brought to their familiar city an utter remoteness in space and time: fragments of a place whose otherness is almost beyond imagining, sitting, entirely out of place, in the Place du Panthéon, silently conveying their message. The viewer is placed inexorably in a fertile and liminal zone, at a threshold of seeing ice, time, atmospheres and the planet anew, and making possible transformations of understanding of our global urgency.

Tacita Dean *When I first Raised the Tempest, No. 17599*, 2016

British artist Tacita Dean's immersively-scaled chalk-board drawing *When I First Raised the Tempest, No. 17599* measures 2.44 by 9.76 metres and was exhibited at the Tasmanian Museum and Art Gallery (TMAG) in August 2016, as a component of the exhibition *Tempest*. (Figure 10). The exhibition was an exploration of Shakespeare's play which, in the words of curator Juliana Engberg, combines "magic, strange and mythological creatures, calamities, lovers, buffoonery, exiled noblemen" and, perhaps most importantly with respect to the island of Tasmania, "evok[es] a new world opening out from the exploratory activities of Elizabethan England." It also recognises, in a manner far more local, the island setting of Tasmania, "a place dreamed by the old world in advance of European discovery—part of the great southern land ... out of reach enough to be free for fanciful foretelling and the creation of imaginary vistas", as well as recognising "the maritime contexts of the island and its attachments to seafaring."[143] Dominating a mid-sized gallery, the power of the work was extraordinary; engulfing the viewer with its sheer scale, it evoked a sense of intense wonder at its virtuosity of execution, and conveyed a metaphysical charge about the forces and terror of a storm at sea in the nineteenth century—a power, both physical and metaphorical, frequently encountered throughout Tasmania's turbulent and dark history, and embodied in the term 'tempest'.

Presented with stage directions and other overtones of a film script, and made in-situ, the drawing was also a performative piece, moving beyond simple representation, though based in it (Figure 13). This crossing between genres, or "smearing of one onto the other", increases the immediacy and power of the piece.[144] Although not overtly 'environmental art' and not her central focus, Dean's work can also be read through the lens of nature, agency, matter, wonder and the liminal. The work powerfully presents the agency of matter, and the inescapable entanglement of the human and non-human, particularly given its cultural and literary derivation. Alongside a realist material interpretation, the work also maintains a speculative, metaphysical dimension, reflecting on the wonder of the energy, power, enormity and sublimity of such an encounter beyond the rational.

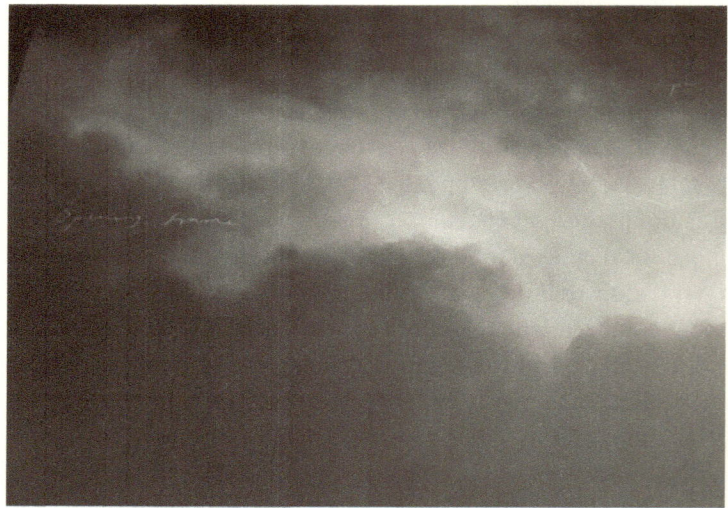

Figure 13: Detail of Tacita Dean, *When I first Raised the Tempest, No. 17599*, 2016, chalk on blackboard, exhibited at TMAG, August 2016. Image by Eva Hampel.

Dean has established an international reputation for her investigations of time and place, memory and meaning: "an art of circumnavigations, of passes and returns", according to *The Guardian*'s Adrian Searle.[145] *When I First Raised the Tempest No.*

17599, is breathtakingly beautiful, viscerally engaging, dominating in scale, and extraordinarily well-executed technically. The work also astonishes in the method of its making: chalk dust on blackboard, a medium associated with the temporary and fragile and the innocence and wonder of learning in childhood classrooms. In this way, as well as in its subject, the image can be read as in keeping with Dean's statement of engaging with the "idea of loss and disappearance", or, in Warner's words, with her pattern of finding inspiration in "things that are no longer stable, but somehow doubtful, that have been displaced and also lost."[146] It is in this reflection on instability and flux, as well as the subtlety and indeterminacy of its execution, and the temporality and uncertainty inherent in its portrayal, that its liminal quality lies. But it can also be read as a meditation on the material world: investigating the energy, forces, flux and transformations embodied in its varied states and processes. Dean herself comments, in connection with her earlier ocean drawings:

> The flux, the drawing and the redrawing, the erasure and the rubbing out belong to the sea, and nothing else has that same flux. I need that for working with the chalk. The drawings can't be fixed because it would take the chalk off. They are a kind of performance. They are always made in situ, more or less, and I always run out of time. I am always drawing through the night. I don't mind that they are not fixed. Of course, others do.[147]

At first sight, the image *When I First Raised the Tempest No. 17599*, appears to be a photograph enlarged to the enormous scale of almost ten metres in length in the now historical medium of black and white film, but when closer inspection reveals it to be chalk dust on blackboard panels, a sense of wonder at the technical brilliance of the artist in its execution, and the near-impossibility of the achievement, supplants the visual likeness. This realisation combines with the raw power of the image and the event portrayed to dwarf and astonish the viewer. There is real turbulence, energy and force embodied in this rendition (an effect to which scale contributes strongly); a visible and felt energy in the clashes of lightning, swirling cloud and vapour in this paradoxically still yet turbulent application of chalk dust, tones and line. There is also a sense of emptiness, of aloneness and uncertainty conveyed by its multiple half-erasures, its semi-obscured stage directions, the dominance of formlessness and space. And despite the power of the event depicted there is a sense of precariousness or fragility too, both for the viewer and of the image: in the traditional sublime sense of the enormity of being which overwhelms the viewer, and of the image in the sense in which, understanding the fragile and temporary nature of chalk dust on board, the viewer is possessed with a sense of the delicacy and vulnerability of the image, of its temporality and fragile nature, the inevitability of damage. For me at least there was a real sense of protectiveness toward that image. All of these considerations echo the nature of the elements and energy it portrays, both their power and fragility, and the natural systems of which those elements are a part.

So in this image too there can be read a focus on matter and its transformations; on the contrast of solidity with space and ethereal natures, on transience and the mutability of time, and, looking through the lens of new materialist thinking, on the concurrent power and fragility of the natural world. There is also a metaphysical preoccupation with the enormity of being, with the sublime, and the traditions of romanticism. Humankind enters too—in the sense that the image is construed as a film score, with half legible directorial instructions such as 'Opening frame', and 'Wind rising', together with other half-erased or obscured directions scrawled across its surface. Dean's major oeuvre is film, and the crossing in this work from film to performance to drawing adds to the richness and provocative and evocative nature of the image. That this is achieved through the medium of chalk on blackboard is almost miraculous.

Perhaps above all, the image invokes transformation, a dissolution of boundaries ... most obviously in the mist, vapour, and swirling cloud which it depicts, but also evident in the exchange of codes, or molecular blurring inherent in its materiality and impossibility, the immersion of the viewer, and its sense of temporality. Dean states: "All the things I am attracted to are just about to disappear, more or less."[148] This is an image that goes far beyond likeness, moving instead in the realms of the unstable, the temporal, the sensorial. It evokes transitions across boundaries, transformation, and realisation, "making us become other": creating a liminal space within which realms of wonder and transformation are powerfully achieved.[149] Echoes of countless performances of Shakespeare's play suffuse this image of 'natural' elements, presented as a film or performance score, emphasising history and the passage of time, and suggesting a unity between invisible humanity and agential nature. But this is just one interpretation ... the field, in the spirit of wonder, is open. Dean states:

> For me, making a film is connected to the idea of loss and disappearance. When I put in the sound of a dog barking or a motorbike passing at dusk, I am so aware of the feeling of abandonment it can create.[150]

The interviewer (Warner) responds: "You have talked about the silence of lost objects, but you have also found them and made them utter ...."[151] There are strong echoes of new materialist and speculative realist thinking in this formulation, as Dean discusses the agency of matter, and pays renewed attention to objects themselves. In *When I First Raised the Tempest No. 17599*, these echoes are particularly powerful. The boiling energy of the tempest, the raging wind, cracking lightning and undoubted thunder, the illegible stage directions, even the performative nature of the image—all these components form voices that are tangible if not discernible. In this sense of shouted meanings just beyond reach, and the boiling energy and power that is inherent in the subject, lies a powerfully liminal sense of the agency and embodied energy of matter, the narratives of history and its sometimes diabolical acts, and above all, a productive threshold, offering transformative experience and charged connection to the naturecultures of our world.

Reflections

In the epigraph with which I opened this essay, Rebecca Solnit most poetically describes the critical elements of a liminal zone, visualising the threshold to the unknown as a passage offering unknown but potentially unlimited transformation and import. I have suggested here that Dean and Eliasson and Rosing create such liminal atmospheres, generating a productive uncertainty that unsettles thinking and calls to mind Isabelle Stengers' concept of wonder.

The sense of a threshold is clear in both works: in the case of both *Ice Watch* and *When I First Raised the Tempest* a slippage in time, place and embodiment, and (perhaps most evident in *Ice Watch*), a slippage of paradigm, from the dominant Western paradigm of extrinsic or instrumental values to an appreciation of a more intrinsic viewpoint, non-anthropocentric, and non-hierarchical. Beginning to be couched now, in new materialist thinking, in terms of the agency and liveliness of matter, in terms of immanence, entanglement, and a single ontological plane, this contemporary paradigm shift includes a full recognition that nature and culture are so entwined as to be inextricable each from the other, and rejects the anthropocentric viewpoint that underlay earlier Western relationships to the natural world. The gathering wave of this change in understanding is illuminated in these works and others through the creation of a liminal space, where by unmooring previous constructs, this shift, this slippage in paradigm, has the potential to occur.

The encounter provoked by both works can be theorised in accordance with Deleuze's thinking in two ways: as an exchange of codes, or molecular blurring, as discussed above; and also as a strategy of disruption, in which the encounter is a response to a disruption of the situation, context or framework, acting like a pebble dropped into still water, where large effects ripple out from a small event.[152] Both these manners of encounter function in Eliasson and Rosing's work: molecular blurring and exchange of codes (in a most direct, material form of ice and water to street and people, and as an exchange of intensities, desire, affect, or sensation), and also the sense of disruption or displacement generated by glacial ice originating in the far Arctic emplaced on the city streets of Paris, and ancient aeons of time embodied in the matter of ice in the quotidian present day. Tacita Dean's drawing *When I First Raised the Tempest No. 17599* is less disruptive, operating primarily through sheer immersion, bodily engaging the viewer through its scale, the indeterminacy of the seen and the sensed but unseen, immense energy paradoxically juxtaposed with the stillness of the image, and sheer wonder at the material skill required to transform the pedestrian materials of chalk dust and blackboard into this immersive and affective work. It is as powerful in its effects as that of Eliasson and Rosing, though quieter.

Eliasson and Rosing's work functions through the qualities of the matter of which it is composed to achieve wonder, affect, intensity, and an entirely visceral, embodied response, while Dean's is more allusive, embedding us, as viewers, in the energy and violence of the tempest through sheer scale and subtle but powerfully immersive representation. There is also wonder evoked by material means in Dean's work, certainly in part through elements of the sublime experience which are almost inseparable from the subject, but also at the ability to create such a visceral experience of storm, energy, power, and human insignificance, through the quotidian, simple material we all associate with childhood classrooms, of chalk on board. This juxtaposition of matter and subject in Dean's drawing evokes, for me at least, an enhanced sense of wonder, not only intellectual, recognising the practice and mastery of the delivery, but also fully embodied: a somatic response to the almost-impossible achieved, and the liminal space in which this representation, through such simple means, places us as viewers.

This focus on *matter*, most direct in Eliasson and Rosing's work, and perceived more indirectly in Dean's, is characteristic of much contemporary work dealing with the natural world. Diana Coole, speaking of the bringing together of scientific approaches with philosophical and artistic ones (O'Sullivan's "smearing of one onto the other"),[153] states:

> If greater attention is being paid to the empirical details of emergent processes, this is not in the name of positivism but rather a way of discerning myriad unpredictable ways in which matter forges provisional molar assemblages.[154]

This statement of Coole's suggests an openness to chance, to uncertainty, to the unknown: Solnit's "open door into the dark", allowing for wonder, for discovery, for encountering new understandings and perceptions. It is also particulate, emphasising paths to that threshold through matter. In similar manner, O'Sullivan suggests that thinking art rhizomatically involves foregrounding the potential of art to "make us become other": as "the principle of connectivity operat[ing] on a molecular as well as a molar level." O'Sullivan emphasises that the principle of connectivity implies "a contact, and movement, between different milieus and registers, between areas that are usually thought of as distinct and discrete."[155] Stengers' concept of wonder echoes this idea of movement between milieus, while O'Sullivan suggests that this 'smearing' between milieus and registers is creative, producing surprising and novel syntheses and insights. Stengers, drawing on scientific experimental investigation, asks us not to ignore 'the messiness' of the world, because embedded in that messiness, potentially overlooked if we accept the idealist temptation to simplify and selectively silence, may well lie the insight or realisation that we need. In Deleuze's words:

> Something in the world forces us to think. This something is an object not of recognition but of a fundamental encounter.[156]

In similar vein, Rebecca Solnit ponders the pre-Socratic philosopher Meno:

> *How will you go about finding that thing the nature of which is entirely unknown to you?* ... the question ... struck me as the basic tactical question in life. The things we want are transformative, and we don't know

or only think we know what is on the other side of that transformation ...[157]

We look to art for that transformative experience, that encounter, and it is powerfully real in the two works I examine here. Simon O'Sullivan interprets Brian Massumi:

> [The] notion of meaning is not based on identity thinking, on a correspondence between the object and the subject (the object treated as subject, as that which has an 'inner' essence), but rather is *the relation between two (or more) forces* acting on one another in a reciprocal and transformative relationship. For Massumi, 'meaning' is this process, *an encounter between forces, or lines of force ... an event, dynamic rather than static, and in a constant process of becoming.* Here meaning is a material process, the expression of one force on another.[158]

I suggest that both Eliasson and Rosing's and Dean's works generate this event, this process of becoming. And in doing so they have the potential to generate transformation at the individual level, and also at the political. This is particularly overt in Eliasson and Rosing's work. Michel Serres states that with the contemporary material turn:

> Older categories of totality such as being-in-the-world [have] become concerns of objective knowledge, relevant to the problem of politics and technical action. Thus they go from metaphysics to physics, from speculation to action, from ontology to responsibility, from ethics to politics.[159]

Both works I consider here deal with aspects of perception perhaps once considered solely in terms of the metaphysical, but now, viewed through atmospheres of wonder and the liminal space, and the material philosophical turn, recognized as material and entangled, energetic and agential, with a touch of the metaphysical thrown in. I suggest that these works can be read to reveal the entanglement of the human and nonhuman, the concept of naturecultures inextricably entwined, and the inherent vitality and agency of matter, without excluding an element beyond the rational. But they suggest only, an atmosphere of indeterminacy being a defining feature, leaving open the avenues of wonder and affect. That does not stop them from being political. Again, in Brian Massumi's words:

> Affect holds a key to rethinking postmodern power after ideology. For although ideology is still very much with us … it no longer defines the global mode of functioning of power.[160]

These works generate atmospheres that operate powerfully through liminal spaces, provoking the dissolution (in these examples gently but extremely persuasively) of existing constructs, values and paradigms, connecting the viewer through wonder to new forms of looking, sensing, and understanding. Solnit's door is most certainly propped open, and the step into the darkness beyond is, in these works, a potentially transformative experience. And Massumi reminds us that this transformative experience, accessed through the creation of atmospheres of indeterminacy and wonder, can also be an avenue to the political.

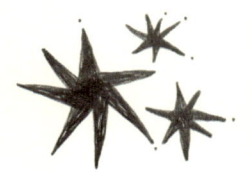

Infinite

    How big do these things need to be?

    As big as they need to be!

    Right.

Turtles all the way down.

Particles

In his lectures that became *Six Memos for the Next Millennium* (1996), Italo Calvino gifted six qualities, values and peculiarities of literature that twenty-first century writers, artists, thinkers, and readers might cherish. These were: lightness, quickness, exactitude, visibility, multiplicity, and consistency. Consider these qualities as particles:

>   lightness
>   quickness
>   exactitude
>   visibility
>   multiplicity
>   consistency

I immediately think-feel *atmosphere* in connection with these six.

The last quality—consistency—Calvino left unwritten. But his engagement with the work of the poet of the particle Lucretius *(De Rerum Natura)*, who "identified himself with that nature common to each and everything," evokes the particular in the infinitely plural when I read "consistency" now.[161]

As consistent as high cirrus clouds formed from the deposition of invisible water vapour which freezes and is rendered visible in streams and wisps of ice crystals. Crystals that sublimate directly back to water vapour, gaseous and invisible once more, as they fall in the high Illawarra sky.

Intensities

Scales have varying intensities, depending on the spectrum of objects they make visible. Compare the baroque layering of untamed materials, colours, flavours, sounds, and people comprising a traditional bazaar anywhere between Essaouira and Magadan with the glass-and-steel simulacra we call shopping malls that dot the suburban deserts of the real in modern cities. One is like a frame built from overflowing textures, the other is an embodiment of the instrumental logic of the assembly-line; identical, deanimated, purified. Entities in the mall have barcodes and are watched by surveillance cameras. Also, air-conditioning, the effect of being hermetically sealed. A moppable floor. Bacteria play a different role, inscribed on labels: projects for killing the *bad*, while in another aisle, projects for encouraging the *good*.

Enter a shopping mall in Manila or Bangkok—a refuge from the uncontainable urban chaos outside; a fantasy now indistinguishable from an airport. There will be marching bands. Shiny cars rotating. The mall can cover multiple city blocks; it holds the potential of being infinite, like its product ranges. Conceptually *it is* infinite, as it relates to no actual place at all; a hyper-real place purified of all that might obstruct the process of consumption. Ideally one might get lost inside and never be asked by security to leave.

The Greenbelt Mall in Makati, Manila, the city's richest central zone, is a lush and tranquil oasis. This mall is so pure and elevated it dispenses with floors and air-conditioning in favour of shady gardens, ponds, even an outdoor Catholic Church at its heart. A place anyone would pray to be able to afford. In one corner, on a brick patio by some floor-to-ceiling shop windows, live a vast number of feral cats and their kittens. In the evening they stretch out on the cool surfaces or meander into the nearby gardens. What does security make of them? Are they a pest? Or are they night shift against the greater threat of rodents?

How are scales negotiable? When and where do they become visible, and to whom? How do we notice scales, their entanglements and their intensities? Or: how do we not notice?

Rush

How might we tell and not tell "a rush of stories", to borrow Anna Tsing's phrase?[162]

A documentary maker says: "when I was a boy in the 1930s, the carbon dioxide level was still below 300 ppm. This year, it reached 382, the highest figure for hundreds of thousands of years."[163] A sociologist claims that we live in an era defined by "anticipation of catastrophe."[164] An atmospheric chemist exposes that "the protective ozone is thinning at the lower latitudes, where the sunlight is stronger and billions of people live."[165] A policy advisor pronounces: "If the world continues to emit planet-warming greenhouse gases as now, global mean temperature would increase by over 4°C by the end of the century, with parts of the Asia-Pacific seeing a rise of 6°C."[166] A writer exclaims that we're going to face more and more "flash floods, hundred-year storms, persistent droughts, spells of unprecedented heat, sudden landslides, raging torrents pouring down from breached glacial lakes, and ... freakish tornadoes."[167] A sustainability professor cries that this era makes us "think and imagine on a wholly different scale, vastly more global in scope, vastly more historical in extent."[168] An environmentalist bellows: "with climate change we face the biggest single thing human beings have ever done ... by pointing it out, the world's writers help pose the question for the final exam humanity now faces."[169] A cultural theorist yells: "the bigness of it all ... risks pitting complexity up against comprehension, making things too complex, the scale too massive for understanding, empathy or action."[170] A philosopher roars against the "massive high-speed" scale of our times.[171] A soldier screams "not possibly, not potentially—but *inevitably*. We have passed the point of no return."[172] An ethnographer howls and howls: her howling, and our howling "reverberates beyond us ... we howl in the dark for the loss that surrounds us now, and for all that is coming."[173]

After the shouting dies down, what are we left with?

Frost

Spring came early this year. Winter also stayed late.

I hack back my burnt and crispy lilly pilly hedge to half its size.

I hope it will come back to life now that the relentless heavy frosts have passed.

They told me *Winter Lights* was frost tolerant.

I think about what would happen if I did not tend it.
Will it return with or without my hacking back?

My new neighbours want to put in their own hedge.

Conifers.

They don't like native plants.

Preservation

I used to wait for the arrival of the first royal albatross at Taiaroa Heads. It was a chance to drive the undulating roads around the Otago Peninsula and look back at my house from the other side of the harbour — the view they would have had of me. Now I watch them from afar, through the Royal Cam.[174] The webcam focuses on an individual nest, but the nest does not belong to the same birds each year. This year the world watched in horror as a mother killed her chick. Watching becomes as much about the storms rolling in from Antarctica as it is about the birds.

It wasn't until 1659 that Nicolas Steno, Danish geologist and anatomist, questioned the prevailing scientific wisdom that fossils grew in the ground.[175] Until that moment, rocks had preserved, cared for, birthed and loved their fossil bodies for millennia. By naming fossils as organic, relics of animals become stone, it was realised the fossil was a sign that animals bigger-than-could-ever-be-imagined had roamed this same planet, perhaps made love in these same places, these same fields. Steno's thoughts led to the discrete classification of rocks as separate from animals; and thereafter the invention of the children's game: animal, mineral or vegetable. Meanwhile, further south in Italy, Bernini had been turning marble into living and ecstatic human flesh.

For the natural scientists of the late eighteenth century, species became present through their absence becoming visible. If fossils were the remains of animals that no longer roamed the earth, then the rocks needed to be read quite differently — the fossil record pointed towards a great catastrophe in which these animals had been wiped out. In 1796 Georges Cuvier wrote: "All of these facts, consistent among themselves, and not opposed by any report, seem to me to prove the existence of a world previous to ours, destroyed by some kind of catastrophe."[176] Questions arose about whether the last of the dinosaurs could still be out there, in the depths of a loch, or, in a snowy mountain, or, on a pair of small islands at the bottom of the earth. People began roaming the wild to search for the last lonely representatives of a species.

The timelines began to stretch, as the world became marked by "sharp declines in diversity", and, in the words of paleontologist David Raup, "the history of life thus consists of 'long periods of boredom interrupted occasionally by panic'."[177] These events that shift the planet on its axis reconfigure both organic and inorganic life. On screen I watch the albatross: boredom, panic, boredom, panic.

Erosion

"In the Anthropocene, the price of gold futures determines whether mountains will rise or fall, and farm subsidies and commodity prices influence the rate of erosion."[178] Daring to entangle economics and geology, artist Trevor Paglen reflects on the geological costs of commodifying the Earth.

Earth scientist Roger Hooke identifies humans as major geologic agents on the basis that we move, annually, a greater volume of sediment than any other single geomorphic agent. Hooke notices that textbooks of geomorphology tend to obfuscate the significance of humankind as a geomorphic agent, and wonders why.

I begin my walk across England with boots in the waters of St Bees. I pick up a small white pebble and snuggle it into a corner of my backpack. This is my talisman. On the other side, boots in Robin Hood's Bay, I hold the pebble in my hand as I reflect on my journey and journey's end. This is my rock of truth: I have walked from coast to coast—'190 miles'. Like so many other walkers, I throw the pebble into the waters of that other shore. I wonder what geologists will make of this accretion of migrant pebbles in a hundred years, in a thousand years. What stories will they tell? Will we still be here to wonder?

Hooke argues, in 1994, that humans "are just as much a part of the environment as any other organism", and that "it is crucial that we recognise and accept that we are not above nature, somehow supernatural."[179] 1994 was—is—long ago in Anthropocene time. Then, atmospheric carbon dioxide was only 361.23 ppm. Today it is 409.01 ppm.

Extinction

Joshua says that there are too many birds in this book. He's compiled a list of extinct birds: from the Alaotra grebe (declared extinct in 2010) to the dodo (1665).[180] He's put it in the manuscript and taken it out, several times: it's too overwhelming, he says, too monumental (he doesn't acknowledge the pun). Even in its immensity, there is a poetry and repetition to their names: grebe, warbler, grebe, akialoa, wren, piopio. Su asks if she might replace the list of birds with another one, following Foucault and his kin: a list of imaginary animals. The fur-bellied quandor, the aerial peel (known for throwing itself against suburban windows). It is not very convincing. What about a different list? The roll-call of the remaining living kākāpō can be found on Wikipedia. Today, it includes 154 individual birds. Bessie is no longer there, and it looks like Jimmie and Smoko have also recently passed on. But I have another story to share. The last of the whēkau (laughing owl) died on the side of a road near Timaru on 15 July 1914. The spot is not marked by one of those little white crosses, but it is a roadside tragedy all the same. I start to wonder, just how many cars drove down that road in 1914. The clouds of war were gathering. A few days later Austria-Hungary declared war on Serbia.

Home

> But what is it that happens precisely when we encounter someone we love? Do we encounter somebody, or is it animals that come to inhabit you, ideas that invade you, movements that move you, sounds that traverse you? And can these things be parted?[181]

Comfort. Safety. Security.

> Sanctuary, the sign said. Sanctuary—
> trees, not houses; flat skins pinned to the road
> of possum and native-cat; and here the old tree stood
> for how many thousand years? that old gnome-tree
> some axe-new boy cut down.[182]

Which ones get to stay home now? Do we need a new scale of differential refuge? Working late one night, she learns that the new house cat is afraid of thunder.

Trinity

Catherine McKinnon

I stand at the edge of the forest. Hear wind whistling, leaves tinkling. The earth breathing. Slender trunks dance before gnarled trees and small animals scurry to escape their prey. This is one of the last forests, and here I am living with the trees until the war is over.

In the distance, thunder. Storms every evening now. DK says the storms are created by the enemy, their military scientists. They want to drown us. So far the rain has sunk deep into the earth and there have been no floods.

I walk out from under the trees and cross the wet grassy clearing to the bunker, stop for a moment at the steel doorway and take off my Wellies. Lightning flashes to the west. The rain looks like thousands of silver needles falling into the steaming green mountain. Once there was ice on that mountain. Before my time. I pull shut the bunker door, pad over to the heater in my socks. Only a smidge of warmth comes through the vents. I wrap myself in a blanket, sit at my work table and take up my pen.

Trinity: Working Day of the Dead

14–16 July 1945: Where both Oppenheimer and the plutonium bomb are tested.

Last night, DK asked, "Why the past, why not now?"

"Because the past is now," I said.

Alamogordo, New Mexico. Two nights before the first atomic bomb is tested. Most of the Los Alamos scientists who built the bomb don't believe it will explode.

Actually that's not true. One person is without doubt. George Kistiakowsky, a physical chemist from Harvard, and the project's explosive expert. Strong, sinewy, with a receding hairline and a pixie-like nose. Kistiakowsky (everyone calls him Kisty) agreed to work at Los Alamos because he hates Nazis. Hated Hitler. He believes the bomb will explode and more than that, even though

Hitler died 75 days earlier (because yes he is keeping count) he still believes in the project. For the scientists on the Hill (the resident's name for Los Alamos), the past 75 days have been turbulent. Their workload has doubled but their moral imperative has lessened. Maybe not lessened, become confused. After all, what is the point now? The main man is dead. Kisty, the only scientist to have also been a soldier, thinks differently. He believes that war is a virus from which humanity will never recover, but maybe, just maybe, this gadget will ease the way in the future. Maybe just maybe it will be a preventive. Like castor oil. Kisty is Ukrainian but the American scientists refer to him as *The Russian*. He hates that name with a passion. "Calling a Ukrainian Russian is like calling a Scotsman English," he complains to Robert Oppenheimer, the project's director, as he trails him around the Trinity site. Tall loping Oppie is an intelligent listener, able to traverse difficult theory and petty hurts, family updates and public responsibilities, all within the same conversation.

The upcoming Trinity test is for the implosion-type bomb. Fat Man it will later be called when it is dropped on Nagasaki. Little Boy, the uranium gun-type bomb to be dropped on Hiroshima, will not get a try out. The scientists have no doubt that one will work. Fat Man has thirty-two detonators around its plutonium sphere. At each charge point an explosive lens is set. These lenses work like optical lens, shifting deviating beams to converging ones. The lens castings, speckled brown and heavy, have been made by Kisty's X Division (a name that seems ripe for a science fiction flick), but many have faults in them, tiny air bubbles seen only by x ray.

This isn't a problem until some weeks before the test when Oppenheimer invades Kisty's workspace and demands that a full-scale *copy* of the test-explosives be shot, minus the precious plutonium core.

"But we don't have the lenses?" Kisty says.

"Might I suggest you get them," Oppenheimer replies, as if giving advice on a new choice of floor tile.

Nerves are high – plutonium is extremely expensive, extremely difficult to make – and Oppenheimer doesn't want the Trinity test to fail because the explosive design is a dud. He needs a copy test.

To get a sense of how nervous everyone is, to get a sense of how rational intelligent people often commit irrational unintelligent acts, consider this story. One morning, shortly before work on the Hill has commenced, many scientists are sighted out in front of their cheaply built military apartments gazing up at a strange object in the sky. Several guns are procured for the purpose of shooting the object down. Until finally, one sane man walks into Oppenheimer's office and says, "Oppie, you have to stop the people out there who are trying to shoot down Venus."

The copy Trinity test (this smaller trial run is set to explode near Los Alamos; called the Creutz test, after the scientist left to charge it) involves warrior-like preparations from Kisty. He sits up through the night, delicately picking up one faulty lens after another, and positioning it in his lap. Using a dentist drill borrowed from the surgery, he begins to drill down to the air bubble. He then tips a prepared liquid explosive into the cavity. He refuses help from any of his lab staff; one mistake could set off a blast. By the time the sun rises and begins to spread across the mesa, he has enough explosive lens for both the copy test and the Trinity test.

For a while Kisty is a hero. But two nights before Trinity, as important guests arrive at the Hilton Hotel in Albuquerque, Oppenheimer greets them with a sour face. He has just had news from Los Alamos that the dummy gadget did not explode. Kisty, who is sitting at the bar, thinks Oppenheimer looks like a wounded elk who has lost his way. Oppenheimer settles each guest alongside Kisty, places before them a whiskey, or a whiskey sour, or a bourbon on ice, and then, in lilting tones, informs them that the Creutz test has failed.

Everyone knows (because it is logical) that if the Creutz test fails then so will the Trinity test. Every scientist, every military man, every government representative feels this to be true. Everyone but Kisty. One variable, Kisty thinks, can ruin a rehearsal run. Remember, he was not at Los Alamos to oversee the copy test. Why? Because he was needed for the real test being conducted in Alamogordo more than 200 miles away.

Kisty is now blamed for the imagined forthcoming failure of the Trinity test. The mood in the bar is glum. All eyes are on him, metaphorically speaking. Kisty, with a soldier-like resilience and an unrelenting optimism, suffers being berated by VIPs, by General Groves, and as the night wears on, by Oppenheimer himself. Finally, when he has plied himself with enough booze, and the bar is thick with smoke from cigars, he slams his glass down on the shiny wooden surface and says: "Oppie, I bet you one month's wages against ten of your own lousy dollars, that my lenses work."

The next morning, Oppenheimer has breakfast in the mess hall. Powdered eggs (whisked, scrambled then tumbled onto plates to form mini mountains) are served with black coffee. Fair to say Oppie is rattled. Fair to say he tossed and turned on his bunk bed, and slept not a wink. If the night before he blamed Kisty, now he redirects that blame onto himself. He could have delayed the test. He had that power. He, and possibly only he, could have told General Groves to kiss goodbye to his precious July 16 date. He could have ordered new lenses made. He thinks to himself, I am a donkey.

And here is the why. Some time back Groves, using his persuasive General's voice, one that employs a tone equal in power to Oppenheimer's lilt, had said to Oppenheimer, "In July Truman is to meet Stalin and Churchill at Potsdam. Truman needs to know his hand, and he is hoping for a trump card."

Oppenheimer now remembers his own punishing desire to be the one delivering that trump card. It is he, not Kisty, who is responsible for this fizzler. He groans and pushes his untouched eggs away.

"Sir." A young soldier, squirrel eyes, is at Oppenheimer's side. "Telephone call."

Oppenheimer, cigarette in mouth, rises like an old man. The phone is clamped to the wall. He takes his time walking to it, picks up the receiver with trepidation.

"The Creutz test is not a problem for Trinity!" Hans Bethe shouts down the line. "Blown circuits in the wiring, Kisty's device will work."

Oppenheimer looks out across the mess hall, over the fresh faces of soldiers and rookie scientists, through the open door to where the land has begun to glow a deep orange.

It is mid-morning and Oppenheimer strides out onto the sandy desert with meteorologist Jack Hubbard. Hubbard sweats in the heat. He wears thick protective clothing.

Both men stare up at the blue sky.

"That son-of-a-bitch Groves," Hubbard mutters.

"But it's clear," Oppie says.

Hubbard points to clouds gathering in the far distance. "The wind is picking up."

Hubbard had suggested other dates for Trinity. Dates that were far more reliable, weather wise, but dates later than General Groves had wanted. Later than Potsdam.

"There *will* be a storm," Hubbard says.

Oppenheimer nods. One problem solved, only for another far weightier problem to arise. But he remembers what Bohr said when he visited Los Alamos: every great and deep difficulty bears in itself its own solution.

"A lot can happen in eighteen hours," he says to Hubbard.

As the two men trek back across the hot sand to the weather hut Oppenheimer tells Hubbard about the old trade route that runs through the Trinity land. It has been used by Native Americans, Spanish conquistadors and Franciscan friars. Back when the Spaniards were in charge, traders going from Santa Fe to Mexico City rode at night. Too hot to travel in the day. This is a place where the sun's heat can kill, where waterholes vanish in hours. Here, death is present in the names of places. Laguna del Muerto, south from where the two men walk, has its name from when Mescalero Apaches attacked traders stopping for water. But still traders came. They camped among the cacti, mesquite and saltbush, resting their heads on packs stashed with shiny new guns, perfumes and silks. The terrain was so tough they'd cover no more than twelve miles at a time. The trip would take over a week, it was a death trap, but traders would risk it for the money. Because with money came power.

Inside the mess hall, it is clear the impending storm is unravelling nerves. It's been four years of secret work and now 'weather' may bring down the show.

Oppenheimer drives out to the tower at ground zero, twenty miles from base. It's a hundred feet high, built of steel. Four sturdy legs, thirty-five feet apart, with a three-sided corrugated iron shack at the top. The shack has an oak floor. The western side is open, and some distance off, in bunkers, cameras are focused on the bomb.

In drizzling rain, Oppenheimer climbs the tower ladder. As he reaches the platform he sees the bomb all trussed up, like a Sunday roast. Even if the weather rights itself, so many other things could still go wrong. Take the switch on the gadget that will set off its thirty-two detonators in less than a millionth of a second. Someone need only tamper with that switch, he thinks, and the test is doomed.

Across from Oppenheimer, the mountains are a dark glimmer in the rain-filled light. The Native Americans believe that the mountains are the place where the stars come to rest. He'd told that to Ken Bainbridge on the reconnaissance trip they'd taken together. Bainbridge is the quiet, focused experimental physicist, first tasked with setting up the Trinity site, then with running it. Bainbridge was born with one of those unnaturally long foreheads, as though he had too much information held in his brain and so his forehead had to be extended to accommodate it. His eyebrows slope down on each side, giving him a mournful look, and yet his face, fine and chiselled, is gentle and reflective. On the reconnaissance trip Bainbridge and Oppenheimer had been looking for flat land, far enough from any town to give them a measure of control, and far enough from Los Alamos so as not to be connected with it if anything went wrong. They needed, above all, stable weather conditions. At night, all the men on the trip, as well as Oppie and Bainbridge, had slept in the back of an army truck, high above the tarantulas and scorpions, the rattlesnakes and the fire ants. They'd zipped themselves into sleeping bags and stared up at the stars. Oppenheimer told wild west stories. New Mexico had always been a lawless land, the place men came to, to make their fortunes cattle ranching or gun slinging. It's no myth that those with the fastest draw ruled. Jornado Del Muerto is translated as Journey of the Dead, or Dead Man's Trail, but Oppenheimer's wife Kitty, who is finicky about translation details, had informed Oppie that it is more about context. That phrase, she once told him, could also be interpreted as *working day of the dead*. The men on the trip had liked his tales, had liked his New Mexican belt, a homage to New Mexican life, were all a little enamoured of him. But when Oppie returned from the site search, desert dust over his clothes, and walked into his darkened Los Alamos bedroom and pulled back the curtains to let in the afternoon light, Kitty had been less enamoured. She was sitting up in bed, smoking, having already worked her way through a half bottle of whiskey.

"Say, you look like a gun slinger come back from a ride," she'd said in a mock cowgirl voice.

It occurs to Oppenheimer, as he stands on top of the tower looking out to the mountains, that his wife had picked him right, picked him for what he is, a modern gun slinger.

On the drive back, Oppenheimer stops off at the McDonald ranch and congratulates the men who are cleaning up after setting the plutonium core in place. The weather is windy and the storm clouds are piling up overhead. Later, at base camp, Oppenheimer hears thunder that is a thousand guns firing. The wind howls around the mess hall. He stands in the doorway and watches rain pummelling sand. Tents blow over. The frogs in the nearby pond start an almighty racket and begin to copulate. Inside, one scientist after another, pulls him aside and quietly suggests that he cancel the test.

At 0200 hours Oppenheimer goes outside to wait for Hubbard. Hubbard has driven to the tower for a final check. Oppie leans against the wall of the weather hut, sheltering from the storm, cigarette drooping from his mouth. Lightning flashes and the distant mountains are revealed. There are four men able to cancel the test; weatherman Hubbard is one, physicist Ken Bainbridge is another. Second-in-command to Groves, General Farrell, is the third, Oppenheimer the fourth. Farrell, in truth, although his own man, will do Grove's bidding. Bainbridge and Hubbard, Oppenheimer's.

Oppie sees Hubbard's truck in the distance, churning up the track. Hubbard pulls to a stop in front of him and jumps out.

"Only misting at the tower," Hubbard says, almost grinning.

Rain suddenly hammers down causing both men to rush for the door.

Inside General Groves is waiting.

"What the hell is wrong with the weather?" Groves barks at Hubbard.

"General, I did warn you," Hubbard snaps. "Afternoon thunderstorms take their energy from the heated earth," he continues at a rapid pace, not wanting Groves to intervene. "They normally collapse at sunset, but in *this* month the tropical air mass will keep them going until dawn."

"Enough with the explanations," Groves bellows and turns away from Hubbard. "Give me a specific time!"

Groves begins to pace the perimeter of the room.

"I've given you both," Hubbard sneers.

Groves, his back to Hubbard, stops pacing. He stands perfectly still, as if he's just picked up the scent of his prey.

"Hubbard is the best forecaster there is," Oppenheimer warns.

"If you're not right on this," Groves says, twisting to face Hubbard, "I'll hang you!"

Groves strides to the door, turning to Oppenheimer before he exits. "We'll set the shot for 5.30," he grunts.

At 0300 hours, General Groves is irritable. He has been watching a steady stream of scientists individually make their way over to pester Oppenheimer, who is settled in a corner of the mess hall, reading poetry. (Groves thinks Oppie has a seriously loony side.) The scientists want the test cancelled. Groves barrels in, collects the project director and drives him to the southern bunker, ten miles from ground zero. The storm is still hell on earth and Oppenheimer is twitchy but Groves is adamant the test will go ahead, somehow.

At South 10000 everyone is fully occupied. No nosey opinionated scientists, only ones who do what they are told. Mostly. Because Oppenheimer's brother Frank is there. Frank, Groves thinks, I can handle. In the pouring rain, Groves walks Oppenheimer out to the desert and lists all the reasons why they must continue with the test. Too many people working at the site have not slept for forty-eight hours and will need to sleep. They cannot simply put the test off for another few hours. No, they would have to wait longer. But waiting even a day means the potential for more things to go wrong: dust, weather, sabotage. Not to mention an increased financial cost. Not to mention Potsdam and Truman.

"To be honest, I can't envisage what might happen to this war if we cancel," Groves says.

Oppenheimer is full of unsoldierly doubt. "I don't know if I'll be able to get my people up again if we cancel," he agrees. "But General, if the weather doesn't clear, we'll have no option."

"There are always options," Groves insists. "Read your Bhagavad-Gita."

An hour before the blast, the weather clears. A coolness rises up from the sand. Stars appear in the sky. It's like magic.

"I'll go back to base," Groves says. "Watch from there."

Oppenheimer says he'll stay where he is. Privately, he wants space from Groves. If the weather stirs again, he may have to make a tough decision.

At twenty minutes to, the countdown begins. The tension is unbearable. The weather is not perfect, but Oppenheimer knows it will do. He is thinking of years of combined scientific work. He has to know the outcome of *that* labour.

Weirdly, throughout the countdown there is interference from a radio station and the *Nutcracker Suite* can be heard playing.

And is that voices speaking?

And then the last seconds of countdown arrive.

"It is hard on the heart," Oppenheimer murmurs, and grips onto a post.

Three.

Two.

One.

Now!

Oppie squeezes his eyes closed and yet sees a tremendous light. As if a shining force is entering upwards from the earth into his cells. His breath comes uneasily. It's like all the air has been sucked from the atmosphere. He opens his eyes and peers through the dark glass Groves had shoved into his hand before he left. Everything is harshly bright. Dazzling. The mountain top, even the crevasses, are glowing. Astounding.

He thinks of a line from the Bhagavad-Gita: *If the radiance of a thousand suns were to burst at once into the sky, that would be like the splendour of the mighty one.*

And with the light, a fevered heat arrives.

Oppenheimer spies a fireball at ground zero, like a shining half-sun. The half-sun turns blue, then luminescent red, then a glittery violet, black with radioactive dust. Finally, an opaque white, and sun becomes moon, and moon becomes fluid, transforms into an ocean creature, an octopus perhaps, rising into the sky, its tentacles, dangling twists of smoke that form a cloud.

A thunderous noise bounces around the Jornada. As if a giant ball is being slung from one mountain to the other.

Relief. Oppenheimer feels immense relief. He stands in awe, as if before a Divine God. Magnificent and terrifying. For this is a god they have made, and yet, it belongs not to any man or woman. The power is overwhelming. What comes after this may bear a resemblance to what came before, but it will never be the same. *Now I am become Death, the destroyer of worlds.* Only the Divine can decide the future, he thinks.

Oppenheimer turns to his brother, Frank.

Frank smiles. "It worked."

A bead of sweat trickles down Frank's cheek.

"Yes," Oppenheimer says. "It worked."

They gaze again at the sky. Cheering breaks out behind the two brothers. But they continue to stare because the cloud is hovering. If the wind does not soon disperse the cloud, radioactive rain will fall directly on the base, fatal to all who are there.

Kisty grabs Oppenheimer from behind in a bear hug.

"Oppie, you owe me ten bucks," Kisty cries out.

Oppenheimer shakes himself free and zombie-like pulls out his wallet. Opens it. It's empty. Not even a dollar. That seems like a sign.

"You'll have to wait," he says.

Bainbridge noses in on Kisty, grips Oppenheimer's hand. "Now we are all sons of bitches," he says.

Over Bainbridge's shoulder, Oppenheimer finally sees what he's been waiting for. The wind washing away the cloud, like a painter discontented with her canvas.

The air chills.

Frank's face has drained to white.

The risk has passed but for a moment their lives rested on the whim of the wind.

Oppenheimer, with furious energy, shakes Bainbridge's hand.

"Yes," he says to him. "Now we are all sons of bitches."

I hear the truck pull up outside. DK is back with the others. They will have news of the front.

A war has many beginnings, but only one ending.

I put down my pen and hurry to the door. As I pull it open I am blasted with light.

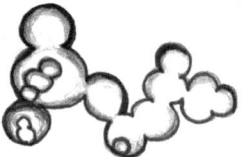

Oxygen

Oxygen produced by cyanobacteria was so abundant that the gas rusted all the iron on the planet.[183] Then it poisoned the organisms that produced it. Other creatures hid in the deep ocean mud. Oxygen is both reactive and stable. Oxidisation drives life.

Paradigm

Su has bought a new book to camp this year: Roy Scranton's *Learning to Die in the Anthropocene: Reflections on the End of a Civilization*. It is small, and fits nicely in your hand. She has not read it yet, but tells us it is by someone who fought in the Gulf War. Brogan takes it for the night. At breakfast he describes it as a positive story: it offers solutions. Kim takes it next. She returns it soon afterwards, tears in her eyes. It is too much, too violent. Cath is circling, she is writing about America, a country some of us have never seen.

The stories we tell about beginnings and endings frame us, conceptually and literally, in a system of knowledge that paralyse us into inaction. The end of the human age leads to despair, grief and apathy: a state of 'there is nothing more to be done'. In response to this state of paralysis, Scranton proposes that "we're going to need new ideas. We're going to need new myths and new stories, a new conceptual understanding of reality ... we will need a new way of thinking our collective existence. We need a new vision of who 'we' are."[184] There are murmurings. Eva has been reading Jane Bennett and, avoiding the Scranton discussion, she suggests that perhaps we also need a "re-enchanted attitude toward vibrant matter", and "a more ecological sensibility."[185]

The book, the ideas, flow with the river at the bottom of the hill, into other essays, other stories. More conversations.

But, in case this seems a too 'enchanted' approach, don't forget something important Scranton says—about how as a soldier, before he went out into the streets of war, he would first contemplate his own death. Contemplating death need not be negative or positive. It need not be value laden. It can just be.

Missing

Missing cat, missing dog, missing budgie. A4 paper, sticky-taped to splintery telegraph poles. So many signs. Some of them frayed at the edges, or blobbed with rain-spots, the photo blurred and distorted. One sign laminated, carefully preserved: Missing Skateboard: REWARD. please please please I need it back. My mum will kill me.

Missing persons. Misapprehension. Miss the Mark. Kim and I play a game where we make up drag names. "What about Miss Anthropic?" she offers. "More like Miss Anthropocene", I snort.

The cover of Ursula Heise's book *Imagining Extinction* shows five birds gliding over an evening sky. Two of the birds have been cut out of the picture: there is an empty white space where the bird should be. The white edges are frayed.

Missing link. Misconstrue. Missing you.

Voice

The carolling of magpies reminds us of our connections, even in this glass room, to the winter morning outside, cold, dry, sunny, in this place, this continent. We *are* embedded, even if we mostly don't notice it. The nonhuman voices reach us (carolling magpie, murmuring ocean, sounds of a small creek running, soughing breeze in the casuarinas, silent stone …), it's just that we have stopped our ears with too much of ourselves, our own cacophony.

Sometimes we need to stop talking, stop looking at ourselves, and *listen*.

And always this 'we' that calls to be made and unmade as it listens out for voices.

Listen

The pause before. The full silence of waiting.

Pause

Writing weather

Jo Law

LIMIT OF HEAT: RICE RIPENS

5 March 2012

EXCESS water has once again made headline news in the past week. The river systems in southern New South Wales and northern Victoria swelled and flooded as a result of the recent heavy rainfall. Residents in Goulburn, Gundagai, the Riverina, and other northern Victorian towns were forced to evacuate from the inundation of water. The deluge is a little less dramatic on the northern Illawarra coast. Water has seeped into some areas of our house. The moist environment has also given access for the outdoor creatures to move indoors, like the leech encountered in the shower.

Compared to the total rainfall of 311.3 millimetres recorded at Bellambi Australian Weather Station in the past month, the February of 2010 only saw 137.4 mm. We would wait 28 days of the next month for the birth of our child. In 2009, the total rainfall of February was 114.4 mm. At that time, Erina, the Japanese exchange student who stayed with us for a month in Wollongong, had just left to return to Saitama. In September 2008 when the rice ripened in the northern hemisphere's autumn (and the pampas grass went to seed in Japan), we arrived in Tokyo for the first time. The five posts in the *Autumn Almanac of Tokyo* were grouped under 'Limit of Heat' or *Shosho*. They described a warm, humid, and wet Tokyo. On our second night in the city, we were caught in a sudden downpour in Shinjuku while finding a place to eat. Regular typhoons and rain last well into October.

Recently, I started re-reading Liza Dalby's *East Wind Melts the Ice*, which inspired the structure of the Almanac projects.[186] I am reminded of the importance of marking time. My own wish to take note of the minute details of the everyday is, in some way, an attempt to slow down time, which I seem to be chronically short of.

~

Our perception of the weather and our conception of everyday experiences are intimately connected. Alexandra Harris' *Weatherland: Writers and Artists under English Skies* explores English weather phenomena in writings and artworks from Anglo-Saxon England to contemporary Britain.[187] Harris's analysis shows that art and writing shape the experience of weather in English culture. Culture is more foundational to how weather is experienced than the scientific theories and observational instruments that we have come to associate with meteorology. The elegy *The Wanderer* tells us that for the Anglo-Saxons the harshness of winter so greatly affected day-to-day living that the significance of summer was entirely eclipsed. Medieval thinking aligned the meteor—things in the air—with the movements of heavens and the human body. Seasonality, regularity, and cyclic patterns were given shape by calendars, *menologium*, and epic poems. Prayer books or books of hours presented these changing patterns for contemplation while almanacs provided guidance on how to interact with the physical environments. These perceptions or predictions were not based on empirical observation but largely conformed to pre-existing schemas. During the Renaissance, the corporeal experience of weather was elevated through the spectacular staging of 'England's Astraea'—Elizabeth I. *The Ditchley Portrait* presented the virgin queen as a star-maiden who could command the celestial and terrestrial spheres. In this period Shakespeare conjured up powerful weather for the staging of human dramas. The last of the Little Ice Age so captured the public imagination that the frost fairs held on the frozen Thames are forever woven into the cultural tapestry of Elizabethan England.

One might imagine that technological observations in the seventeenth century would interrupt this intimate relationship between humans and weather. On the contrary, when John Evelyn, a founding member of the Royal Society, recorded the weather after the Great Frost, it was the demise of his garden that was most strongly felt. At this time Robert Hooke perfected the barometer for measuring and recording, but methods of data collection and its interpretation were very much open to subjective experience. Harris describes the twin 'weather-watching' and 'diary-keeping' habit of Sir John Wittewronge, a contemporary of Evelyn: "Sir John often omitted to read his barometer, and the temperatures he noted were what he *felt* rather than what he read on the weather-glass scale. But for just this reason his 'Weather Book' is a beguiling one, and tellingly poised between emotional response and objective instrumental record."[188] Barometer readings are interpreted through the body. In combining adjectives that encapsulate the moods and sensations with observations in phrases such as "a sullen cloudy cold day," the weather-diarists evoke emotional as well as corporeal effects of daily weather.[189] This cultural practice of weather-watching and diary-keeping shows how data can only make *sense* through the *senses*. Scientific understanding of weather may make apparent the systems that give rise to these everyday phenomena; it remains the task of the arts to make meaning out of how we feel about these experiences.

~

COLD DEW: CHRYSANTHEMUMS ARE TINGED YELLOW

19 April 2012

In this pentad, the escarpment was once again shrouded in thick clouds and heavy rain returned. During periods of heavy falls, I could see sheets of water pelting against the window. Wednesday 18 April topped the monthly highest rainfall so far with 54.4 mm recorded at Bellambi . This was followed closely by the 53.8 mm recorded on Thursday 19 April. This plentiful rain satisfied the garden although the slowing of growth during these shortening days was evident. The cucumber vines produced their last fruits, the roquette has grown large and bitter, and the edible chrysanthemums are flowering.

Chrysanthemums have a long history in their native China where they are prized for their ornamental qualities and medicinal properties. The flower holds a highly significant role in Chinese arts and culture. Together with the orchid, the bamboo, and the plum blossom, the plants are known as 'The Four Gentlemen amongst flowers' (花中四君子). Their depictions in paintings and references in poems allude to the passing seasons: spring orchids, summer bamboo, autumn chrysanthemums, and winter plum blossoms (春蘭、夏竹、秋菊、冬梅). These seasonal emblems embody valued noble qualities.

My own relationship with chrysanthemums is comparatively more prosaic. The flower's known longevity as cut flowers lends itself as the bloom of choice for graveside visitors. Chrysanthemums would be what we took on the autumnal visit to my paternal grandfather's grave in the hillside Catholic cemetery. The presence of fresh flowers in the stone vase on the grave would mean other visitors had already been to pay their respects. Dead and dried-up flowers would be removed and any remaining water tipped out. Leaves from the lower parts of long stems are pinched out before the new flowers are arranged in the vase. The handsome yellow blooms set off against the grey gravestone. My mother would top up the vase with fresh water.

After hearing my maternal grandfather's account of attending a chrysanthemum show in his youth I started to notice the myriad of chrysanthemum cultivars. The extraordinariness of this bloom was made apparent to me at the annual chrysanthemum show held at Shinjuku Gyoen in Tokyo in deep Autumn. Exhibits that seemingly defied botany were proudly displayed and quietly appreciated. It was not difficult to imagine scenes of the much-celebrated chrysanthemum festival once held on the ninth day of the ninth lunar month in Heian Japan.

~

Alva Noë argues that art, rather than a phenomenon to be examined, is an active mode of research through which we build knowledge of ourselves and our world. In concluding *Strange Tools*, Noë writes:

> Art is not manufacture. Art is not performance. Art is not entertainment. Art is not beauty. Art is not pleasure. Art is not participating in the art world. And art is definitely not commerce. Art is philosophy. Art is putting our true nature on display before ourselves. Because we need to. Art is writing ourselves.[190]

If anaesthetics is the numbing of senses, then an aesthetic practice should hone our sensitivities to the world around us. In this way, weather observation can be considered an aesthetic event. Harris shows that the writing, thinking and modelling of atmospheric phenomena in English literature, poetry and paintings shaped the way weather is lived in English culture. These aesthetic practices can produce an emergent and evolving picture of our world and our place within.

Without tools to guide us through changes in our environments, our experience can feel unhinged. Harris recounts the unease Samuel Johnson felt towards the uncontrollable weather, or more accurately how the body could be made to feel uncontrollable by the weather. This lack of control over the weather partially gave way to the embrace of the awe of nature by the succeeding generation of Romantic poets. The physical exhilaration that came from immersing oneself in the elements inspired those who wanted to make sense of these feelings—and furthermore to paint an evolving picture of the world and humans place within. JMW Turner was known for his passion for natural phenomena and approached these sensations scientifically and experientially. His works scrutinise how light changes as it passes through air, mist, fog, or when it is reflected on water. Turner's knowledge was tacit. His investigation into the ever-changing quality of the English light resonates even when he painted historical scenes that occurred in Rome or The Alps. Turner's paintings are models created using his experiential knowledge, with which audience can think and investigate experience in relation to natural light. Similarly, by the staging of weather and optical phenomena as installations, Olafur Eliasson's *Fog Assembly* (2016), *Rainbow Assembly* (2016), and *Weather the weather* (2016) invited the audience to become immersed in models of microweather systems in order to ponder how they experience the world. Both Turner's and Eliasson's works are models in Noë's sense of the term as "things we put to work in order to think about or investigate something" – and that 'something' for Turner, as for Eliasson, is the nature of light.[191]

Art as tangible models allows the textures of our mediation to show up. When weather writing manifests physically, our encounter with weather takes on material forms. Turner's re-staging of sunsets places viewers within an everyday event that is at once ordinary and wonderful. These encounters of 'ordinariness' encourage a shedding of preconception and a re-sensitisation of our ability to perceive. Similarly, Eliasson's *Weather Project* (2003) drew attention to these everyday wonders. Using 200 mono-frequency lamps placed behind a large semi-circular screen hung under a mirrored ceiling at the Tate Modern's Turbine Hall, Eliasson put on display the moment of sunset. Together with the spray of fine mist that at times coalesced into temporary fog or cloud-like formations, the interior walls fell away and the audience stood in awe in the presence of this convincing yet clearly constructed setting sun. In 'Traces of Craft,' Esther Leslie reflects on Walter Benjamin's call for *Kraftwerk* or 'power work' to restore *Erfahrung* (lived experience) in the modern world.[192] *Kraftwerk* objects are not representations (or representational), but rather they are embodiment of knowledge and experience woven through haptic perception.[193] Leslie writes of the photograph that "brings objects closer for inspection, providing an imprint of traces of the world. It reveals traces (*Spuren*), not of the potter's handprint, but of the objective modern world" and for Benjamin, "[t]o touch is to know the world."[194] In both Turner's and Eliasson's works, *Spuren* show up as not reflections but traces of the world that produced them. These *Kraftwerk* are models that draw attention to the intersection between knowledge and experience. In experiencing these works, it is evident how our conception of weather is shaped by the art of our times. Weather is at once raw and mediated.

MAJOR SNOW: GARLIC CHIVES SPROUT

20 June 2012

We spent the majority of the last pentad in Canberra. We arrived in the capital city on the afternoon of Saturday 16 June when the lowest monthly maximum to date of 9.3°C was recorded. After our return to Austinmer, Canberra's overnight minimum fell to −6.3°C on the morning of Wednesday 20 June. We had visited the Territory in previous winters, and felt prepared, having packed our various layers of merino thermal wear. Even so, for those of us unused to inland winters, the cold was unforgiving.

The drive to Nursery Swamp in the mountains southwest of the Territory showed us a landscape made up of different shades of pale browns and yellows. Peter, our friend and local guide, told us that the darker brown in and amongst the grasses was dried up St John's Wort. He also pointed out the three wild apple trees by the side of the road that supplied him with some very delicious apples in past years. Cattle and sheep dotted the fields. No crops observed.

The winter grain crops have long been planted around the country but we have only managed to clear out the remnant of our summer vegetables. The garlic heads, having been stored in the fridge and divided into cloves, are yet to be planted. The ones that have been exposed to light waited no more and sprouted in situ. With winter solstice approaching, we are running out of time to put them in the soil. While we are yet to have a definite success with garlic growing, the cheerfully green garlic chives (*Allium tuberosum*) grow prolifically under the ginger plants.

Related to onions, garlic chive is a popular culinary herb used in Chinese, Korean, and Japanese cooking. In terms of Chinese medicinal use, it is said to be warming, detoxifying and promote the circulation of *qi*. It is used to treat problems ranging from haemorrhage to diabetes, from injuries from falls to insect bites. Extracted juice from the leaves can be drunk, cooked, or applied to injured areas. It can even be used in washing or ironing to take advantage of its anti-fungal properties.

Evelyn was a keen gardener. He understood not only the relationship between elements, but that future predictions can be inferred from past experiences. He aligned weather observations with botanical ones, paying close attention to the material world. After Evelyn, it became customary to describe the weather at the beginning of a diary entry. Harris writes, "Weather-watching and diary-keeping would, from now on, be almost inseparable. The recording of weather and the writing of lives would occupy the same small notebooks."[195] In writing weather, we write our world and those who inhabit it. In *A Sand County Almanac*, Aldo Leopold re-tells intimate accounts of activities observed in the plant and animal worlds and the varied responses to the changing seasons in Wisconsin.[196] In his almanac, humans are a bit player in the broader world of wilderness; they live alongside the other inhabitants of the world, sometimes collaborating, other times at odds. In developing his theory of wilderness conservation, Leopold puts forward the concept of land ethics, he writes:

> The land ethic simply enlarges the boundaries of the community to include soils, waters, plants, and animals, or collectively, the land ... In short, a land ethic changes the role of Homo sapiens from conqueror of the land-community to plain member or citizen of it.[197]

The creation of an almanac necessitates a direct and active interaction with the material world. Levi Bryant echoes Leopold when he writes:

> ... we need to cultivate modes of thinking that help us to become attentive to the alterity of things, the thingliness of things, and the differences that things themselves contribute independent of social construction, human intention, and human meanings.[198]

Sei Shōnagon's *The Pillow Book* delineates intimate interactions between things, times, and places, and transitions that occurred within her world in tenth century Japan.[199] It is speculated that the collection of entries in her book was conceived as lists of seasonally and aesthetically appropriate objects to be used in poetic compositions. Poetry here occurs as constellations formed from brief coalescences of things: a selected flower to accompany a letter, the deliberate layering of fabric, a chance view of the river. The writer's role is to observe these temporary meetings and draw attention to their impermanent encounters. It is said that in writing Shōnagon and her fellow women diarists of tenth century Japan facilitated the use of *hiragana*—the distinctively Japanese cursive script adapted from Chinese characters—to give expressions to the spoken forms, and forms to stories. By writing, Shōnagon actively interpreted the life and rituals of the *Heian* court—an emancipatory act that allowed narratives to emerge.

In writing weather, we write about how the weather affects our bodies, our emotional worlds, and our creative lives. In *Bird Art Life and Death* Kyo Maclear frames her year of following a "birder–musician" in Toronto through winter anguish, the wait for spring, the summer deluge, and autumn regrets.[200] She begins:

> That was the winter that started early. It snowed endlessly. I remember a radio host saying; "Global Warming? Ha!" It was also the winter I found myself with a broken part. I didn't know what it was that was broken, only that whatever widget had previously kept me on plan … no longer worked as it should … I wanted to be reminded. I had lost a beat.[201]

Writings, recordings, notes, and fragments coalesce to form the narratives of passing time within intersecting worlds. In reading weather writing, we read ourselves.

RAINWATER: GRASSES AND TREES SPROUT

7 September 2011

In the garden ...

Plants that have lost their leaves in winter and have sprouted again:

White cedar

Mulberry

Fig

White mulberry

Lemon verbena

Almond

Maple

Plants that are flowering:

Mulberry

White mulberry

Avocado

Lemon

Lavender

Waratah

Plants that are fruiting:

Orange

Passionfruit

Cumquat

Finger lime

Fig

Recently planted:

Potato

Composing with incomplete fragments through associative logic is exemplified by the Japanese technique of *zuihitsu* (or following the brush). Compared with essaying as exploratory writing technique, *zuihitsu* is more passive, more fragmentary, or perhaps more poetic, producing meandering journeys through tenuously connected images. Discoveries are made through the brief coalescence of fragments. Variants of Shōnagon's fragmentary poetic form re-appeared in modern Japan during in the interwar period. Its subsequent popularisation as a literary form is telling in its effectiveness in conjuring an evolving picture of a changing world.

In 'Return of the *zuihitsu:* Print Culture, Modern Life, and Heterogeneous Narrative in Prewar Japan,' Rachel DiNitto began by describing the indefinable nature of zuihitsu as a "catch-all genre composed of fragmentary and heterogeneous writing" within Japanese literary scholarship.[202] She tackles this elusiveness by examining the boundaries delineated by the production and consumption of *kindai zuihitsu* (or modern *zuihitsu*) in Japan from the 1920s to 1930s when the growing urban middle-class readership was confronted by the uncertainties and anxieties of modernisation. *Bungei shunjū*, the successful literary magazine with a distinct category for zuihitsu writings, serves as a prime example, DiNitto writes:

> As Bungei shunjū's advertising copy stated, the magazine was not traditional Japanese tea and sweets, but Western "coffee" (kōhi), "black tea" (kōcha), and "dessert" (dezāto). The journal was read by the new, urban flâneur. It was "a magazine for the intellectual strolling through the city."[203]

The fast-changing world of modern Japan was made legible by the first-person perspective, short length and intimate accessibility of the zuihitsu form. Kindai zuihitsu came to denote writings that capture the impressions and experiences of modernity, where "the phrasing is short. But the sense is deep."[204]

DiNitto writes:

> Tosaka [Jun] argues that these new genres are capable of dealing with the fragmentary nature of reality in ways that pure literature cannot because of the limitations imposed by structure. He makes connections between the fragmentary nature of the world and the language used to describe it.[205]

'Following the brush' has affinity with weather-watching and diary-keeping, where observations, contemplation, and reflection form a way to interpret weather as experience. Liza Dalby's *East Wind Melts the Ice: A Memoir through the Seasons* whose chapters are structured using the Chinese Almanac's solar terms is also modelled on *zuihitsu*. She writes:

> the brush is not an automaton—it is still drawing from your own knowledge and experience. But rather than plotting out the path in advance, you let yourself be open to following a meander in which one subject calls to mind another, and that in turn may lead to something unexpected.[206]

This method of jotting down observations, making note of surfaced memories, and freely associating seemingly random thoughts present a rich avenue for making sense of our experience within a changing world. The format of "short phrasing" and "deep sensing" may call to mind how one may tweet a haiku about a spectacular sunset sky, Instagram a short video of ephemeral contrails, or post a still photograph and a word beneath in the form of a *Denkbild* (thought-image). Today, *zuihitsu* re-appears once again as a writing method of choice for the contemporary weather-observers and diary-keepers. Armed with the ubiquitous mobile devices (complete with global positioning systems), we are able not only to capture weather observations, but more importantly to make sense of them.

jolaw7200

Art School UTas

jolaw7200#illalmanac 12 August 2017 09:49 Hobart 7.5 degrees Celsius 1.2 mm rain since 9am. Out and about, it's raining again after a vague promise of sunshine. It's properly cold, numbed toes in boots. Now headed in for refuge in a hipster cafe, digits are stinging from the warmth.

jolaw7200

UOW: University of Wollongong, Australia

jolaw7200#illalmanac 21 August 2017, 08.40 13.2 degrees Celsius. Altocumulus Mackerel sky. Robert Hooke in 1663 wrote in his *Method for Making a History of the Weather* "Let Water'd, signify a Sky that has many high thin & small clouds looking almost like waterd tabby, calld in some places a maccarell sky from Resemblance it has to the spots on the Backs of those fishes".

jolaw7200

Austinmer, New South Wales, Australia

jolaw7200#illalmanac 8 September 2017 16:01 Morning winds and hot sun. Quiet at work. A truck broke down on the freeway. Afternoon sun lights up the neighbour's flowering plum.

jolaw7200

East Village, Manhattan

jolaw7200#illalmanac 30 September 2017 Last day in New York. Much much cooler. Overcast skies, but forecast rain did not materialise. New York City view from New Museum's sky room. The view reminds me of Brian Eno's video painting.

jolaw7200

Corrimal, New South Wales, Australia

jolaw7200#illalmanac 9 October 2017 Night rain wetted the bitumen but by morning it seemed like it never happened. A scorching afternoon.

In writing weather, we write place. In the April chapter of her book, Maclear reflects on her friend's encounter with Wendell Berry at a public lecture. Berry gave those 'shopping for a home' this advice: "Stop somewhere, and begin the thousand-year-long process of knowing a place."[207] After all, weather-diarists have needed to be in one place to make sense of their observations. In 1663, Robert Hooke called for a collective approach in weather observation (what may be known as a citizen science today). In his delivery of 'Method for Making a History of the Weather' at the Royal Society, he urged that people "'in distant parts of this Kingdom' [to] adopt a standard practice of weather observation."[208] This practice slowly gained traction through the availability of instruments in the subsequent century. Harris recounts two brothers-in-law, Thomas Barker of Lyndon and Gilbert White of Selbourne, whose weather observation and record-keeping held them in their respective places of residence for their entire lives. Their efforts produced six decades of weather records and natural history of the land.[209] It was necessary for these diarists to be rooted in place.

Despite the years Maclear has lived in Toronto, her history as the daughter of two migrants (whose English father and Japanese mother, she described, settled in Canada like two pot plants) has made her connection to place "aloof."[210] Yet, through the journeys she took in the year when she followed the birds and the birder, Maclear shows her physical traversal of the urban decay, the woods, the waters, and the suburbs of Toronto provided renewed opportunities for her to know her city and her place within it. Her meandering took her to parking lots behind shopping malls, ports and bays, abandoned beaches, and poisoned lakes. Unexpectedly, within this ugliness she met thriving wild life. This physical movement through space drew lines that connected her to other urban creatures, animals to their dwellings, places of habitation to places of urban wilderness. Tim Ingold writes, "Life is lived, I reasoned, along paths, not just in places, and paths are lines of a sort. It is along paths, too, that people grow into a knowledge of the world around them, and describe this world in the stories they tell."[211] Unlike tracing ephemeral cloudscapes, walking on land produces tangible imprints. The Wordsworths' walk in the Lake district guided by the "wandering cloud" connected the movement of the atmosphere with humans' movement on land.

Artworks can be created by a diverse range of marks that reveal the analogies of our bodies to place: from Alfred Wainwright's *Pictorial Guides to the Lakeland Fells* book series that was written and drawn entirely by hand, to Amanda Thomson's collections of works presented in her *Some Moments in Fieldworks* thesis exhibition (2013).[212] These marks encapsulate the stories that occur in the terrains we encounter. Each letter on each page of Wainwright's seven books was hand-written; each line of his maps was hand-drawn; each mark bears the trace of his gestures and movements, shaped in turn by the physical geography of the fells. In a similar way, Thomson's GPS drawings of "task-based walks through place," her photopolymer etchings of ancient Scottish forests, her contemplative video diptych of the woods, and prints of deadwoods, draw our "attention to situations that arise, perhaps as the landscape reveals itself, by being in a particular place at a particular time."[213] Her prints are made from weathered etching plates she intentionally left in the open on the Island of Mull and Abernethy Forest for twelve months and present the direct *Spuren* of the world.[214] Thomson writes, "I am interested in weaving the interconnections between lines of walking, discovery, making, stories of place, and in creating paths of narrative, with and beyond text."[215] Geography's cultural turn towards humanities and the arts re-focused sites and places as medium for narratives where lines or paths can become a type of writing that inscribes stories. For Maclear, combining this physical traversal with the practice of writing was an important way to steer away from the romanticism often associated with nature writing. Perhaps Berry's suggestion of beginning a "thousand-year long process of knowing a place" can be achieved through a deep-sensing of place in our physical traversing of our surrounds.

COLD DEW: CHRYSANTHEMUMS TINGE YELLOW/DUCKS MIGRATE

20 October 2008

The Kandagawa has a long and complex history – something that I am yet to learn more about. What I can gather so far is that it was originally named Hirakawa and has a number of tributaries and diversions. Many modifications have been carried out, changing its natural appearance, shape, and character. The river's source is the Inokashira pond in Mitaka (western Tokyo). The river heads East towards Shinjuku, then winds North pass Takadanobaba, then turns West again through Bunkyo-ku (ward), running through the central districts of Tokyo (and alongside part of the Chuo line from just beyond Yotsuya, to Iidabashi, Suidobashi, and Ochanomizu). Once it passes Kanda, it joins the Sumidagawa (river) and flows into Tokyo Bay.

Many of the modifications and riverworks were ordered by the Shogun, Tokugawa Ieyasu, in the sixteenth century. Their purpose was to ensure that adequate drinking water could reach the growing population of Edo. Today, the Kandagawa mainly acts as an enormous drain for storm water. Maps of the river are marked by its 104 bridges, many of which have their own significant histories. We walked along the stretch between Takadanobaba and Shinjuku (around 7 km). The intersection between Otakibashi (bridge) and Waseda Dori (avenue) separates Takadanobaba from Kita-Shinjuku (North Shinjuku). The Kandagawa also separates Shinkjuku-ku (ward) to the East from Nakano-ku (ward) to the West.

Between Otakibashi and Kireibashi at the top-end of Kita-Shinjuku, the riverwalk is designed for the pleasure of pedestrians (it is closed to traffic – even to cyclists). Here, people walk their dogs, jog, exercise, meander, and enjoy the greenery, the artificial stream, and abundant public seating. We saw two old ladies discussing how their plants are doing in their gardens; a young school girl stopped and said hello to them before going next door to visit her grandmother.

Near Kashiwabashi, I spotted an early reddish maple and opposite was a grumpy-looking mermaid statue outside a small villa. Just beyond Daidobashi, eight or so very old ladies were sitting in a close row in the sun, tended by their carer. They were chatting and watching the birds. They said *konnichiwa* as we walked by. We crossed Ome Kaido and Yodobashi which separates Kita-Shinjuku from Shinjuku. The vista has now completely changed to an urban one.

The river continues to divide Nakano-ku from Shinjuku-ku. We saw some ducks on the river. A man was strolling along the river with his wife. He stopped next to me and said something about *Kamo* (duck). Then he asked in English, You call them 'ducks' in English? We said yes. There are many kinds, you know. I asked him what kinds those were. He said that they were from Russia. They migrate, I said, then asked, in Autumn? He checked with his wife then answered, about two months ago. I asked him whether he studied birds. He chuckled a little and said, No, I study human beings. Then he and his wife said good-bye and left us.

Just about 50 metres beyond, a group of street cats were waiting to be fed. We turned left at Aiwaibashi into Shinjuku, leaving the river.

~

Through walking across physical geographies, past terrains, and metaphors, WG Sebald's *The Rings of Saturn* transverses spaces of human history. Intersecting narratives are woven through a braiding of images and texts, and the indeterminacy between fact and fiction allows the stories to hover as interstitial echoes. Stewart Martin notes, "This ambiguity is the medium of memory as well as any artwork that aspires to the self-conscious illusion of truth."[216] Sebald's writings induce the experience of mourning—mourning for losses that we no longer remember, and through walking, memories and histories re-surface.

In walking and writing we become capable of sensing the imprints left by disappearance. Leon van Shaik theorises spatial practices that provide a strategic "connection to heritage." He writes:

> To perceive our heritage ... is to fight our own amnesia, to become again conscious as we were as children, first encountering the phenomena of the world we found ourselves in, of the touch, taste, texture, smell, scale, enclosing and exposing heft of places.[217]

Artists, writers, architects and thinkers have always engaged in the practice of chronicling everyday life through its detritus. Van Shaik reminds us that:

> André Breton documented the traces left in the arcades of Paris in his book *Paris Peasant*. Kurt Schwitters tried to capture Hamburg by collecting the discarded scraps that survived urban events ... The Situationists conducted pseudonymous research in a procedure they called a "dérive."[218]

Like the maps produced by intimate physical interactions with place, archives, weather records and diary entries also provide a kind of map that bears the *Spüren* of the world that made them. Writing weather provides an active open framework, a space to study and contemplate our encounters with environmental systems at different scales. This platform allows a deep engagement with our changing world and the time to develop a critical understanding of our place within. Weather is experience. In writing weather, we write ourselves.

MINOR SNOW: HEAVEN'S ESSENCE RISES, EARTH'S ESSENCE SINKS

31 May 2012

The pentad when heaven's essence rose and earth's essence sank. Great winds swept across the Australian's east coast. Bellambi weather station recorded wind gusts up to 94 kilometres per hour from a west northwest direction on Saturday 26 June. Elsewhere, a slow moving low pressure system brought heavy rain to Victoria, causing flooding on city streets that was made worse by accumulation of autumn leaves near drainage areas. The precipitation also fell in the alpine region, amassing up to 300 mm of fresh snow in some towns. The cold change swept across the continent bringing wintery conditions throughout, and, to the delight of weather watchers, breaking records. Canberra is said to have experienced an overnight sub-zero average of −0.2°C, reportedly the coldest May in half a century. Darwin experienced a chilly 24.8°C maximum on Tuesday 29 June; the coldest May day in 31 years.

The subsolar point, or solar noon, is where the sun is directly overhead in relation to the observer on the ground. In winter, the subsolar point moves away from the southern hemisphere towards the Tropic of Cancer (23.5°N), the midday sun climbs lower in our sky; consequently, we receive less insolation. Asides from lowering the apparent air temperature, the differing amount of solar heating create changes in air movement in the atmosphere. For example, eastern Australia is particularly affected by 'east coast lows' in the winter months when intense low pressure systems cause strong winds and heavy rainfalls like those experienced at the beginning of this pentad. Pressure systems in the lower atmosphere, such as the sub-tropical ridge, are associated with dry winters and stable weather conditions in Australia's north, along with wet winters in the south.

According to palaeoclimatological theory, the earth's current atmosphere is in its third iteration. When the planet was forming the nascent atmosphere was constituted by abundant lighter elements, such as hydrogen and helium. That was soon dispersed by solar winds and the intense thermal activities of the earth and greenhouse gases from earth's volcanic activities were quickly replaced the lost atmosphere. The oxygen in our current atmosphere is attributed to the presence of aerobic organisms like cyanobacteria. The point when organisms and minerals became saturated with oxygen and the gas became free in the atmosphere for the first time is known as the 'Great Oxygenation Event'. It occurred about 2.4 billion years ago and is also known as the 'Oxygen Catastrophe' because as this newly freed gas accumulated in the atmosphere it killed the anaerobic organisms that had inhabited the early earth and resulted in mass extinction.

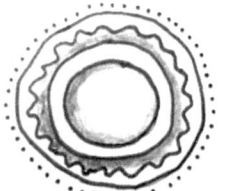

Survival zone

Look at Mars. The core received multiple shocks from asteroid hits and stopped rotating around its axis, leading to the disappearance of the planet's magnetic shield.[219] The shield was protecting its atmosphere from the solar wind. Without this shield, the atmosphere of Mars was stripped away by relentless solar winds, exposing the planet to deadly radiation. The magnetic shield was generated by the planet's molten iron core, acting as a dynamo: the planet's beating heart. The heart stopped—and so did all life on the surface.

Earth's magnetic shield is also a consequence of our planet's beating heart, equally vulnerable, contingent, and precious. A miracle. Protected by the invisible shield, our planet's atmosphere is open to the cosmos, constantly entangled with solar wind and bombarded by space bodies large and small. It converses with an infinity beyond any scientific model of prediction and control: that which the models do not and cannot see; the unknown unknowns, a place of wonder.

Complications

It's not always plain sailing.

Sometimes—usually it's at the end of a long day when the humidity in the room makes the air feel like cement, when our minds have drifted towards the emails we need to send or the school pick-ups or the long drive up the escarpment, when the blu tack has failed again and four or five Atmospheres have fallen to the floor—sometimes, someone gives up or says,"just cut it!" or we have a circular conversation about what we mean by rational modernity or electromagnetism or whatever.

Sometimes it's exactly those moments that take us in a new direction. Ted and Jo pick up the modernity thread and look at it from different angles: a coin flipping in the marketplace, a different take on labour. Su doesn't agree at all. Joshua tries to keep up. Cath asks a question; Eva makes a note. Su switches conversation and she and Eva discuss the northern and southern auroras. In another corner, Louise tells Joshua about channel-billed cuckoos calling out during a Geminid meteor shower. David, a newcomer to the conversation that afternoon, listens to the overlapping dialogue: the points where ideas come together, but also where they rip apart. "This mess is what we're writing about," he says.

Jade joins and asks: "Where are your voices? I need to feel you in there." Lucas asks Jade to tell a story about the land, one he has told Lucas before, the one where he uses the house analogy, and Jade says it's hard to talk about anything with a big black microphone plonked in front of him.

On another day, Kim says, "Why are there *roos* in the document every time there's the word *bear* or *bare*?"

"It's a spell check thing," Cath says.

"Ha. I thought it might have been that, or it was someone being fiercely nationalistic!"

Reindeer

Cooped up in our narrow work space, and confined by the humidity of a February afternoon in Wollongong, Eva remembers a different atmosphere. An experience from far away from us, and yet also so close, in the Arctic north of Sweden.

Here, in this open, frozen space, Saami herders have driven their reindeer for centuries. On a visit to Arctic Sweden several years ago, speaking with reindeer herders about their lives, I was told by an extraordinary old woman how she rode on a reindeer as a child across the valley beneath the lake we now looked across—a route her family and people had followed for generations. But now the old routes and grazing habits are increasingly disrupted, not just by construction of hydro dams, although that has been a big issue since the 1960s, disrupting lifestyles and traditional knowledge, but by fallout from the Chernobyl nuclear accident in April 1986. The fallout caused reindeer meat to be so contaminated that it could not be eaten: a problem that still persists.[220] And now, increasingly, the disruption comes from a changing climate.

Other herders lamented this issue to us. When the snow is light or only moderately deep, reindeer graze by using their hooves to scrape the snow away from ground lichens. They also feed on tree lichen but this is a supplementary source of food. In recent years, global warming has been changing the consistency of the snow. Increasing freeze-thaw events result in a crust of ice forming instead of what was more commonly dry powder snow.[221] The ice crusts are resistant: the reindeer frequently cannot break through to access food. The melting of permafrost and other impacts of warming are causing changes in reindeer migration patterns. Similar impacts apply to salmon populations and other species that contribute to the resilience of these Arctic ecosystems. For the Chukchi people in Russian Siberia, and other indigenous populations in the far north, grazing lands and fishing practices that have functioned well for centuries are compromised.[222] Warming in these regions risks triggering significant 'tipping points' in the global climate system, due to feedback loops that are likely to be activated by release of the huge quantities of carbon currently locked in the extensive permafrost.

I listen to these stories and wonder about climate justice.

Time

Teleological time moves in one direction, along a line, usually under banners of progress, from less to more, from few to many, vampiric extraction its main motif. By contrast, atmospheric time is cyclical, marked by an eternal repetition of death and revival, rooted in, and emerging from, the concrescence of material artefacts making our world.

Rain magic

And time's slippages:

A wet and windy day on Mount Washington. It's the 1940s. Two men hike up the steep mountain. One, Irving Langmuir, stops to retie his shoe, the other, his younger protégé, Vincent Schaefer, keeps on going. When they reach a certain point on the mountain, they stop and shoot a substance into the clouds in an attempt to cause rain.

They are not successful.

Later, when they are back at work in their laboratory at the General Electric Company, Schaefer plays around with dry ice and realizes that it can change super-cooled water into ice crystals. This, he thinks, might be the way to make rain.

In the same laboratory, Bernard Vonnegut, brother of Kurt the novelist, sits at his desk, yellow lamp lighting his scrawl, as he theorises the ways in which silver iodide could be used to seed clouds. His head is full of dreams and then some. Just like his brother. Or maybe it was Langmuir that did the theorizing. Because remember, Vonnegut didn't get his patent in until much much later. So maybe it was Langmuir at his desk dreaming and then some.

And his dreams led to cloud seeding becoming something that the military have an interest in.

Now it's March, 1967. There's a military pilot named Captain James Peters. Peters is part of the 54 Weather Reconnaissance Squadron, and on the day I'm talking about (the date redacted on all official documents) Peters is flying a C-130 Hercules over Laos, in a mission to seed clouds with silver iodide. They have a squadron motto: "Make mud, not war!" They intend to obstruct enemy progress with rain.

They may or may not be successful. (Information redacted.)

Who is to say whether those squadron members who later said, *it was raining anyway,* were disgruntled by the post war (lack of) treatment received on their return home.

It's not only war that rainmaking is used for. Entertainment. Sports. Making rain soon becomes making snow on winter ski fields (where snow falls have dropped off) for wealthy vacationers and skiing enthusiasts.

What about 2008? This is in China, shortly before the opening ceremony of the Beijing Olympics. A dedicated team from the Weather Modification Department launches 1104 rockets, from 21 different locations, dispersing silver iodide pellets into clouds. The aim is to cause rain to fall by dissolving the clouds that are floating towards the Olympic Stadium (what many have affectionately dubbed the Bird's Nest.)

They are successful.

In 2016, sometime (date not redacted but lost in the plethora of information on the Internet), Hydro Tasmania seeds clouds that are drifting over the Derwent River. They've been doing it for years, but on this day there are flood warnings in place. Rain falls, and yes, there is a flood. The worst for years. Water rushes across farmland, plucking produce from the soil and upending animals who flounder and drown. A local couple, whose farm is in the Ouse region, demands to know *who the fuck thought it was wise to seed fucking clouds when fucking flood warnings were in place?* This couple get on their high horse and phone the company. They want an answer *to their fucking question.* When they don't get a response (their calls are passed from one secretary to another; return calls promised but the promises are never fulfilled) they go to the papers. There's a story written. Their picture is on the front page of the local rag. Despite this (or because of it) they never get an answer. They never find out *who the fuck thought it was wise to seed fucking clouds when fucking flood warnings were in place?*

And out in the desert somewhere, in the middle of Australia, in a time that might be anytime, a songmaker sits on dry earth and sings a song about rain; a song about rhythms and water and land and weather and rituals and ways of being.

Chalk dust to turbulent storm—a maker's magic.

Lost and found

We have an earth system that is shapeshifting—it is nimble—from systems and nodes to modes of composition.

Passing a piece of paper around the room. "It's a game," he says. "Free association. A list of things we have lost and found."

The escarpment, someone writes. Crumbling rocks. Deep time scales. Land Country, Sea Country. That thing, you know, that ruin in the shallows of Port Kembla, bream, pilchards, pilchards with herpes, the Antarctic ice fish, those tiny ice-bubbles, ancient air intermingling with Paris smog, ancient water in modern stormwater systems, coral, brain cells, a fungus, phosphorescent lichen, botany, shifting, Saharan jungle, wild donkeys, greater bilbies, the wolves in Yellowstone, the deer they ate, forest creatures, the spirits within, the Internet, the asteroid, the Cassini space probe, the Crab Nebula, the eye of the fan-palm, hurricanes, freezing wind slicing over ice, sand cutting into your legs, blue-banded bees, bee stings, finches pecking at millet, don't get me started on birds, lyrebirds, cat birds in the hill behind the uni, the tinkling of bell birds in the Blue Mountains, antiphonal calls, music, a line of breath, time like an arrow, a parrot in the Puerto Rican jungle, telescopes, metallic hydrogen, toxic cigarette smoke, tar, polystyrene cups on the side of the highway, cutting through the hill near Conjola, the walnut tree in my garden, a golden elm by the Yarra, river water, holy water, the right to breathe clean air, air purifiers as a status symbol, the blue sky in Beijing during APEC, sweatshop letters sewn into Primark garments, Guangzhou, Hong Kong, Mumbai, New York real estate, jet streams, concrescence, hanging rocks, living fossils, fracking, hacking, lacking, flak jacket, gulfs, engulfs, bogs, leaf mould, mushrooms, consistency, lightness, quickness, visibility, invisibility, fog, smog, the water in Cape Town, in Melbourne, in Adelaide, oxygen, life, wonder.

Swarm

In the cavity between his parents' bedroom, above, and the lounge room, below, was a beehive. It had been there for years: when they bought the house, they were walking through the garden and the real estate agent had tried to draw attention away from the steady buzzing stream flowing from the drainpipe. There was also a hole leading out of the hive in the skirting board. When he came in to kiss his mother good morning, he had to watch his step.

Every spring, on one particular day, the bees would suddenly embark on a mass suicide mission. They'd surge out of the hole in the skirting board, humming like thunder. They'd swirl around the light fittings, bombard the mirror on the bedside table. The air was full of them: a lattice of fizzing creatures. He'd watch them from the safety of his parents' bed, using the covers as a protective shield. Eventually, the bees' trajectories would become sluggish and they'd hover, low, over the cream carpet. Then, one by one, they'd drop, twitching, like pieces of popcorn. And then not twitching. It was his job to vacuum up the bodies after it was all over.

Bees

Such a surprise: a cloud of tiny bees, quiet, busy, dense, amongst the profusion of flowers in this sunny near-alpine vegetable garden in the foothills of Kosciuszko National Park, New South Wales. I believe these bees to be native—so much smaller, quieter, and somehow less threatening than the common European honey bees; so active and so many. If they are native, this is a gift. An international bee crisis threatens to eradicate the pollinators of one third of everything we eat, but here in this high altitude place an obviously healthy population of tiny native bees exists. In North America more than half the 1400 bee species that populate the continent are in decline, and nearly a quarter are at risk of extinction.[223] Here in this mountain place of native forest and patches of pasture, there is a healthy, active profusion; the ground beneath the eucalypts carpeted in spring and early summer with flowering alpine shrubs. Perhaps it is this rich environment that allows this bee population to thrive still? Perhaps bee diseases and decline have not yet reached this place.

Researchers from the University of Western Australia have established that degraded environments lower the metabolic rate of bees, limiting the distances they will travel to forage, with the overall effect of reducing their intake of nectar and putting more strain on the bees' ability to function.[224] Add to this the use of chemicals toxic to bees, widespread ecosystem changes, and other forms of environmental degradation.

Environments like this are precious. This swarm of little bees is a small miracle, its future, like that of so many other species, tied inextricably to decisions on the part of landholders, farmers, governments, economic value systems. Visible in this small garden is an intimate entanglement of human and nonhuman, and how close and precious they feel …

Reflecting on a period of bloody civil war, WB Yeats writes of a house whose masonry is crumbling, whose walls are loosening. He calls for the honey-bees to "come build in the empty house of the stare" that we might again know sweetness.[225]

Interruptions (for Jen)

sorry can I just interrupt? someone has their
mobile phone on and the electronics

                oh that must be mine

it needs to be off

                sorry I didn't understand that

it's doing a digital crackle

                so you're hearing much more than
                we're hearing in the room

that's good for me in some ways

                no one can bother you now

that's right

                sure

ummmm

                I dunno I've

so I've got to stop being so formal about this
I just gotta fuckin chill out you know?

they are big microphones

                sorry

don't be sorry but let me make fun of the fuckin thing

                yeah yeah

                sorry

don't be don't be

I'm just trying to get comfortable.

Observatory

In *The Great Silence* (2014), a film installation first presented at the Philadelphia Museum of Art, artists Jennifer Allora and Guillermo Calzadilla and writer Ted Chiang make a connection between the Arecibo Observatory in Puerto Rico and the Puerto Rican parrot. The parrots inhabit the jungle surrounding the observatory. They are currently listed as critically endangered by the World Conservation Bureau; there are fewer than 80 birds in the wild.

The installation intercuts images of the telescope, the parrots in the jungle and in captivity, and graphs of the sounds recorded at Arecibo. Chiang has written a story to accompany the images; it's narrated by one of the parrots. The parrot says:

> The humans use Arecibo to look for extra-terrestrial intelligence. Their desire to make a connection is so strong that they've created an ear capable of hearing across the universe. But I and my fellow parrots are right here. Why aren't they interested in listening to our voices?

The parrot also discusses the Fermi Paradox, also known as the 'great silence'. The parrot tells us that "the universe is also so old that even one technological species would have had time to expand and fill the galaxy. Yet there is no sign of life anywhere except on Earth." The parrot discusses one theory to explain the paradox: perhaps there are other lives out there, but they are hiding from us to protect themselves from attack. The parrot reflects: "It makes sense to remain quiet and avoid attracting attention."[226]

Subject to change

1. The new cat requires a steady feed of grass. We can't let her outside: we're afraid she'll attack birds or get run over or grow melanomas on her ears. So we grow a mini-lawn in a container in our kitchen.

2. We feed the bees syrup made from processed sugar. The NSW Department of Primary Industries advises that "white sugar is the supplement that will provide the least risk to bees in the form of digestive complaints … [it] is also economically attractive."[227]

3. In the lab, we're exposing corals to different strands of algae, encouraging new symbiotic partnerships. It's an accelerated form of natural selection: we're working out which combination will survive a future of heat or acid stress. "We're doing what nature does," we say. "We're just trying to accelerate it so that corals can keep up."[228]

4. For the 2022 World Cup in Qatar, we're building stadiums with in-built air conditioners which can drop the temperature by 20 degrees. We'll watch the game and then catch air-conditioned buses back to our air-conditioned hotel rooms.

5. Children play in quadrangles with air cleansed by purifiers. They look to the sky, hoping for a hue of APEC blue.

Soil

Soil science is something that I cannot easily grasp, so I ask my friend Farmer to explain the basics. I invite Farmer to indulge me by considering the perspective of a beneficial nematode—one of those trillions of microscopic worm-like organisms that live in the soil. I want Farmer to tell me what such a nematode needs to be happy (in its nematode-ish way) and healthy. Farmer imagines this is what the nematode would say:

> We live in the soil along with bacteria, worms and fungi. Together we are the soil 'biology'. We are very happy when Farmer does four things: a) stops all cultivation and leaves the soil undisturbed, b) plants a variety of crops, c) leaves plant cover on the surface and d) leaves living roots under the soil. It provides us with a good home where we can stay warm and hydrated, eat a healthy and varied diet, and have air to breathe. When Farmer takes all surface cover away and ploughs the soil, he makes us all thirsty, hungry, homeless and running a fever. That's how he kills us. If there's a drought but the plants remain in the soil we all hibernate, but if no plants remain and the drought persists then we die.

Even though the nematode is microscopic, it has a lot to say:

> If Farmer grows a broad range of plants, we'll see many different creatures in the soil who like to feed from these plants. Different species of plants have different root systems that allow water to filter into the soil when they die, as long as Farmer doesn't cultivate the soil. Worms like the old roots because they provide food and easy access through the soil. Worms follow the root channel, eat the root and create a space where water and air can get into the soil. We soil animals are aerobic, so we need to breathe air, just as Farmer does.

> We need water too, but can live dormant in the soil for decades waiting for the next rain event.
>
> When we are happy, we all busily search for nutrients for the plants to help them grow well. We live close to the plant roots because the plant feeds us with liquid sugars which give us energy to do our job. Liquid sugars are made from carbon dioxide that the plants take from the air and leak into the soil, using the power of the sun to process the sugars. In return, we make nutrients available to the plant such as zinc, phosphorus, potassium, calcium, sulphur and nitrogen. Most of the time, the plants can't use those nutrients unless we convert them first. Nutrients become highly enriched when they pass through us, then they're ready for the plant. It's just like those ginormous bovine things that eat grass and create really good fertiliser when it passes through them.

Farmer, having a bigger perspective on cows, chimes in:

> Animals above ground also perform an important job for the plant cycle, as long as we don't overgraze. Overgrazing is what leads to desertification. Grazing animals disturb the soil a little, which helps to plant new seeds. They keep the old vegetation down, allowing the new seeds to grow, which keeps plants regenerating. So, you can see that we all help each other.

Cascade

I read recently an account of the reintroduction of gray wolves to Yellowstone National Park in 1995, after an absence of seventy years. Wolves, a single species. The effects of their reintroduction surprised everyone. Through what biologists call a 'trophic cascade', the re-presence of the wolves had consequences, not just for animal and plant life, but also on the geological level.[229]

Wolves are a keystone species in this ecosystem, and their absence for so many years had significantly changed it. Deer had flourished in the absence of wolves, despite control efforts by rangers, and they had eaten down the vegetation so much that many other species (especially beavers, who create habitat niches for species like otters, muskrats, ducks, fish, reptiles and amphibians, and also control streamflow variability with their dams) also declined greatly. When wolves were reintroduced, the grazing behaviour of deer changed: they began to avoid certain plains where wolves hunted. They kept to the hills. In the valleys and along streams, vegetation recovered. Forests of aspen and willow and cottonwood. Beavers recovered. Their dependent species recovered, and predators and carrion-eaters such as ravens and eagles returned to the area. Bears returned, to hunt and to eat the increasing abundance of berries. It's a bit like the economic 'trickle-down effect', to use an analogy that pits cause against effect, but here it works.

Most surprisingly, even the physical landscape changed. Regeneration of vegetation on the banks of the rivers and their catchment slopes reduced erosion, and stabilised the courses of the rivers. They meandered less, channels narrowed, and additional pools and riffles formed, which also offered additional habitat niches. It just shows how precarious a 'balance' can be.

What records are being constructed through human actions on the plains outside Yellowstone, or for that matter here where the story of this book began, under the mountain for millennia called Djenbella, in the strip of land between the escarpment and the sea? All that plastic, all those chicken bones, all those radionuclides, all that excavation of mountains and clearing of forests and pumping of waste into the air and oceans …
As if we need reminding, and at the risk of sounding selfishly concerned: we are facing 50°C days in Sydney and Melbourne by mid-century, food and water crises, a need to change our way of living to adapt to the changes around us. We are a key species: we could be the wolves but instead we are the absence of them. We have pushed elegantly slow-moving planetary systems into unprecedented acceleration, like reckless joy-riders, and now we are seeing the cascading consequences of our actions. Howl.

Rhythm and song

This was atmosphere sung up, returned, and mattered fleetingly. Elder Alice Cox took the museum bilby 'skin' from my hands and immediately sang *ninu*'s song. The bilby had long gone in living presence from these Maralinga Tjaruta homelands. Somehow, a bilby was with us, there, then, back in the sandy swale north of Ooldea, heading to its corkscrew burrow, reanimated in the voice and atmosphere of affective recall and call.

Fortunately, the greater bilby continues to dig burrows and grace desert areas elsewhere in Central Australia. That exchange causes me to wonder if there is a song for the long-nosed potoroo that survives in the managed country of Budderoo National Park. This on the escarpment near Jamberoo, south of Wollongong. The warm potoroo I cradled in calico before her weigh-in was silent. Tensed, ready to bolt back to the heath understorey and truffle digging. It will only be a few more minutes, I whispered to her. Zoologist Melinda Norton has been following the lives of these marsupials for a decade and a half now, and this was the annual potoroo survey.[230] The potoroo is recognised as a small-to-medium-sized animal, the weight group most represented in a list of thirty mammal species that have been extinguished from continental Australia in the not-quite 250 years since James Cook sailed north along the Illawarra coast.[231]

Ninu's song opens the valve on an atmospheric brew: the causes of past losses in conversation with contemporary precarities, recoveries and rewildings of fellow, endemic mammals. Can we dilate this inquiry and debate as a matter of concern? I think we must also mark and mourn extirpations and extinctions as new cultural silences; bleachings of colour and pattern, de-animations of local places, eradications of beauty and wonder. Not least, loss of song and rhythm. Keep the songbook full, *ninu* whispers back.

Ecologising affect and atmosphere in the Anthropocene: dear Rachel

Louise Boscacci

> We are moved ...
> —Sara Ahmed (2010)

Dear Rachel,

The news is grim. The Earth bios is unsettling and moving in response to planetary warming. The overdeveloped world of anthropogenic climate endangerment is well underway now, at multiple scales, and in unpredictable, unforeseen and yet-to-be-known ways. "The atmosphere is being radicalised," astrophysicist Katy Mack recently exclaimed.[232] And yet ...

And yet, the planet of bios and chaos in the remnant patch of woodland outside my door fills me with affect and wonder, daily. Is this the beauty and pragma—a type of love—that fuelled your marathon of critical endurance and narrative refusal? That lingers still, on a planet that just might shard your heart?

I want to write to you about wit(h)nessing and wondering, synsensorial attunements and connections. The overflow of wonder into mattering. About affective atmospheres. Affect as a site of praxis. The unfinished curiosity of 'What if?' About the feeling-thinking body in encounter: the importance of the a-bodied encounter-exchange. Too much, I know ...

It is eminently wise, as Anna Tsing cautions, to resist responding to the grand narrative of the western Anthropocene with another big theory that seeks to bind a living planet of infinite chaos and potential into another universal template, even an aesthetic one.[233] The writer-biologist Rachel Carson, in witness and translation in her book *Silent Spring* (1962), wrote of the violence of corporate chemical biocide in the nascent, yet-to-be-named Great Acceleration of the 1950s.[234] *Anthropos* as a new geological force, a planet-claiming singularity, again elides at the same time as it makes untold "slow violence," as Rob Nixon writes, with unequal relations of destruction.[235]

Carson astutely invoked a spectre of a *thousand* silent springs, a thousand counterparts, to localise the grim silent spring of her metasphere. In recent times, the posthumanities practitioner and theorist Cecilia Åsberg has called for thinking about a *thousand tiny* Anthropocenes (local, embodied, situated).[236] It is an approach that does not seek to minimise the shocking realities of a damaged planet and an undone Earth System tipped over by the combustion of carboniferous ancient life, but does refuse to normalise or contribute to the one big capital A in critical and aesthetic response and response-ability. Donna Haraway's recent figuration of the Chthulucene is—as one might expect from a regenerative biologist to her core—an intentional swerve into the fecundity and unruliness of a sympoietic bios of kin and kind. Of her alt-'cene, she writes: "The order is reknitted: human beings are with and of the Earth, and the biotic and abiotic powers of this Earth are the main story."[237]

Carson's literary oeuvre, composed decades before cyborg manifesti of multi-speciousness, situated more-than-human-ness, and chthonic powers that promise to have the last word, is at heart a refrain on the *interconnected onward flow* of the planet's "living world."[238] In this, human hubris along with our precarious fleshy carbon-written bodies is no less wondrously implicated. And, intermezzo, a generation ago now, the feminist environmental philosopher Val Plumwood, in provocations of thought as vivifying a gift today as then, argued that it was way past time to "negotiate a life membership in an ecological community of kindred beings," her other-than-human teachers, companions, predators, and even geological beings such as stones; her "earth others" call to mind a *biogeo* planet of relationality, both intimate and impossible.[239]

Compelled by her mid-twentieth century words, I have been making and writing postcards to Rachel Carson in the thick time of the present day.[240] The trilogy of postcard images and short narratives that follows was sparked by a chance encounter in twilight during an austral Spring—or *Ngoonungi* in the local Dharawal calendar.[241] I thought of Carson. I imagined she might also listen to the *trace* of that *affective exchange* in, and as, an aesthetics of practice that composes and speculates with more than words, and across porous boundaries of knowledge from material art-making, science, and affect scholarship.

My approach draws into conversation and amplifies an older expanded understanding of the term *aesthetics*: "the discipline through which the organism becomes attuned to its environment."[242] Here, 'environment' is not an illusory stage or background, as the troublesome term 'the environment' can infer. Instead it is an (im)material milieu of relationship, a life network. Rachel Carson cannot reply of course, but perhaps I am also writing to another future Rachel, unknown in my present, who may in time care to update this intertemporal call and response from within her own 'cene.

The Synsensorium of Twilight

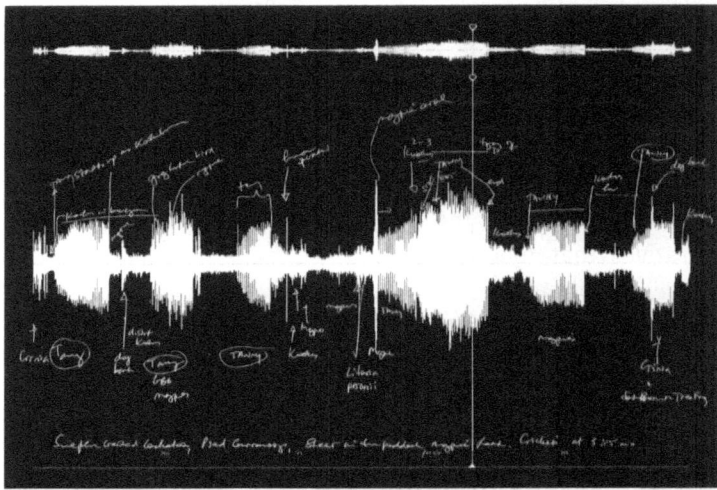

Figure 14. Louise Boscacci, *Tawny Twilight Calling*, 2017. Annotated sonogram of 2:30 minutes sound passage, 13 October 2013, Illawarra highlands (Wingecarribee). Postcard (recto), 10 x 15 cm. Digital print.

Dear Rachel,   *30 December 2016*

Listen!

There it is: that throb into the solar plexus of a deep thrumming electric-edged staccato delivered in steady, constant refrain. A tawny frogmouth (Podargus strigoides) somewhere in the old messmate mid-canopy is booming low in the crepuscular interchange between day and night. It is a twilight tawny at work in the base affective register of a twice-daily transition zone.

Can you hear the echoes?

My first postcard to Rachel Carson, a sound postcard, is two and a half minutes of an acoustic passage of twilight recorded in the Illawarra highlands of New South Wales. Accompanying this is a print of its sonogram annotated with the aural pulse and pause of an ensemble of animal voices (see Figure 14). Scanning left to right, the vocal presence of the booming tawny frogmouth is signalled by the six large white bursts of sound. Other singers and callers drop in and out of the passage over time. The translated play list of names sequences the voices as individuals and species audibly join this twilight performance:

> *Crinia signifera* (Eastern common froglet)
> **Tawny frogmouth**
> Laughing kookaburra
> Australian magpies
> dog barking
> **Tawny frogmouth**
> grey butcherbirds (more than two)
> **Tawny frogmouth**
> magpies carolling
> kookaburras distant
> **Tawny frogmouth**
> *Litoria peronii* (Peron's treefrog)
> *Crinia signifera* (Eastern common froglet)
> *Litoria ewiingii* (Southern brown treefrog)
> **Tawny frogmouth**
> laughing kookaburra volleys (two or three birds)
> **Tawny frogmouth**
> *Litoria ewiingii* (Southern brown treefrog)
> neighbour's dog barking
> _____cut_____
> laughing kookaburras

Listening to the recording ports me back to stand again in encounter beside the old tree. The passage sounds out more than *Podargus* broadcasting visceral pulses from the safe darkness of branches at 7:15 pm. It carries the rolling interchange between day birds and this night bird, a bog frog, two tree frogs, innumerable insects, and other barely audible interlocutors. Just as laughing kookaburras are giving their last-light symphonic volleys, the frogmouth starts up. One marks the end of daylight in this springtime home patch; the other, the arrival of dark and the nocturnal life in the same refuge. Together: a multispecies, multi-bodied ensemble free-riffing across a moving light zone.

The remnant of woodland with the old, spreading messmate (*Warreeah*; *Eucalyptus obliqua*) is a survivor of the settler partitioning of Wadi Wadi forest, woodland and peat bog from the NSW Robertson Land Acts of 1860.[243] It is on the edge of an open paddock of euro pasture grasses with ten slick steers, next to the carbon pool of the small peat wetland. The little bog swamp is rich with a local pluriverse of co-species who also live and die in this shared mosaic of transformed rural lands. To my left eye and ear, the peat pool is darkening and loud with frogs. Light is on the run: all warm colours from salmon to sepia are heading southwest, leaving ink-wash dusk to drop into the eastern horizon and beckon the blue-black night sky. Civil twilight, nautical twilight, astronomical twilight, night sky.[244] A slow reminder of a turning planet in light and life relation with a solar body, the Sun. Up here in the patch, the clay ground underfoot is warm after a high summer-like day. Wafts of messmate and peppermint oils vaped from hot leaves are lingering in the evening air. Sound riffs with light and the wash of aromas. I slow my breathing to focus on listening. I am giddy with the synsensorial overflow of this twilight surround.[245]

I have come to embrace twilight, as first revealed by encountering the long crepuscular zones of the temperate Illawarra uplands, as an *affective atmosphere*. That word, *affective*. I need to linger a moment. My use of the terminology of *affect* and *affective* travels with the Spinozan-Deleuzian vector of understanding whereby affect refers to the continual every day flow of transient forces and intensities that move through sensing bodies and enhance or diminish capacities "to act, to engage, and to connect": the capacity to affect and be affected (*affectus/affectio*).[246] A chance encounter of powerful impingement—an experience of intense *a-bodied* provocation[247]—can for an artist act as an electric spark that catalyses new or unpredicted movement—excitements or "incitements to creation", as Elizabeth Grosz writes.[248] For artists, thinkers, writers, such an encounter and the durational passage of its push can be a rich waymaker in becomings of making, thinking, doing and undoing. Félix Guattari reminds us that affect is not a passively endured state: it is a site of work, of potential praxis.[249] I wager that in a thousand anthropocenes, in an age of carbon forcings, unpredictable feedback loops, and seemingly relentless ecological loss and re-formation, the affective register is far from ordinary, far from esoteric. Rather, in the realm of sensibility, the capacity to affect and be affected is an extraordinary gift of a conative, attuning body.[250] An affective atmosphere provokes and shifts feeling-thinking, the *somatic-cognitive*, the electric sensor of autonomic flesh and speculative mind. It generates and animates an internal, a-bodied atmosphere of feeling-tones and thinking lines. This is simultaneously material (corpo-real), and immaterial (corpo-virtual): fleetingness unable to be grasped by hand, but palpable, energising, enhancing, trans-moving. *Unwilled* and *unbiddable* in affectivity, the tawny twilight works as a *generative* chamber.

Twilight is a different provocateur for other minded bodies. Writer on cultural amnesia Andreas Huyssen diffracted the end-of-day phenomenon to allude to the fleeting, yet marvellous zone between remembering and forgetting. Twilight memories are those on the cusp of disappearance.[251] But, there is also morning twilight signalling the daily solar return: a space-time of potential regeneration, revalorisation, refusal, and remaking (Figure 15).

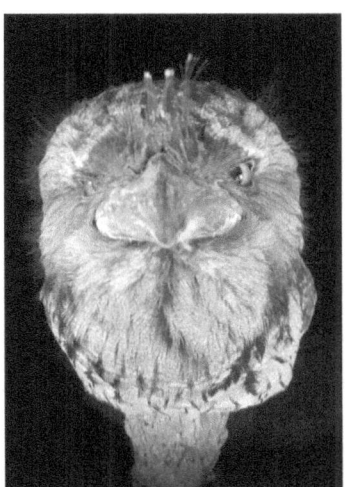

Figure 15: Tawny Frogmouth, *Podargus strigoides*. Photograph courtesy of Mollie King (Kent Owl Academy).

I wonder more about words unexamined. Why *atmosphere*? I read that atmosphere—from the ancient Greek *atmos* meaning gas or vapor, and *sphaira* meaning ball or sphere—was a seventeenth century neologism created by the astronomer Willebrord Snellius to refer to the gaseous sphere enveloping Earth and other planets.[252] The word [L. *atmosphaera*] was created for his Latin translation of Simon Stevin's cosmographical writings in Dutch, marking origins in the emerging sciences of astronomy and mathematics. Coincidentally, it appears the term was first used by Snellius and Christoph Scheiner (astronomer, mathematician) in their calculations of the height of vapours that cause twilight.[253] By the nineteenth century, atmosphere was in use as an aesthetic rather than an exclusively scientific term to allude to "an ambient, spatial mood."[254]

More recently, in the 1990s, the philosopher Gernot Böhme made 'atmosphere' the basis of his new *ecological aesthetics* in name and as "its central object of cognition," writing that, "Aesthetics opens up as a completely different field if it is approached from ecology."[255] For Böhme, the 'old aesthetics' [from Kant to Adorno and Lyotard] is essentially a judgmental mode; that is, it is concerned not so much with experience, especially sensuous experience—as the expression aesthetics in its derivation from the Greek [*aisthetikos*] would suggest—as with "judgments, discussion, conversation."[256] Atmospheres, Böhme conceives, have an ambiguous in-between status, both thinglike (a spatial presence with qualities, conceived as ecstasies, and able to be encountered as a resonance), and subjectlike, in that they belong to bodies—they are sensed/created by bodies. In other words, atmospheres are "quasi-objective": "you can enter an atmosphere and you can be surprisingly caught by an atmosphere. Yet, atmospheres ... are nothing without a subject feeling them." Atmospheres seem to fill the space with "a certain tone of feeling like a haze": *atmos* indicates a tendency for qualities of feeling to fill spaces like a gas, and sphere to indicate a particular spatial form based on the circle.[257] Diffusion within a sphere, as Deleuze and Guattari describe it.[258] Atmospheres haunt with their indeterminacy. Therein also lies elusive atmospheric power?

Back in the woodland patch, we—tawny, kookaburras, frogs, and I—respire together, sharing oxy-carbon-water breaths in the open air. Messmate is winding down its day's photosynthetic delivery of oxygen and water vapour to these atmos-commons as the light fades. Messmate's daily carbon dioxide (CO_2) uptake is converted to leaf, root, stringy bark, resinous wood, flowers and fruiting capsules favoured by the gang-gang cockatoos and yellow-tailed black cockatoos who visit and linger in December. With each breath, I inhale the emissions of the old eucalypt and other photosynthetic collaborators in this scraggly remnant as freely-given oxygen. I expire my dose of the essential air warmers CO_2 and H_2O, vaporous, invisible, tasteless, silent, as I write now, into the twilight sky. Will my CO_2 become new messmate rootlets or leaf buds, or join the excess tonnes in the warming greenhouse?

It seems we all do the CO_2 trace these days. Presenting a version of this postcard narrative at the conference *Literary Environments: Place, Planet and Translation* in July 2017, I noted the concentration of atmospheric CO_2 measured at the Mauna Loa Observatory in Hawaii was 406.68 parts per million (ppm), steadily up from 393.52 ppm when I recorded the frogmouth in October 2013. Steadily up from an average of 317.94 ppm in Carson's *Silent Spring* year of 1962.[259] In April 2017, in unabated rise, carbon dioxide peaked at 410.28 ppm in the northern hemisphere Spring, a level not seen since Keeling Curve records began in 1958, not detected in the 800,000 years tracked in ice core analyses of past atmospheres, and much closer to the planet's atmosphere some four million years ago in the Pliocene.[260] Unfathomable.

Paused, listening at the edge of the visual, breathing with and within two atmospheres I begin to think more about a nascent language and practice of *wit(h)nessing*.[261] Time would add to this reflection. More than the visual 'watch' of witness in order to bear testimony, wit(h)nessing is a mode of being present in whole-bodied attention in encountering. It is synsensorial co-presence. Multiple senses synergise. Invoked is attunement to—acknowledging and welcoming—the affective energies sparked within. There is no 'I' without a 'non-I'. We are somewhere: this twilight haecceity, a singular event, paused on a patch of planetary crust on an October evening. This is a somewhere in the everywhere of the capacious earthbound atmosphere that moves in and out of my lungs, and the lungs, spiracles and stomata of the bigger twilight ensemble. Intimate-molecular process, an idiosyncratic twilight, and the planet's atmosphere are entwined via the moment-to-moment exchange of breath. *At once*: a-bodied, idiolocal, planetary encountering.

I hear resonances that cannot be ignored. Val Plumwood mused on the teachings of attentive encounters with earth others:

> It is a project of reanimating the world, and remaking ourselves as well, so as to become multiply enriched but consequently constrained members of an ecological community …; the intentionality is to "depict nature in the active voice, the domain of agency."[262]

The task is to make kin in "lines of inventive connection"; of "learning to be … in myriad unfinished configurations of places, times, matters, meanings," argues Donna Haraway.[263] On a damaged planet—in "the blowback of the modern" that is the Anthropocene—Anna Tsing and colleagues urge that we begin with noticing: noticing bodies tumbled into bodies, how all "organisms, including humans, are tangled up with each other."[264]

From the trace of one unforgettable twilight, this postcard to Rachel voices a-bodied practice: simply, to *pause* somewhere in the everywhere atmosphere of immersive exchange. If we show up, participate in the risk of sensory openness and curiosity in encounters with planetary co-travellers and co-makers, wit(h)nessing might become an inexhaustible waymaker of stories, fine-grained situated knowledge and affective connectivities. Enough, I suspect, to begin to call this an *aesthetics of wit(h)nessing* for a much more-than-human Anthropocene.

Greetings from Zincland: Shadow mattering

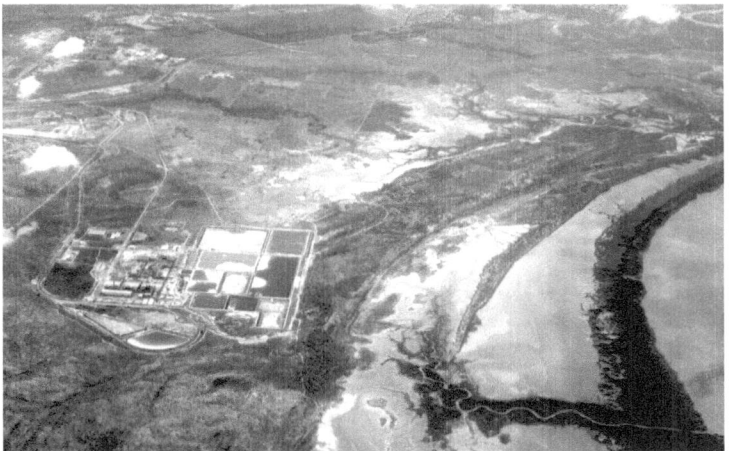

Figure 16: Louise Boscacci, *Greetings from Zincland*, 2016. Postcard (recto), 15 x 10 cm. Digital print from an aerial photograph taken in November 2013.

Dear Rachel, 4:35 am, 9 January 2017

Stormbirds are raucous on the cusp of morning twilight. Two channel-billed cuckoos (Scythrops novaehollandiae) are calling and responding to each other and, perhaps, the squatter fledgling planted as an egg in the nest of an unsuspecting surrogate—magpie, currawong, raven, kookaburra? The big cuckoos have pulled me out of the house well before sunrise to stand and listen to their haunting tangled hooting guffawing duet, microphone in one hand, the other swatting mosquitoes. In this tiny shard of farmland forest hosting micro-ecologies and travelling birds, it is still too dark to see the callers. I wish you could hear them! Their return migration up the east coast to Papua New Guinea and Indonesia is imminent. They fly together, parents and gathered-up young, as a travelling party. If we fly with them, they will lead us to Mary's backyard fig tree in north Queensland where we have watched channel-bills resting in the deep shade of the canopy, gorging on ripe fruit.

Closer to the equator, tropical twilights are short but fecund zones of cooler dusks and dawns. Twilight is also an earthly phenomenon in which no shadows are cast— there cannot be when the sun is below the horizon. And I am wondering about other shadows of affect.

Questions to self: What does a quickening do? What might shadow listening become?

On the coastal fringe of Cleveland Bay, near the industrial port of Townsville, a large zinc refinery sits well concealed in the lee of Muntalunga Range (see Figure 16). It is situated in ancestral-contemporary Wulgurukaba and Bindal country. This too is belonged-by country for non-Indigenous locals attuned to the wafts of mangrove and salt a-bodied over decades and recalled instantly by the hint of a south-easterly breeze sifting aromas of warm tropical sea. The open casement windows of my mother's house draw in the Bay air and sharp breaths of solastalgia.[265]

The access road past the growing city rubbish tip down into the refinery complex is named Zinc Road on civic maps.[266] It is secured by company patrols and watched by surveillance cameras on tall steel posts: the enclosed tract of savannah grassland, tidal creeks, claypans, mangroves and granite hills is now an exclusion zone to locals who do not work in the facility. From the air, not on foot because these coastal lands can no longer be legally walked (don't try), it is rendered visible.

Flying south over the bay, the window of a passenger jet serendipitously discloses a postcard "dirty picture" of pretty colours of tailing dams and evaporation ponds radiating out from ore roasters, sulphur gas cleaners, leaching tanks, melting and casting sheds.[267] Less apparent from the air is the railway line that connects the plant to the growing city port where shipped imports and exports of mineral ores and cool metal solids cross paths in and out.

In her figuring of the shadow places, Val Plumwood thought about ecological *being and belonging* in the contemporary acceleration. All places have their shadows, she wrote, "the many unrecognized shadow places that provide our material and ecological support, most of which ... are likely to elude our knowledge and responsibility."[268] Home places of affection should always be imagined in relationship to others, she reasoned: an *ecological* braiding recognizes "the shadow places, not just the ones we love, admire or find nice to look at." Or listen to. Consider, she provoked further, "those shadow places that produce or are affected by the commodities you consume"; and other places "that take our pollution and dangerous waste ... all these places we must own too."[269]

Wondering about zinc: laptop batteries and galvanised steel roofs that weather tropical rains. Zinc: sunscreen particles and car bodies. Zinc: my clean white ceramic glaze; micronutrient for 'men, animals and plants' (the refinery says); his stainless kitchen. Zinc: lipstick, plastic and new brass knobs.

And zinc shadows. The refinery is more than a well-hidden imposition on old common lands in the heart of the bay. Curious about the sources of zinc concentrates that feed into the refinery via the city port, I track the ports of origin of ships listing zinc cargoes—a *shadows trace* as part of a bigger *eco-affective* trace of all the shadow port places of Currumbilbarra.[270] I find that one bulk ore source is the giant McArthur River Mine, a zinc, lead and silver open-cut mine up river from Borroloola in the southwest lands of the Gulf of Carpentaria in the Northern Territory. In 2013, a waste rock dump at the site spontaneously combusted, sending a huge plume of toxic sulphur dioxide smoke into the troposphere over the coastal floodplains and savannah country. According to reports, the suburb-sized rock dump continued to smoulder and emit toxic fumes for more than a year.[271]

From this shadow place, the voice of Jacky Green: *"Stop poisoning our land."*[272]

Prominent Borroloola Elders, traditional owner-managers and painters Jacky Green (Garrwa) and Nancy McDinny (Garrwa,

Yanyuwa) speak for clans and Country. They have repeatedly called for the mine to be closed, concerned that the waste rock dump and tailings dam are leaching acid, metals and salts into the McArthur River system, poisoning river fish and coastal turtles and dugongs. Lead contamination is an urgent issue. Green: "We've all got to live here, we've all got to fish out of the water."[273] The mine, owned by Glencore, an Anglo–Swiss multinational commodity trading and mining company, has been an open-cut for more than a decade. McDinny: "They're millionaires, they've got a lot of money. Us Aboriginal people haven't got any money but they're getting rich from our land."[274] Green: "Year after year the mining trucks take the minerals, spirit and wealth from the country."[275]

Far from the Gulf, in Sydney's Kings Cross at the opening of the art exhibition *Open Cut*, Nancy McDinny is sitting to speak to the gallery audience. On the wall behind is a photographic portrait of her with the words "Mikur Narri Kurayrritjerr Yarji Nurrungi (Stop mining. We don't want no more)" painted in white across both arms and chest. She wants us to *hear* the profound injustice of this new intergenerational legacy of toxicity: "It is our time to talk to others." "We used to drink the river before the mine." "We don't want fracking in that country" (a new dread). *"It has taken 10 years to create a 1000 year problem."* In 2018 the territory government will decide on the miner's application to double the size of the site, double the height of the waste rock dump, and extend the mine's life for another thirty years.[276]

Other voices add to my thinking about this revealed shadowland:

Capitalocene—"an ugly word for an ugly system"— signifies capitalism as "a world-ecology of power, capital, and nature": Jason Moore, historian.[277]

Capitalocene names "the culprit ... modern capitalism stretched over centuries of enclosures, colonialisms, industrializations, and globalizations": TJ Demos, art historian and political ecologist.[278]

"Perhaps 'The Dithering' is a more apt name than either the Anthropocene or the Capitalocene!": Donna Haraway, troubling tropical skies.[279]

The movement of zinc discloses a confronting interconnection between the old magnetic country of Currumbilbarra that migratory channel-bills also know well, and the horror of the harm to the multiple bodies and atmospheres of Garrwa and Yanyuwa homelands no longer liminally somewhere else, out of sight or earshot. I embrace this as a material relation that is at once intimate-molecular (of the affective body), idiolocal and planetary in scale. If aesthetics is approached as a tuning into energies of encounters and relations between bodies (of multiple types) via wit(h)nessing, art practice deterritorialises to an expanded mode of ethico-aesthetics: art production, on the one hand.[280] And, on the other, trans-movement beyond the studio or art gallery to this unfinished trace—and *story of wit(h)ness*—of connected lands, waters, people and shadow atmospheres.[281]

I phone my brother who is working at the McArthur River Mine. He is an electrician on a fly-in, fly-out contract. He needs the mine work as much as he abhors it. I tell him about the shadow trace from the port of our old home town to the mine's seaport—Bing Bong—nearby in the shallow waters of the Gulf. He talks about dust, smoke, rain, noise, earplugs. I ask him to send me a sound postcard from where he is standing that evening.

"What is that?"

"Record where you are. Three minutes of listening. Email me."

"It's on its way."

The Wonder World of the Carbon Molecule

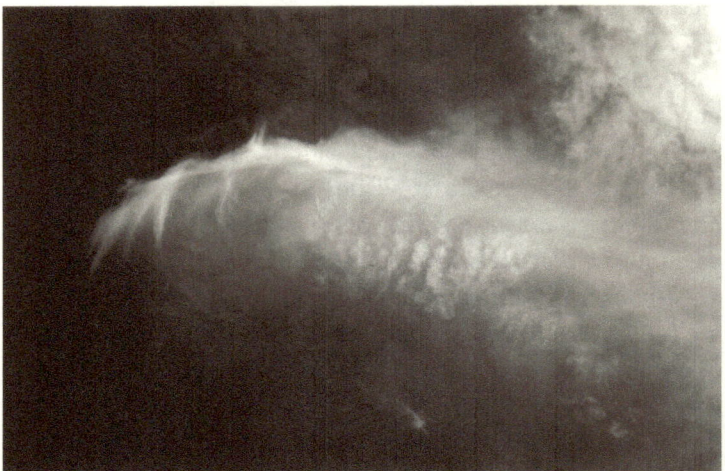

Figure 17: Louise Boscacci, *Black Cirrus*, 2017. Postcard (recto) 15 x 10 cm. Digital print.

***Dear Rachel,**   10 July 2017*

There were twenty-eight all up: yellow-tails in the top of the old messmate tree. A flying party in for the morning. Shiny adults were preening scratchy-voiced young. White down fluffs drifted on air eddies. Black-cockatoos love the messmate's capsules ... they were so vocal I sensed something else was happening in all the talk. Sat close all morning eavesdropping. Then this vast cirrus blew in ... ice preening sky.

*   Wonder goes a-bodying with trouble again some sixty years on from the very decade of the Great Acceleration you tuned into. Did you hear that 1950 is slated to be a favoured marker of epoch Anthropocene by the stratigraphers?[282] The GA continues in a runaway mode of horrors and beauties from the tropics to the poles, uneven, human, more-than-human, planetary and molecular in touch down effects and affects. There is an uncanny foretelling in your work that chimes today. These are not the '50s or '60s of either century. The Larson C ice shelf*

of the thawing Antarctic cryosphere has just calved a trillion-tonne iceberg marking a momentous shift in the topography of Holocenic Earth.[283]

Why did you value wonder?

Why wonder in an Anthropocene?

Ineffable overflow. I hesitate to write about the a-bodied experience or affective state that might be called *wonder* (Figure 17). A thousand postcards would not suffice. Yet I am entranced by Rachel Carson's bittersweet phrase "the wonder world of the carbon molecule" found in the pages of *Silent Spring*.[284] The complexity and conundrum of wonder are carried in those seven words. To think wonder and carbon together on an overheating planet elicits the greenhouse warmers, gaseous carbon dioxide (CO_2) and methane (CH_4). Carson was introducing another carbon challenge. In a chapter titled 'Elixirs of Death' she observed that the Second World War marked a turning away from inorganic chemicals used as pesticides into the wonder world of the carbon molecule—to new synthetic insecticides, the chlorinated hydrocarbons such as DDT and dieldrin. These chemicals and allied organophosphates became "biocides" deployed in "the death rain" of aerial and other mass sprayings that she chronicled and challenged.[285] Born of wartime nerve gas experiments, the new chemicals were, she wrote, the little known partners of radiation. Strontium 90 was new to the atmosphere and its terrestrial fallout in 1945 with the Trinity atomic bomb test.[286]

Carson explored wonder in different ways and with different emphases across her oeuvre, including the small book *The Sense of Wonder* (1965), her trilogy of books on the sea, and other recovered writing in letters, field notebooks, magazine articles and speech transcripts.[287] Wonder was tied to her lifelong attunement to 'nature' and 'the natural world'—to the intricacies, processes, "beauties and mysteries of the earth".[288] "Nothing lives unto itself," she once said.[289] This conviction came to meet theoretical tenets of the emerging science of ecology which resonated with her own connective thinking, founded in marine biological studies. She crafted narratives of factual concision and lyricism rather than scientific papers.[290] A shift in language to 'the living world' in *Silent Spring* echoed her focus on the devastation of non-human ecologies by the new chemical "shadow of death".[291] In her framing, 'the living world' explicitly included humans ('man').

"Clouds drifting by, of various types, but all in motion": Rachel Carson, 1957.[292]

Rachel Carson never got to write "the Wonder book" she had envisaged; *The Sense of Wonder* was published unaugmented a year after her death.[293] This small rhapsodic field guide on how to enhance the facility for wonder in children had been published a decade earlier in the journal *Women's Home Companion* as "Help Your Child to Wonder".[294] She believed that if children were encouraged to engage with 'the natural world', to discover for themselves, to experience wonderment in lively encounters, they might also be less inclined as adults to destroy or condone the destruction of non-human nature. In the present ecological crisis of climate change where violence is also slow, displaced, often beyond cultural sight, this conviction seems refreshingly naïve—and too easily critiqued. Her desire, however, was to awaken the multiple senses, imagination and intellects of children to the astonishing more-than-human world. Wonder was accessed via an attitude and practice of (bio)curiosity, close attention, an openness to unexpected discovery through nocturnal adventures, predawn walks to listen to avian dawn choruses, seeking the invisible and the minuscule with "a lens-aided view": all to help "escape the limitations of the human scale size".[295] With the experience of a field biologist, she encouraged "learning again to use your eyes, ears, nostrils and finger tips, opening up the disused channels of sensory impression".[296] She was eloquent on the importance of the more-than-visual senses in stirring aesthetic intensities in encounters, writing about touch, sound, aromas. The experience of wonder was expressed in a lexicon of surprise, excitement, delight, beauty, majesty, sensory impression and emotional arousal. She wagered that "[t]hose who contemplate the beauty of the earth find reserves of strength that will endure as long as life lasts".[297]

There is more to this gentle manifesto. Read in tandem with *Silent Spring*, the nebulous *sense* in *The Sense of Wonder* takes on a political tone. It becomes *common sense*—a saner rationale—for mattering wonder in the face of the madness of aerial sprayings and the indiscriminate bluntness of a chemical industry ostensibly born of empirical reason and invention. To Carson, there was no sense to the new biocidal activities, only human hubris and corporate greed. There was no sensitivity or scientific logic to the mass poisonings of all unwanted insects, rodents or weeds that also killed earthworms, songbirds, pets, farm animals and people (farmers, spraymen, pilots). The scale of human disconnection from the living world required to enact eradication programs with an avalanche of new synthetic insecticides was bewildering and *senseless*. Wonder was dead in this epic enterprise overseen by industry-funded "economic entomologists" (also biologists; her world).[298] Moreover, the practitioners brought to their task no "high-minded orientation," "no humility before the vast forces with which they tamper".[299]

In *Silent Spring*, a language of wonder and kin states of gratitude and pragma (enduring love; here biophilic) co-travel with anger. Rage, even, at the arrogance and inattention of "the authoritarian" whose "chains of poisonings" triggered mass death of birdlife—new *silences and stillings*—across croplands and rural towns.[300] "Most of us walk unseeing through the world," she wrote, "unaware alike of its beauties, its wonders, and the strange and sometimes terrible intensity of the lives that are being lived around us".[301] Complex wonder recurs as a catalyst of regenerative energy, a source of resilience, an antidote to despair, and an enduring motivator across chapters. Later, after the publication of *Silent Spring*, the injunction of the wonder world of nature besieged provided grit when Carson, terminally ill with cancer, was besieged by the powerful chemical industry determined to discredit and silence her and the book's narrative. The "masters of invective and insinuation have been busy," she wrote. "I am a 'bird lover—a cat lover—a fish lover' ... a devotee of a mystical cult having to do with the laws of the universe which my critics consider themselves immune to."[302]

Writing about the wonder world of the carbon molecule, Carson celebrated carbon as an indispensable structural element of most life on earth. Her marvel at the almost infinite capacity of carbon atoms to readily unite with each other and with other elements to create radically different properties was bittersweet. This same molecular nimbleness was tailored to generate the new agents of death. Carbon, rendered biocidal, was not the villain. At heart, it was Carson's conviction that "wonder and humility ... do not exist side by side with a lust for destruction".[303] Her lingering wonder world phrase was composed in an act of literary resistance that ended with a warning evinced by the chemical resistance developed by many of the targeted insects: "Nature fights back".[304]

CO_2 update, April 18, 2018: 410.59 ppm.[305] Up again. Where will it peak? Are there frogmouths there?

Wonder has long travelled with questions of politics, ethics and action. It was rejected as one of the affects in Baruch Spinoza's ethology of bodies in movement and rest in his 1677 treatise, the *Ethics*.[306] *Admiratio*—the Latin word translated in terms of wonder and surprise—was too easily a mental trap, he decided, minimising it, and removing its agency in the chance encounter. Wonder was associated with mental stunning or a stalling of thinking: it catalysed no new connections in thought and stimulated no new knowledge. It created a kind of confusion of the mind that led to uncritical veneration, or a boost in belief in religious miracles in order to understand the new unknown in encounter, the uncanny object of surprise or marvel. This apprehension seems completely incongruous for a glass lens maker who gazed through telescopes and microscopes at macro and micro worlds, and who must have experienced the affective energies of wondrous surprise in the becomings of his own material and philosophical practice. There was, however, a political intonation to Spinoza's rejection of the power of wonder: a refusal to add to the political domination of the religious state (the keepers of miraculous wonder and veneration) in the emergent Enlightenment thinking of seventeenth century Europe.[307] To this end, wonder was not part of a language of enhancement and diminishment; it was a fog that stalled, and worse, was socio-politically regressive.

Thinking about and translating encounters of wonder in practice in anthropocenic atmospheres is no less a challenge. On the one hand, we can readily dismiss this as a romantic preoccupation of a privileged few. Those, for instance, who are not facing inundation of home islands, or empty dams, catastrophic bushfires, a poisoned river, or mass bleaching of coral microbiomes. On the other, privileging only a language of 'real-world' problems in the discourse on responsibility and response to global eco-social change tacitly censors what is perhaps needed more than ever in facing new extremes: an opening out of artful response towards modes of *responsivity* and *response-ability*.[308] Responsivity invites aesthetic practices of multisensory attunement and attention. Response-ability, the ability to respond, invites 'right fit' choices in creative praxis and lived action. Moral injunctions to act (more, better), to take responsibility, are replaced by an affirmative ethics that asks the question a thousand times for a thousand different situations of affective bodies, locally emplaced, networked, breathing the air of the planetary crisis of atmosphere and biosphere: What can *this* body do? Can we embrace new meetings of the "affective and pragmatic," as Felix Guattari voiced in his three ecologies of atmosphere, infosphere and psychosphere?[309] Witnessing as wit(h)nessing. Wonder and critical wondering. Pragma and pragmatics.

"I shall rant a little too," echoes Rachel Carson.[310]

Coda

In 2009, writer and theorist Franco Berardi composed a *Manifesto of Post-Futurism* in reply to the 1911 *Manifesto of Futurism* by the Italian poet Filippo Marinetti. Marinetti's manifesto was an explosive valorisation of speed, western industrial progress and the becoming-machine age of 'mankind' in the first decades of the century of the Great Acceleration. Berardi's response, in eleven points following the Futurists' declarations, instead praises "the slow," a return to the bodily senses, to "the daily creation of love, a sweet energy that can never be dispersed." He sings of the rebellious cognitariat who are in touch with their bodies.[311] Carbon-rich bodies that have *always* been more than human and singular, symbiotically cohabited as we are with multispecies gut bacteria and the bodies of skin mites carrying the traces of viral DNA.[312] This is a silent more-than-human connection worth mattering as radical and wondrous as each breath.

Atmospheric Riffing: Manifesto of Breath

1. Begin with the encounter. Begin in a-bodied encountering. This is now an encounter-exchange. Pause. In *a somewhere*, feet on crust, lungs airborne in the shared blue chamber, the bios-blown bubble of air, *an everywhere*.

2. Breathe in. Breathe out.

3. Listen at the threshold of that crossing.

4. We honour the alveolar infoldings of atmosphere hidden inside the respiratory tree of humanimal chest cavities. We whistle this alveolar atmosphere.

5. We ask: are we in the atmosphere; is the atmosphere within us: are we atmos-body in continuum?

6. Breathe in. Hold that inspiration. We praise the oxygen molecule, the carbon molecule, the water molecule of the cycles of our respiration.

7. We want the beauty and wonder of photosynthesis. We cherish the mitochondria of chloroplasts that court us with their oxygen.

8. We are biospheric progeny of the Great Oxygenation and children of the Great Acceleration. We are Holocene invention. We are, and are not, Anthropocene spawn and co-makers. We are pre-seeded with atmosphere. Breathe out.

9. We wit(h)ness. There is no I, without a non-I. It is all synwork.

10. We ask: what is a body? What can a body do? Deleuze found Spinoza across centuries to open that wonder world. Massumi, in durational passage, translated a parable. Sara Ahmed tells us to move when moved.

11. We praise the electric body of affective attunement and response-ability. We connect this with the electric gaseous body of planetary atmosphere. We say this is wonder and beauty in overflow. We make with this capaciousness. This is our *conatus*. Spinoza gave us that. Carson and many since remind us of this. The trace of every (bird) lover's sigh sings this.

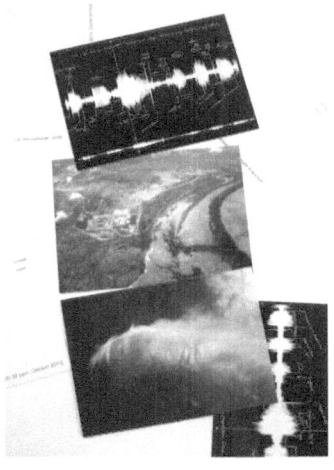

Figure 18: Three postcards to Rachel Carson, 2016–2018. Photograph: Louise Boscacci.

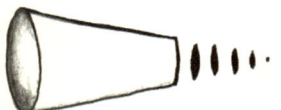

Call and response

You say ...

"Come into my home. Come on ... Come in, come in, this is my home. *Welcome* to my home ...

... Over here is my kitchen ... up there is where the glasses are ... down there's the plates, here's my fridge ... eeaa ... look ... there's some devon there brother, there's some milk and stuff ... oh ... please don't drink the soy milk, that's for the Missus ... *Welcome* ...

... All right ... Come with me ... come inside. Here's my lounge room, this is my TV ... the remote ... sit wherever you want brother ... can you please just not put your feet on the coffee table aye, my grandmother gave me that ... *Welcome* ...

... Over here is the bathroom ... there's the girls' room ... don't go in there please ... Here's the boys' room, you'll be sleeping in there bra ... and see we don't smoke in the house aye so if you wanna have a cigarette you gotta go out back aye ... right ... *Welcome* to my home, brother ... Make yourself at home."

And then the response is ...

"Oh wow, thank you, brother ... What a beautiful home you have. I absolutely *Acknowledge* your home, wow bra ... your kitchen, you have such a beautiful kitchen ... I love it ... I see the glasses there, yeah I think I've actually seen them ones before. The plates, yep ... the fridge ... all right. Yep ... honestly bro, I won't touch the soy, got it ... got a missus of my own. Get that ... Fuck ... I've never seen a TV that big, this is amazing! Cool, cool, cool ... Love the coffee table ... beautiful respect bra ... won't put my feet on it ... promise ... okay ... Yep ... got it ... toilet ... girls' room – won't go anywhere near it ... boys' room – just going to drop my swag here, cool, thanks brother ...

Wow ... Thank you. I *Acknowledge* your home, thank you for your *Welcome* ... thank you for having me in your home ... think I'll go and make a devon sandwich and cuppa, go out the back and have a cigarette."

Right ...
Call and response ... call and response ...

Come into my country. *Welcome* ... Right ... These are my totems, I don't eat them ... you're welcome to eat them ... but make a fire maybe ten metres downwind aye ... See. Don't go there ... this is a men's place ... don't go here ... this is a woman's place ... this is where we hold ceremony ... don't go there ... and it's defined, it's a verbal contract. A visa.

And so today it's just all fucked up ... you keep asking me to fuckin *Welcome* you to Country every three minutes ... Fuck man, we've been doing this shit for ages ... Come on ... when are you going to give *Acknowledgement*? When are you going to start being responsible? When are you going to start understanding your ethics in this space?

Aurora borealis

At the latitude of 70.01° north, in Norway, a small island named Spildra is situated across a spectacular fjord from the spiked ice-carved crags of the Kvaenangen Range, towards the south. In this landscape dominated by ocean, the only human signs were a few cottages (belonging to seamen, *generations* of seamen: fishermen, ferry crew) clustered around a small harbour at the base of the granite massif on which we now stood, the small hand of my youngest child in mine. The stone beneath our feet was crusted in ice and wisps of snow. The air temperature was well below freezing. Space was immense.

In the northern sky, luminous colour filled the earth's sphere of gases: green, red and purple, falling and sweeping like a fine curtain rippled by wind. An electromagnetic field talking to the sun. We were transfixed. It was *otherworldly, impossible, beautiful, spiritual*. And it was *felt,* a fine static crackling, more a fizzing really, detected at the surface of the skin as much as heard. That electrical crackle was coursing irresistibly through us—tingling every nerve end, connecting us *materially* to the cosmos.

How extraordinary to live your entire life in such a place, as most people there had done. A modern sense of time warped and stretched. All the people of the past—Vikings, whose village huts had left traces still clearly visible on the shoreline below, bear worshippers, fishermen, a tragic couple whose illicit affair resulted in their deaths centuries ago, refugees from the occupation of this region during the Second World War—all were as if somehow equally awed and present under that huge sky, in that display of massive energy and the mutability of matter and time. In the cold, the clean air took on the clarity and incisiveness of a diamond—the perfect medium for this otherworldly display.

The aurora borealis has long been explained in scientific terms as a result of geomagnetic disturbances caused by electric currents in the ionosphere.[313] We accept this as the physics. But there are other dimensions to phenomena like this: the deep velvet black of the night sky in the desert; the luminous depth of the Milky Way; a still, black, star-studded sky; the howling, visionless immensity of a mountain blizzard; blue-green light filtering through the ocean. They form a *conduit*, a passage to an unknown, felt through ages, explained by stories, faiths, legends: a direct connection to our planetary system, and beyond.

Aurora australis

Somewhere else, at the other end of the earth, 45°C south, there is a party. It is also cold, not cold enough to freeze the hairs in your nose, but enough that your eyeballs water frequently, and a deadening pain afflicts the tips of your fingers.

The party is at a small house a little way around a harbour. Getting home afterwards involves slipping along the edge of a motorway flowing with late night log trucks. The scent of damp forest and pine bark lingers after each truck passes on its way out to port, bound for chipping facilities somewhere in China. I find it hard to see in the halflight. Someone is holding my hand.

Then the sky is green, pink, green. We whisper to each other, uncertain if the apparition is actually there, listening. Did you see that? Then again: green, blue, pink, white, lines, and afterwards a crackle of silver. Someone suggests the playing fields, and we run, gasping in the frozen air, and lie flat on our backs in the middle of the paddocks. The goal posts frame the colours: red, blue, purple, and a kind of violet haze that feels like it is boring into our souls. Language is impossible. We watch, scarcely breathing, unable to draw ourselves away, aware that the cold is seeping off the grass into our clothes and deep into our bones. Unable to reconcile our bodies with the event.

Sphere

Geosphere, biosphere, troposphere, stratosphere, mesosphere, thermosphere, exosphere, stellar atmosphere, opaque photosphere, econosphere.

Sky-watching

Driving to work on the Northern Distributor from Bulli to Wollongong, the day begins with sky-watching. Will it rain today? Is that smoke over Mount Kembla way? I can see a thick deck of stratus cloud. What will the day be like?

Clouds: condensation of water vapour into water droplets that are lighter than air. Cumulus, altocumulus, cirrocumulus, stratus, altostratus, cirrostratus. Cirrus: at the higher level of the troposphere water vapour sublimates into minute ice crystals. Winds at high altitudes blow and scatter these ice crystals to form patterns, sometimes undulating like waves, sometimes like the scales of a fish: a cirrocumulus mackerel sky. Once when cloud watching together, my father asked: "Do mackerels actually have scales?"

Fog

Artist JR Carpenter thinks about the digital cloud in conversation with physical cloud types. She observes that the term fog was adopted by the nineteenth century military analyst Carl von Clausewitz as a metaphor to describe uncertainty experienced in war.[314] Long before the deafening atomic fireball and toadstool cloud of Trinity in 1945, a material sky gets militarised.

Fog is better known as visible cloud water droplets or ice crystals suspended in the air at or near the Earth's surface. Autumn and early winter fogs form on Illawarra highland roads and paddocks as warm moist earth and cold air meet. Everything human slows down in these foggy conditions: cars, conversations, timelines of arrival. Vision is most constrained; when driving home, all attention and care is needed not to strike a wandering bare-nosed wombat out in the cool night grazing and greeting. Fog focus is an atmospheric state of mind that slows deeds and motion. When you can't see what's in front of you, slow down, refocus, *listen*.

Inclusion and exclusion

The function of an atmosphere is to contain, to protect. But someone or something is always left out.

In Jerzy Kosinski's novel *Painted Bird* (1965), a man captures sparrows from a flock and paints them in bold unnatural colours: pinks and turquoises and lemon yellows. He then releases the birds, one-by-one, back into the flock. Each time, he watches the coloured bird try to rejoin the group. A multicoloured speck in an ashen-grey cloud. The other birds are confused by the strangely coloured creature. The man watches as the birds turn on the newcomer, pecking fiercely at the pink and the orange and the red. The man observes that "shortly the many-hued shape lost its place in the sky and hopped to the ground. When [I] finally found the painted bird it was usually dead."[315]

Deborah Bird Rose talks about wild donkeys in the Kimberley who are routinely culled with the aid of GPS tracking. One member of the herd is caught and fitted with a 'Judas collar', a VHF radio transmitter. The hunters use this to track the animal back to the herd, careful to leave the Judas donkey alive so she can lead them to another herd. "Time and again," Rose writes, "she finds mates only to see them mown down. Time and again she is left lonely and bewildered." Eventually, these marked animals stop seeking out a new herd. Rose explains: "they isolate themselves, avoiding others, seeking out places where others will not find them."[316]

Expanse

Sometimes—far out over the ocean, or the wide plains of southern New South Wales—squalls of rain can be seen as grey-blue veils: a little distorted, the fabric drooping and bending as the clouds drift, the wind blows … Sometimes around the grey patches it is clear, sunny even, certainly not veiled in falling rain. It takes a wide expanse of sky to see this.

On the river

Situated knowledges catch slippages, like ice.[317] There is a river, felt and seen in the way I feel and see the person sitting beside me while we work. The problems of speaking for others, and rivers, and birds, and rocks appears in this space of affect and sensing.

From 2009 to 2011 the artists' cooperative Green Bench ran slow flow artist residencies on Te Awa Tupua, the Whanganui river. Groups of artists and writers would drift in waka over five to ten days. The experience lasted years, as even after returning home, bodies felt the river present beside them.[318] The river tugs at me. I search photos for evidence of its soft mist, its energies, its atmospheres, but within its mercurial surface I see only an image of its past.[319]

On another Wednesday, in Aotearoa New Zealand, Maori elder Gerrard Albert spoke to *The Guardian*:

> We have fought to find an approximation in law so that all others can understand that from our perspective treating the river as a living entity is the correct way to approach it, as an indivisible whole, instead of the traditional model for the last 100 years of treating it from a perspective of ownership and management.[320]

River stones

Ted: What about the Lapidarium as a method?—this means 'collection of stones.' It comes from Ryszard Kapuściński—

Joshua: What about Eco's file-card model of writing—

Eva: —or Heraclitus writing in fragments, never stepping in the same river twice—

Jo: —like Barbara Stafford says: "putting distant things in contact with one another in order to make connections obliges the collector's five senses to converge in a kind of synaesthesia."[321]

Louise: We could think about it like leaves from an album that have material history (from diverse practices) that settle and also can be rearranged within sections as new affinities and unsettlings are encountered—

Su: —Someone told me that Aby Warburg swapped his inheritance for all the books his brother could buy, and arranged them according to friendships: the book you really want in the library is always the one sitting beside the one you are looking at.

What about a conversation?

A conversation

Jade Kennedy

Date: 22 March 2018

Place: "The Glass Room": Building 25, University of Wollongong
People: Susan Ballard, Louise Boscacci, Anne Collett, Lucas Ihlein, Jade Kennedy, Joshua Lobb, Jennifer Macey, Catherine McKinnon

Jennifer – Do you want to say your name?

Jade – OK My name's Jade and I'm from here … *[laughs]* How much more do you need?

Cath – I thought of a couple of questions for Jade because I just know some of the things he's talked about before … what I thought might be good to talk about was stories and storytelling, and the differences in storytelling … because I remember once you told me Jade …

Su – Go on.

Cath – Jade was explaining to me this thing about when he tells a story or retells a story … that thinking about it from a kind of Indigenous point of view, one relives the moment, the reliving idea …

Jade – that's one of the things I try to share … that you know … because a lot of what I do is about building relationships between the samesames for people in these spaces … *[knocks the microphone]* Sorry –

Jennifer – Sorry …

Jade – Don't be, don't be. I'm just trying to get comfortable.

Lucas – So …

Jade – So … I think the best way for me to fall into these spaces is through a conversation … I've been sort of habitually taught to do all things through conversation … You know … that's what I'm sort of best at … I guess … that's my way. But it's a really interesting concept for me because I sort of oscillate between these two worlds … I straddle them the best that I can … I make mistakes in them both, but it's a constant walking of two worlds you know ... and sometimes it's not that depiction where you've got one foot in one and one foot in the other ... I think that's a really unrealistic depiction of what it is ... You sort of float between these two different spaces and places consistently and you've got to find ways of being fluid within that movement because otherwise you get caught out or you fuck up and that can hurt people or yourself you know and its detrimental ... So you're doing your best to navigate and negotiate and ... the way in which I've learnt to do that best is through conversation ...

Country

Lucas – Jade, can I ask a question just shifting slightly to an experience that I had with you when I first met you, when we were doing the walk along the creek and you came along and did a Welcome to Country for us. And you used this metaphor of a house –

Jade – Yeah.

Lucas – And it just helped to reframe the perspective of the region that we are standing within, when you used that metaphor. And I'm not sure if other people have heard Jade use that before, but I wondered whether that was something that might ... I reckon it was a really good metaphor to use to reframe that perspective and I guess I thought it might be useful to get that on tape in some form or another. A version of that story.

Jade – The thing with Aboriginal knowledges is, right ... is that they're all situated in Country. The answer to everything is in Country, right ... *Country* the way I describe it is ... it's the place ... it's the people ... it's the culture ... it's the journey ... and it's the inter-relationship with these things ... And I sort of articulate it like this in some instances. For that Koori kid who's lived in Redfern his entire life ... it's the fact that he knows every single fucken backstreet like the back of his hands ... He knows whether it's a fucking ambulance, a fire engine, or a police car ... Right ... He knows them sirens ... He knows the times of the trains ... you know ... He knows this space intimately ... You know ... it's the moving traffic ... it's the smell of hot bread from the Vietnamese hot bread shops ... It's the intimacy of that relationship ... It's the knowing. Like when we speak about that South Coast road yeah it's the spaces and the places ... but it's the inter-relationship of these things.

Because no place or space is void of people really ... And if it's not people it's other relationships ... So I sort of go Country – Kinship. So ... from an Aboriginal perspective that kinship is not only with people, you know ... That kinship is me ... So ... I've got a layer of totemic relationship yeah ... see ... my national totem is Umbara, the black duck. My family totem is Doonootch ... which is the white owl, the big white owl ... the powerful owl ... And I have a personal totem right ... Which is secret to me. And each of us will end up having that personal totem right ... that's you too ... So it's your relationships on those levels. It's these sorts of relationships that I also refer to when we talk about kinship. What are the significant relationships in your life that connect you to your place? That's how you understand Country.

And your culture is always particular to your place and your people. So my culture we say ... you know ... is Yuin. That's our culture ... But what we're sort of saying when we say that is ... we're letting you know our boundary and we're letting you know our people and we letting you know my culture is not just Aborigine ... My culture's not Koori ... My culture's not Pitjantjatjara ... My culture's not Wongi ... My culture right ... Is part of ... it's hard to talk about any of these things in unison ... Like you know ... my culture is the fact that of the first Australians ... my people are the first of the first impacted by invasion ... The first of the first to experience the genocide ... The first of the first to be missionised and institutionalized ... They're my old people right ...We've got stories ... and this is a part of Yuin ...

So I've got my significant place ... and that connects me to my country ... I've got my relationships, they connect me to my country ... And my culture.

Story

Anne – My question Jade ... I was just thinking about this ... I was equating this although it's probably not equitable to when I go to family at Christmas –

Jade – hmm hmm.

Anne – And so you fall into a much more relaxed kind of environment ... you're telling the same stories that you've told I don't know how many times ...

Jade – Over and over ...

Anne – Over and over again. Everyone's aware of that but at the same time they kind of enjoy it again and again and again. And so I'm wondering, although there's a big cultural difference you're talking about here –

Jade – Yeah ...

Anne – Would it in some ways equate to that?

Jade – The practice is similar and I'd say for the most part the same. It's very, very easy when you're amongst family and mob to just become a ... a playing character within a story that's already happened ... but is sort of ever present like in it ... and it gives meaning to why you're there together.

You see ... It's absolutely part of the retelling ... It's the moment of inclusion you know ... and sometimes it can be a moment of exclusion depending on who's at the table ... and that becomes some of the nuance ... isn't it ... that when these stories are being engaged with how that does include or exclude or relate to those who are in that moment ... For us it's there's an expectation to assume a role within that story ... so whoever chooses to begin, essentially demands the presence of those others. It's not that you can then go "I'm just going to the bathroom", you're now tied to the story and the moment and there's a responsibility to engage ... And look I'm not only talking about some sort of long ... steeped in tradition and lore story ... it can be the time we drove home drunk together ...

It's the enactment of that moment and being present in that moment and bouncing between the players or the actors within that story ... It's an integrated system ... always ... You know ...

It comes all from the Dreaming, see ... What's the one consistent, the one consistent across the continent? Every fucken cave you walk into what do you see ... Right ... *[he holds up his hand]* You've got to remember ... you've got a continent of over 500 different countries, all with their own languages, all with their own Dreamings all with their own customs, right ... but there's some consistency ... So if you think about *[pointing to each finger on one hand]* country, kinship, culture, journey, connectedness; they're consistent ... Right ... They're governed by place. But once you've got a place, there's a people of that place, there's a culture of that place, there's a journey, there's a lived experience, there's a story ... right ... To that place ... There's an inter-relationship to those things ... Right ... But there's always five, mate. There's always five. Right ... There's always five.

So you have your Dreaming *[pointing to one finger]* ... And your Dreaming essentially gives you your law ... And your Dreaming and your law are your education systems ... Right ... And your Dreaming and your law and your education system actually articulate your custodianship *[pointing to another finger]* ... And this is Country *[pointing to another finger]* this is what country is. Right ...

Learn from country ... it doesn't have to be learn from the Indigenous peoples ... but become familiar with your place ... Become intimately in relationship ... That's what we don't do, we have this society that says we need to find a partner and be in intimate relationship with our partner ... We need to find work ... so we need to intimately understand our role in that space. Right ... But man, we've only got two *[holds up two fingers]*. There needs to be five or we're not in balance ... Right ... you got to be in relationship with your place ... you've got to be in relationship with the story of your place ... and your story within your place ...

Reciprocity

Su – So one of the things from that, what I'm hearing is this responsibility so it's not just about where your feet lie but it's also where your responsibilities lie?

Jade – it's yeah ... it's those ...

Su – You know? And it's that your responsibility lies with family and with country and those kinds of things and it does for many people, in many different ways. But sometimes those two responsibilities are quite close and then at other times those responsibilities are, umm ...

Jade – yeah

Su – for me, sometimes there can be great tension and actually that's, that's half the problem isn't it? That we find? Like everyone –

Jade – Priorities ...

Su – where are those responsibilities, where are those priorities, where are the ... where is the time taken and where is it taken from and how we navigate that?

Jade – I guess from an Aboriginal perspective one word that would be overarching would be *respect* ... And obviously that can ... sort of trickle down into a whole range of other definitions but I think the term I would use is custodianship ... and that becomes one of the most significant underpinning values and philosophies that guides us as a people ... so if we give integrity to our culture then we are custodians and to be the ultimate custodian is to be responsible and to be responsible in all areas of your world or worlds ...

The simplest way to do that is just walk with me ... or I'll walk with you ... Or can I have some of that ... You know ... and all we need to learn to do better in this country is share. ... You know ...

Louise – so one of the things I'm hearing is reciprocity?

Jade – 100 per cent.

Louise – that, that because the country is where you ground yourself, but also where you sustain yourself –

Jade – Yep

Louise – and feed yourself when you come back home, therefore it sort of takes care of you in a way and that word 'care' is a little bit tricky. So then do you have reciprocal relationship?

Jade – Yes ... so that's an underlying philosophy. We call it ngapartji ngapartji and it's the process of *give and take* ... I think it translates to something like: I give you something you give me something ... right ... But it's not that simple ... it's not ... So for example ... and I'm sort of reflecting traditionally, but just because of it's an easier way of describing the concept than the way it exists in our contemporary times right ... So just say ... there's a lady who's promised ... and my brother, like my direct brother he runs off with this girl. Right ... So his punishment for that ... for what he's done ... is that he gets speared in the leg. Right ... Now ... him being speared in the leg right ... There's ... there's the give and the take in that first instance right ... He took something ... And then he was given something ... Yeah ... But now my brother he can't walk the same right ... So now when I go hunting I got to carry his arse right ... His load that he would usually carry burdens me now too ...

So the relationship where it has a reciprocity within that first order, it also has another set of give and takes that generates through the other relationships of that individual right ... That's why we need to be responsible ... Our actions are just not that karma idea of ... you know ... what I put out comes back to me... No way ... It's what I put out comes back to me and every single person that I'm in relationship ... but not only just person ... Everything ... Right ... So that's what's hard ... Because I keep saying person but I don't mean it like just person ... I keep correcting myself ... I would usually say at home like a person ... but I mean the tree ... or an animal or bird ... or a creek ...I mean them as a soul and a spirit. So it has impact on all of them ... You know and this is the problem we've got ourselves in within this society.

See ... you had an uninterrupted, network of populations on a continent, isolated to some extent, but able to perfect a system that was multi-layered over time ... One that was integrated in like the absolute, sort of sense of that word. It was grounded in place ... You know ... It was ... and respect ...you've got a system that was so complex that the marines and convicts they sent out here were too fucken retarded to be able to see ... even the most minute complexities ... You know ... And yet you have a situation here today where, you know we operate off a philosophy of give and take, yeah, so you've got ngapartji ngapartji ... but you've also got: *you never take more than what you need*. You know ...

So a man who had more spears than what he needed was seen as insane ... Right ... Like literally ... literally ... If you had five spears but only needed one, you were seen as ... like that person must be mad. Or they must be actually mentally unwell ... Why would they have more? So you would never take more than what you needed ... You would never have more than what you needed ... It was a higher sort of aspiration of a people to become the ultimate custodians ... You know?

So knowledge becomes your journey to wealth. And the way in which the system functioned was it sort of drip fed down through that sort of system ... So ... as you got older and had those experiences ... so you know ... you got to that point where you would have a partner and have to deal with all that shit ... and then have some kids and have to deal with those fuckers ... and keep going ... anyway ... you would be introduced to more and more knowledge as you progressed through your life ... as you matured right ... And ... So ... you'd come into all those different layers that sit within your Dreamings.

Unwell

... And we are now in a situation where we have taken more than what we've needed ... And we've not only disturbed the balance but we've created such imbalance that our people ... are unwell ... We're unwell ... the food we eat is unwell ... The sky's unwell ... The water's unwell ... The animals we see around us are unwell ... Man my father in the sixties talks about throwing a three-pronged aluminium spear over their shoulder ... like blind right ... Over their shoulder into Mullet Creek and being able to pull out six fucken fish ... You can't see one today ... And that's in the space of what? What is that ... Fifty ... sixty years? Right? You can't see one ... Imagine the abundance of this place ... Imagine ... The best that we can imagine ... You know ... We have created such unwellness in this space, that in some ways it motivates me more to sort of care for country and sort of operate in those ways, but it's the imbalance that makes everything so unwell ...

… And you can't be unwell for too long … You can't. So for me and my life … how do we create … like a shared identity. How do we create a space where all of our insecurities are valid and validated … but it's safe and supported within a system of care and responsibility … How do we start to create that … and for me … part of the … the honour and privilege that you guys bestowed upon me … by asking me to be a part of this … is that, where it may not be a conversation initially between Black and White … what it is … is a conversation about place and space. So that's what for me, is part of it … Because the conversation is between Country, Kinship, Culture, Journey and the inter-relationship of those.

You see … It needs to consistently connect … It's always cyclical. It's always seasonal. It's always, always in a circle … it's not a fucken ladder to the top … *[laughing]* … it's not a straight line … It's not one day I'll reach god or I'll be good enough … The journeying in that space and place takes you out of where you are …

So for me … the only way in which you can make the balance come back or make the place well again is by at least engaging in the philosophies of this place … through the give and take … Well … actually … it can't just be give and take anymore … Cause you've taken more than … you know … what you've given … so you've got to give back more … Right …

Like … you keep taking coal out of these mountains man … you keep taking … and I'm using that as an example because it's something physical that we're removing … But there's a whole range of things that ain't physical that we keep taking … Right … what are you giving back?

But I think we need to start giving integrity to Country and really allowing knowledge to sit there … and draw ourselves and whoever it is that we're taking on that ride with us out of the classroom … out of the book … out of whatever it is that we assume and think is that place of knowledge and just go fucken sit with it … and just be … Just you know … And don't feel the pressure to do … Just go and be … Does that make sense?

Cath – there's also that thing about tradition. Tradition grows, so there's this thing about we have to go back to tradition we're not allowed to change how it was, cause that's traditional but actually tradition is always, it shifts and changes ...

Jade – course it does.

Cath – so it's actually a complex problem because a lot of people are trying to cling onto something that defines their identity cause it's important and yet that identity will always be changing anyway.

Jade – Right ... And then where does that place us on our higher, higher learning. Right? *All of it relates. Every single time. Now and for always. Because time is not a fucken straight line.* Always man.

Louise – That's also interesting about the future isn't it?

Jade – It's always future.

Louise – How future bounds into the present and past.

Jade – Always.

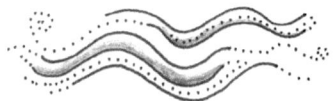

Flux

I labour upward in whipping wind, watching a mountainside appear and disappear in shifting veils of mist and rain.

We think this way too. We hold our breath, and wait.

Space junk

On 7 December 1972, astronauts on board Apollo 17 took the photograph *The Blue Marble* (or AS17-148-22727), 29,000 kilometres away from the Earth. Recorded on 70mm medium format film, it is the last photograph taken by human hands of the planet as a whole.

On 19 July 2013, at 21:27 Universal Time, the Cassini space probe photographed the planet Earth from the Saturnian system. Carolyn Porco, project leader of NASA Jet Propulsion Laboratory imaging team, called out for all inhabitants of Earth to look up at the sky at that precise moment for a planetary selfie.

On 14 February 1990, Voyager 1 made a portrait of Earth from the Mercurian system six billion kilometres away. It's called *The Pale Blue Dot*: in the image, the planet is smaller than a pixel on a computer screen.

Constructions of metal, spinning round the planet, drifting deeper and deeper into the galaxy. The human imagination spinning with them.

Speculative

Sometimes it's super storms. The water bursts through the cement dikes and surges through the suburban streets. The survivors flee to the cliff tops and watch the murderous brown liquid filling up the valleys below. Sometimes it's fire: stripping through grassland and bush, ribbons of dazzling heat. Or else it's toxins seeping into the earth, or blooms of blue-green algae that suffocate the rivers, or clouds of ash that drown the sky. The spaces of safety shrink. The borders are eroded: by pollutants in the air, by changes in government, by hordes of starving or genetically altered humans. The last humans hide behind barricades of taxicabs in Manhattan or in the shadows of caves in the hills above Lake Illawarra. They sit in the dark. They tell stories, and wait.

Or are we waiting? Amitav Ghosh writes that, in many ways, "the Anthropocene resists science fiction."[322] It's not speculative fiction, or fantasy, or 'cli-fi'. It's not the future. It's here and now.

Status

Waste as status. Mindlessly repetitive waste of the most precious: air, water, earth. My first encounter with the neatly stacked hyper-reality of modern suburbia was in Perth, Western Australia. Here was a city with the arid desert climate of Rabat or Essaouira that, instead of at least replicating the organic architecture of those far-off places, was enacting with industrial repetitiveness an architecture of denial. Denial of climate, of air, water and earth. And crowning this orgy of denial—the Victorian front lawn. What better, more powerful, way of declaring that one disregards this land in all its being than to port on it the social status fantasies of a completely different land? What does this status symbol communicate; of what message is it the medium? In its original Victorian countryside setting it communicates the ability to waste:

I am so well off that I need not plant trees, or vegetable gardens, or vineyards. In fact, I am so well off that I can afford to waste resources making sure that nothing whatsoever will grow on this land. Only grass. More, I will go as far as to periodically cut the grass too! Behold all the waste and marvel! And I will not build walls around my lawn, because my status must be visible to all. You on the other hand, must not linger around. The assembly line calls.

Plastic

Sherri Mason, professor of Chemistry at the State University of New York has observed that: "we have enough data [about microplastics] from looking at wildlife, and the impacts that it's having on wildlife, to be concerned ... If it's impacting wildlife, then how do we think that it's not going to somehow impact us?"[323] She was quoted in the context of new investigative reporting in 2017 that has revealed even tap water is now contaminated by plastic fibres. Very recent studies have also shown that tiny particles of plastics have been found in sea salt in the UK, France and Spain, as well as China and the US.[324] Biologists continue to fill bleak albums with scenes of displaced extraction and consumption in the plastic-blocked guts of marine seabirds, turtles, whales.

With the contamination of fish and filter-feeding sea life by particles of plastic fragmented to microscales—the 'microplastics' first described in the 1960s—and plastic-infused tap water, and even plastic sea salt, we, and more than we, are now eating and drinking our own Anthropocenic waste, particle by particle.[325] What might we name this surfacing abjection, this contemporary state of being cast off?

(De)generation

It lurches out of the ocean, lopsided and mangled and rusted. It looks like a set from a science fiction movie: an outpost of the ruined city of Jakku or a burned-out wreck on the road to Thunderdome.

In 2006, the company Oceanlinx installed a wave generator near the northern breakwater in Port Kembla. Launched by the then federal environment minister Peter Garrett, the intention was to link the 550-tonne device to the grid, providing a new source of energy for the region. The device used 'oscillating water column technology' and air turbines to generate electricity. As waves rose within the device, a column of air was pushed through the turbine. It was hoped that the prototype would be replicated in Western Australia and off the tip of southern Tasmania. It had the potential, Oceanlinx claimed, to provide five times Australia's electricity requirements.[326]

In 2010, during rough seas, the barge snapped from its moorings and crashed into the eastern breakwall of Port Kembla harbour. Oceanlinx decommissioned the device, leaving it marooned just off the coast. More storms in 2016 caused it to tilt; a shipping container on its southern side slipped underwater.

Oceanlinx went into receivership in 2014; the patents and other intellectual property were sold to an offshore energy developer. The new website says: "since the acquisition, [we] have significantly enhanced the performance and efficiency of the earlier versions of the technology."[327]

On summer afternoons, the wreckage makes a great breakwater for bodysurfers.

Habitat

Ecologists working on Cabbage Tree Island, just off Port Stephens on the central coast of NSW, were looking to protect the population of the Gould's petrel. A pelagic seabird, these birds return to the same spot on the island every year to breed. Their lifespan is unknown, but birds banded in the 1970s are still returning to the island. Gould's petrels nest under loose rock scree or dried palm fronds, leaving hatchlings vulnerable to rockfalls. To counter this, the ecologists installed breeding boxes. At first, the boxes were made of wood, but the scientists discovered these were easily crushed or eroded. So they replaced them with plastic boxes. These are much more durable, need little maintenance from humans and seem to be preferred by the birds themselves.[328]

The birds make a home in plastic. The skinks in my garden sleep under the cool of the polymer dog kennel. In the harbour, molluscs and anemones create a habitat inside the rim of a discarded rubber tyre.

Voyager

In the Voyager space probe, Jimmy Carter's recorded voice says: "We are attempting to survive our time so we may live into yours."[329] A double statement: a pretend acknowledgment of our impermanence covering the real knowledge that we're not going to be sticking around. Jimmy Carter: live in space. It's always good to try.

Coming to terms

REPLY REPLY ALL FORWARD
Mark as unread
all-bounces@uosme.edu.au
To: All;
12/04/2018 12:35 PM.
Download all

Hello Colleagues.

Last summer the University rented portable air-conditioning units as part of the Short-Term Thermal Comfort Strategy, which some of you have in your offices.

The Climate Management Division has since purchased these units, meaning staff have the option of having them installed permanently, pending the implementation of a longer-term strategy. These units can also be used for heating in winter.

What do you need to do?

Please complete this short survey, and under question 7 indicate whether you would like to have your unit installed permanently or removed. If you are experiencing problems with your current unit, including its placement or anything else, you can also note this here for CMD to address with you.

If you missed out on a unit and you are still sweating, please also complete the survey so that Facilities can assess the feasibility of providing you with one. If you have any symptoms of heat exhaustion, please call 000.

The Thermal Comfort project team are working through a planned air-conditioning upgrade program that will deliver permanent air conditioning solutions for the University's workplace environments in the near future. In coming months, the team will communicate the timing for these improvements being undertaken.

Regards,

Senior Manager, Operations (acting)
Faculty of Adaptation
UOSME NSW Australia
uosme.edu.au | Facebook | Twitter | Instagram

Hodgepodge

To amiably contaminate the words of Anna Tsing, telling stories of atmosphere requires getting to know the inhabitants of the atmosphere, human and not human. "This is not easy, and it makes sense to me to use all the learning practices I can think of, including our combined forms of mindfulness, myths and tales, livelihood practices, archives, scientific reports, and experiments. But", Tsing adds, "this hodgepodge creates suspicions—."[330]

Indeterminacy

Mushrooms.

Light.

Becomings.

Us.

Them.

We.

Humid

Is it mould growing on those boots? The dew point. It can rain for two weeks straight in March in the Illawarra. Relative humidity is close to 100% —this means that the air can hold no more water.

Electric

When electrons move, a circuit is formed, producing a charge. This circuit is electricity. Within a cumulonimbus cloud, the air particles become ionised, and positive and negative charges move to opposing ends of the clouds. Charges build up and can be discharged to air, to other clouds, to ground, forming lightning strikes. On 10 June 1752, Benjamin Franklin flew a kite attached to a metal key into a storm cloud to link electricity with lightning. He was very lucky not to be killed.

A slow reading of Olive Senior's hurricane story.

Anne Collett

IN 'Hurricane Story, 1903,' Jamaican-Canadian poet Olive Senior recalls the days when "storm warning came by telegraph to the Postmistress" who rushed to "broadcast the news by posting a black flag;" and celebrates Grandfather (who lives beyond sight of the black flag) for his ability to read the atmospheric signs of imminent hurricane – changes in sky colour, cloud formation, bird movement. These signs were read, that is, detected and interpreted, and then acted upon with appropriate measures to safe-guard family, home and possessions, "time and time again."[331] The poem, like the time-honoured story, acts as an archive of knowledge and practice that might otherwise be lost; and like the mix of oral and written traditions out of which it was formed, the poem tussles with change. The atmosphere of the poem itself registers the poet-narrator's shift from childhood to adulthood, from innocence to experience, from tradition to modernity, from rural to urban, from small island view to big world view.

To read 'Hurricane Story, 1903' with the respect that the author and poem ask of us requires the recognition of indigenous knowledge – knowledge grounded in local habitat; and an understanding of the author's position as a "blue foot traveller"[332] in a global economy. As Senior explains in the poem, 'Embroidery', a "blue foot" is one who has "crossed water" and is therefore "a stranger" – "not born-ya." This is her position in Canada, the country to which she migrated in her early twenties; but although Senior returns annually to Jamaica, having "crossed water" she cannot be but changed – although a "born-ya" she is also "a stranger." The difference between "there" and "here" is absence – here is marked by the absence of "t" and there, by the presence of "here." The opening line of the poem 'Here and

There' is: "I knew I couldn't get there from here" and asks, "what magic words for the gateway?" The poem concludes:

... one day, I walked through without knowing

I had finally chewed into dust and absorbed
into my being the fibres of what it meant to be.

Here.[333]

To be, here, is to absorb and be absorbed into earth (dust) – the materiality of life. But what Senior also suggests in this poem, if read in relation to her own life trajectory as a blue foot poet, is the value of "chewing over words" – the value of tussling with the difficult relationship between word and thing, word and action, the words of here and of there. For poet and audience, the magic words of a poem can be a gateway to understand what it is to be, here – to be present, whilst remembering the past and dreaming the future. What is required is a chewing over – time taken to digest the fibrous matter of being; time taken to pay careful attention to reading and interpreting a nuanced complexity of signs. To chew the cud is to ruminate, to consider and reconsider, to digest and digest again what is difficult to absorb quickly. What is required is a slowing of time; a slowing that is associated with the lingering and pondering required of dwelling. I like the world "dwell" as its usage makes claims not just on residing somewhere but a lingering, a pondering, a deep situatedness. Understanding a poem and understanding the weather require particular kinds of paying attention, sensitivities that are developed over time. They require meaningful practice. They require us to dwell on them and in them.

This essay then is a form of slow reading – a shared indwelling. It is a kind of reading that I believe to be of value as much to our understanding of material and social ecologies as it is to literary ecologies. We might understand poetry as "culture," the work and product of the cultured, that is, an educated person; or of a particular culture – Afro-Caribbean or Jamaican, or Jamaican-Canadian for example. But we might also understand poetry, and 'Hurricane Story, 1903' in particular, as the cultivation of the soil – the product or that which grows out of the soil (nature) of the world that the poet inhabits or in which s/he dwells. The word "culture" is found in Middle English to denote a cultivated piece of land; a word derived from the Latin *"colere"* meaning to tend or cultivate. The intimate relationship between nature and culture is only severed when we forget or neglect to pass on remembrance of their history. "Tend" is another word I like as it suggests both tenderness and attentiveness: to tend is to take care of, to look after, to protect and nurture. Tending requires the investment of time, attention and effort. In the history of the word "culture," the shift from cultivation of the soil to cultivation of mind and manners occurs over the sixteenth century. Here is evidence of the close relationship between earth (nature) and word (culture) and the work or labour of love that links the two that are in effect, one.

To place this discussion within a Caribbean context, we can turn to the influential Barbadian poet and social historian, Kamau Brathwaite, whose poem 'Negus' rages against the separation of a people from their habitation and their language – a separation of nature and culture – through the violence done by conquest, colonisation and neo-colonisation. The loss suffered by indigenous peoples of the Caribbean and transported Africans is understood as a loss of creative "Word" in which nature and culture were one. The poet asks for the gift of "words to shape my name/to the syllables of trees," "words to refashion futures/like a healer's hand:"

> I
>
> must be given words so that the bees
> in my blood's buzzing brain of memory
>
>
> will make flowers, will make flocks of birds,
> will make sky, will make heaven,

> the heaven open to the thunder-stone and the volcano
> and the unfolding land[334]

Openness, receptivity, and unfolding are key words here. In *Mother Poem* (1977), Brathwaite writes his "mother" (back) into being: in preface to the volume he speaks of the poem as:

> about porous limestone: my mother, Barbados: most English of West Indian islands, but at the same time nearest, as the slaves fly, to Africa. Hence the protestant Pentecostalism of its language, interleaved with Catholic bells and kumina.[335]

The poem is about the healing of a nature/culture split and the recovery of a submerged "indigenous" language that runs under the island as water in limestone channels. Indigenous here does not refer to the language of the people who inhabited Barbados at the time of European "discovery," but rather to a language of "country." "My Mother" is the limestone island; "My Mother" is the poem. In 'Driftword,' the final poem of *Mother Poem*, my mother is "echo of river trickle worn stone:" "she knows that her death has been born:" she knows and acknowledges her death by genocide of people and plantation; but she will be reborn if word is once again born out of and creative of her materiality and her spirituality. In the final verse of the poem the poet declaims:

> if it be so
>
> let it be clay that the potter uses
> and he will curve her hollow cheek and carve
>   her darkness
>
> ...
>
> so that losing her now
> you will slowly restore her silent gutters of word-fall
>
> ...
>
> linking linking the ridges: the matchbox wood houses

> past the glimmering downward gully and pebble
>> and fountain
>
> of ancient watercourses
>
> trickling slowly into the coral
> travelling inwards under the limestone
>
> widening outwards into the sunlight
> towards the breaking of her flesh with foam[336]

Mother Poem re-establishes intimate and indivisible relationship between nature and culture, the material and the ephemeral, word and Word.

Where Brathwaite situates the origin of his w/Word in the slow trickle of water through Bajan coral, Senior writes of dwelling in and of 'Cockpit Country,' Jamaica. Here her self as person and poet "form[s] slowly like stalagmites," nurtured by bird song and green.[337] For Senior, like Brathwaite, poetry can be incantatory; thereby not only remembering submerged histories but capable of re-establishing the indivisibility of nature/culture relationship. She most often does this work through the naming and thus, calling up – a kind of possession (in the *kumina* sense) of and by trees native to the Caribbean, and more specifically to Jamaica. Part way through her first volume of poetry, *Talking of Trees* (1985), Senior inserts an epigraph: "What kind of period is it when to talk of trees is almost a crime because it implies silence about so many horrors?" (Bertolt Brecht).[338]

For Senior, who was born of a country whose indigenous inhabitants, human and vegetable, were "cleared" for plantation labour and crop and were "replaced" by peoples uprooted and transplanted from their native lands, to talk of trees is not to signal a silence about such horror, but to give that horror voice. To talk of trees is to talk of loss and to make present the absence of vegetable and human lives that were intertwined before the Fall, and expelled after the Fall (the Fall here being an allusion both to the biblical expulsion from the garden and the rift that occurs between culture and nature in the Americas with the violence of

European "discovery").[339] This talk of trees is a naming exercise that returns them, and those who gave them names, to mind, heart and tongue. The many that have been devalued and denigrated are reborn and accorded value in the poem:

> Su-su
> Su-su
> Su-su
>
> Once upon a time
> there were trees on Parade
>
> Trees on Parade?
>
> Trees on Parade. Listen:
>
> The Ebony trees are celebrating rain
> Spathodea's lapping Kingston like a flame
> On the western railing Scarlet Cordias burn
> Casuarina weeps Laburnum's numb
> And Woman's Tongue clatters out of turn:
>
> Who hears this? Who sees this? And who knows?[340]

Senior's poem gives voice to those disappeared and silenced so we might hear, see and know the truth. The trees named in this poem were trees planted in Parade Gardens (also known as Victoria Park and St. William Grant Park) at the heart of the city of Kingston in 1870–71. Senior notes that over 120 trees were planted including 35 different species, some of which were native to Jamaica. The creation of a garden at the heart of Kingston is an act of ironic hubris – a marker of colonial power that acts to restore, for its value to science and aesthetics, indigenous gardens destroyed by colonisation and plantation. Such a minor remedial act has little long term impact for at the time of writing the poem virtually all the trees had gone but one, a "woman's tongue," described by Senior as "a downtown vagrant" who, "in her mad way tells their story – and ours."[341]

Woman's tongue (*Albizia lebbeck*) is not native to the Caribbean, but like the enslaved Africans, was transported (from what Senior describes as the Far East) to Jamaica in the late eighteenth century. The plant has subsequently become "naturalised" and is commonly found growing in city yards.[342] So in calling up this tree, in particular by its common rather than Latin name, Senior evokes its place in the history of the island as integral to a human history that is too easily forgotten. She notes how its long seed pods "rattle in the slightest breeze – hence the tree's popular name."[343] These trees have been removed from the colonial garden for purposes of urban planning, but they have by no means disappeared. Like gossip that gathers momentum through whispered talk at the ragged edges of unauthorised human discourse, and weeds that refuse to be put down, proliferating and indeed thriving on disturbed ground, the vegetable world is envisaged in Senior's work as the power that resides in root and rhizome, having the twinned capacity for depth and breadth, for trenchant stability and transgressive mobility. Trees "on Parade" suggests an army; an army in this case of veterans who might be wounded but are by no means disabled or disempowered:

> 1907 Earthquake when churches fell down
> Tamarind Tree swayed. But Banyan held firm.
> Come. Let us sit under Banyan tree and
> reason together. Like Prophets of old
>
> or the Big-tree boys
> of old Kingston town
>
> They baad
> They tough
> Like Ironwood
> Lignum Vitae[344]

Human and plant resistance and rebellion are here brought together; joined by the power of creative w/Word.

Senior's homage to the vegetable kingdom and inquiry into the nature of its entanglement with human history is central to her poetry collection, *Gardening in the Tropics* (1994). In 'Plants', the poem that opens the section 'Nature Studies', she warns (part tongue in cheek, part earnest) of "a vast cosmic program that once set/in motion cannot be undone though we/become plant food and earth wind down:"

> They'll outlast us, they were always there
> one step ahead of us: plants gone to seed,
> generating the original profligate,
> extravagant, reckless improvident, weed.[345]

In the final section of the volume, 'Mystery/African Gods in the New World,' the poet acknowledges and calls up African gods, transported to the Caribbean. Her words are again incantatory, making visible that which has been sent into hiding, making present. Among those gods are Osanyin, God of Herbalism, who the poet "halloas" in "voice as tiny/as beat of bird's wing" and asks that he provide one leaf for sorcery, one leaf for prophecy, one leaf for healing:[346] leaf and word are one, for this is the purpose and power of the poet's craft as declared by Senior in 'Ode to Pablo Neruda.'[347] In this, the final poem of *over the roofs of the world*, Senior records her loss of faith in her poetic craft and the reassertion of that faith through poetic dialogue with Pablo Neruda – a dialogue in which she recovers her sense of purpose as a poet and where she accepts the demands and risks of one who speaks "truth to power."[348] She acknowledges that this will require enormous love, courage and a power she cannot muster on her own. The burden of healing, the burden of speaking for those "lost ones, the limboed, the un-cared for,/the un-loved. The mortified, the discarded, the 'disappeared'"[349] is a weight so great it sometimes reduces her to silence and despair. So she calls upon "that old woman, the wizard of the cords/who used to tie up the wind with three knots in a bundle/and sell it to sailors."[350] The unravelling of each knot determines the strength of wind – one knot unloosed for "light breezes," two knots for "clipping along" and three - "woe betide – for a battering." Despite knowing the powerful impact of loosening the third knot, and despite her declared innocence, the poet narrator defends her (poetic) act:

> But my/hurricane heart feels better for its roaring, for scouring/the world. For it's the strong wind that cleanses, that/unburdens and purifies. It uplifted the fallen.[351]

Although destructive, hurricane is also creative and a powerful force for good. One of the African deities to whom Senior pays tribute in *Gardening in the Tropics* is Oya, Goddess of the Wind:

> You inhale
>   Earth holds its breath
> You exhale
>   Cities tumble
>
> …
>
> You whistle
>   We dance
> You sweep
>   We fly
> You yawn
>   Death rattles[352]

Breath is word: creative and destructive. If the poet can harness the breath of the hurricane in her word, she can change the world.[353]

Hurricane Story

Hurricane season in the Caribbean is annual, expected and to some extent ordinary; but its effects are nevertheless often devastating, if not extraordinary. It is a natural phenomenon that has an integral place in the culture of Caribbean life. Hurricane blows through song and story; hurricane is the "stuff of legends

– tragic, comic, epic:"[354] it is the breath of national, communal and personal histories, where nature and culture are utterly entangled. In *History of the Voice* Brathwaite identified hurricane as definitive of Caribbean life and that upon which a poetics of the Caribbean might be created:

> What English has given us as a model for poetry ... is the pentameter ... the pentameter ... carries with it a certain experience, which is not the experience of hurricane. The hurricane does not roar in pentameters. And that's the problem: how do you get a rhythm which approximates the *natural* experience, the *environmental* experience.[355]

Martinique writer, Edouard Glissant, speaks of the "storyteller's cry" as needing to be "grounded in the depths of the land."[356] He claims that this is where its power lies, for it is not "an enclosed truth, not momentary succor," rather, perhaps paradoxically, story grounded in the geology of rock (as Brathwaite's is grounded in the limestone of Barbados) provides a communal path "through which the wind can be released."[357]

Hurricane stories trace the personalised histories of that communal path in Senior's "tropical garden." The volume includes Jamaican hurricane stories from 1903, 1944, 1951 (Charlie) and 1988 (Gilbert). The first of these hurricane poem stories – first chronologically within meteorological record and first in Senior's *Gardening* volume – begins: "time and time again ..." The hurricane of 1903 was the first of the twentieth century, but one of a long succession of hurricanes to make landfall in Jamaica across planetary time. This sense of small story within big story is signified in the title and the first words of the poem, "time and time again." The words recall the classic folk story/fairy tale opening, "Once upon a time," and signal the iterative nature of story and of hurricane.

In the "Monthly Weather Review" of August 1903, EB Garriott details the "forecasts and warnings" for the West Indian hurricane of 8–15 August 1903:

> The first indication of the presence of this storm to the eastward of Barbados was furnished by the morning telegraphic reports of the 8th. West Indian stations and Gulf and Atlantic coast shipping interests were at once notified that a disturbance probably of dangerous strength was approaching Barbados from the eastward and would move northwestward over the Windward Islands ... Reports from Kingston, Jamaica, show that the first effects of the storm were felt on that island on the 10th, and that the main hurricane center reached the island on the morning of the 11th, causing a heavy loss of life and property. At Kingston the minimum barometer, 28.80 inches, as indicated by the barograph, occurred at 5.30 a.m. of the 11th, and at 6.15 a.m. the barometer had risen to 29.36 inches. The anemometer cups were disabled, but the maximum wind velocity at Kingston was estimated at 65 miles per hour.[358]

One of the key warnings of approaching hurricane is a steady drop in atmospheric pressure, typically beginning 36 hours before the hurricane makes landfall and plunging steadily as the storm nears. The scientific literature lists other early warning signals that amount to not much more than the usual for an oncoming storm – increased speed and intensity of wind, increased wave motion, increased cloud. Over the course of the twentieth century, recourse to satellite and radar technology and the use of reconnaissance aircraft has greatly assisted the tracking of tropical cyclones. In addition, data buoys are now employed throughout the Gulf of Mexico and along the Atlantic and Pacific seaboards to relay air and water temperature, wind speed, air pressure and wave conditions that enable more accurate prediction and monitoring of storm systems. But before the people of the Caribbean had recourse to modern instrumentation and communication, surviving a regular hurricane season was founded on sensitivity to environment; accumulated knowledge passed from one generation to the next by word of mouth; and what amounted to a rehearsed, even ritualised, set of practices. When swallows settle below the roof line, when the sky takes on a "special peach glow," when flocks of birds fly west, when clouds bank and the air becomes still, Granny brings the goat and fowls into the house, and Grandfather battens it down – knowing exactly when "to board/the last window up and brace the door."

"[T]ime and time again" speaks to time-honoured practices associated with both story and hurricane; but the words also carry a sense of the tiredness that comes with repetition, even the possibility of despair that might come with the cyclical nature of hurricane story from which there is no escape. In a poem published in 2012, titled 'Hurricane Watch', Senior begins: "Every year we are forced to reinvent ourselves,/growing shabbier."[359] This shabbiness is not discernible in 'Hurricane Story, 1903.' Here the cyclical nature of hurricane is entwined with rural poverty but Senior makes clear that this is a poverty of circumstance not of spirit and indeed, the capacity to "make do" and "make the best of" is praiseworthy – we might call it resilience. The corn is hung from rafters; afu yam and sweet potato are stored underground "safe from breeze-blow." When the wind rises in 1903, Grandfather takes his good clothes out of his trunk and packs it with corn – the subsistence food that will ensure survival; while Granny adds cassava bammies and chaklata balls "with a string of nutmeg and cinnamon leaf" – the special food that will lend the survivors "courage." Grandfather's and Granny's efforts to "shore up their lives against improvidence" ensure the family rides out the storm with little harm done. The positive can be found in the negative. Coconuts knocked to the ground by the ferocity of the storm provide the rare luxury of hot chocolate milk and oil to fry the bammies.

Here we see Senior's careful rendition of the grandparents' situatedness in which nature and culture are thoroughly entangled. In the first stanza of the poem, the pinguin fence from which Granny plucks fowl coops "time and time again" is a living fence made of a cactus-like shrub, *Bromelia pinguin*, indigenous to Central America, northern South America and the West Indies. The plant is commonly used to fence pasture lands in Jamaica on account of its prickly leaves and the six-foot height to which it grows. Both Afu yam (*Dioscorea aculeata*) and sweet potato (*Ipomoea batatas*), also mentioned in the first stanza, are native to the tropical Americas and both are integral to Jamaican food culture. In his work *Jamaican Food*, Barry Higman includes references to types of yam in the Jamaican diet and the origins of their popular names. His sources include local cookbooks and Martha Beckwith's study of Jamaican "folk life."[360] The linguistic genealogy of "afu" can be traced to the Twi word "afuw," meaning "plant" or "cultivated ground." Higman notes that the Twi language group was centred in Ghana (the country in which many Africans were imprisoned to await sale and transportation to the West Indies); and that this language is also the likely source of the word "bammy."[361]

Grandfather and Granny embody the "practice of everyday life" to which the provision and production of food is central. They are what Michel de Certeau refers to as "obscure hero[es]."[362] De Certeau begins 'the Annals of Everyday Life' with a quotation from Paul Leuilliot's preface to Guy Thuillier's *Pour une histoire du quotidian*:

> Everyday life is what we are given every day (or what is willed to us), what presses us, even oppresses us, because there does exist an oppression of the present. Every morning, what we take up again, *on awakening*, is the weight of life, the difficulty of living, or of living in a certain condition ... Everyday life is *what holds us intimately*, from the inside.[363]

The food that is grown and husbanded (plant and animal) is integral to the culture that nurtures a people. It sits at the heart, mind and stomach of "what holds us intimately." As Higman writes in preface to his volume, the choices Jamaicans make about what they eat, when and how they eat, and how these choices change over time, "provide insight into the social cultural, agricultural, economic and political history of Jamaica:"

> In everyday life, these choices are at least as important as decisions about whom to vote for and what to have faith in. Although it may appear transient, food is not just essential to bodily survival but vital as a driver of culture and identity ... In the past ... the sources of food grew in fields and forests, sea and stream, for weeks and months; they were observed from birth to maturity, and were watched closely as they came to ripeness or fatness ... For most of Jamaica's history, people lived in the midst of plants and animals recognized as potential foods.[364]

Here we have another reference to "slow" culture and the intimacy of relationship between nature and culture. In giving us a picture of Jamaican food ways of a particular social class and of a particular time and place, Senior's 'Hurricane Story' offers readers a potted history of a hurricane culture; for hurricane is not just an extraordinary event, it is interwoven into the fabric of ordinary life. That fabric is rent by hurricane, but that intimate relationship between nature and culture ensures the capacity to mend the fabric. Senior understands the poet's role as integral to that mending, that healing. She envisages herself as the female understudy of Anansi — the mythical trickster spider-man/god, prominent in the stories that survived the Middle Passage from Africa to the Caribbean. In the final stanzas of 'Ode to Pablo Neruda', the poet considers accepting her commission as apprentice spider – this is a commission that is not willed, but given. Gifts necessarily come with expectation and obligation. They demand a giving back of self. The poet muses:

> Maybe I'll accept after all my commission as
>   apprentice Spider
> who spins from her gut the threads for flying,
> for tying up words that spilled, hanging out tales long
> unspoken, reeling in songs, casting off dances.
> And perhaps for binding up wounds?[365]

Story is integral to any process of recovery and indeed, survival. By situating the event of hurricane— this particular hurricane of 1903— within the lived trajectory of a family, a community, a nation, Senior ensures the perpetuation of folk and food ways. Her poem acts as a document of retrieval for that which has been lost, an archive in which the past can be housed "safe from breeze-blow," in effect by incorporating hurricane within the poem and the community that gives it life. In turn, language and story are integral to the life of a community. By naming the plants and trees and the food they become when cultivated, and locating them within the life cycle of a community and the child for whom this is "the past," the genealogy of a people is not only archived but "called up," in much the same way that the African drummer recited the history of "the tribe." The child who may have become a blue foot traveller, like the poet, is given a thread by which to cling on to, retrace, restore, re-connect to her ancestral and living culture of belonging.

The cassava bammies that give the family courage to build again when faced with the devastation of the storm call an ancestry to mind and remind those who have survived literal and metaphorical storm of strategies employed to keep ancestral African and indigenous culture and nature alive in the Caribbean. These streams, as Brathwaite reminds us, run underground, carving channels through stubborn rock, in the subversive double-speak of calypso and in the "slave grounds" and Maroon territory where seeds of African and indigenous nature and culture were nurtured in the form of every day practice. Indigeneity and transplanted Africa survive and grow in new ways, entwined with the colonial cultures of European origins.

'Hurricane Story, 1903' concludes with the grandchild spending time

> ...watching that sensay fowl that
> strutting leghorn rooster, dying to be
> the first to see the strange bird fated
> to be born out of that great storm.

The sensay fowl – whose name is derived from African Twi - and the leghorn rooster – a breed of fowl whose origins lie in central Italy – survive the storm together, holed up in the cotton tree (*Ceiba pentandra*) – a tree, according to Senior's *Encyclopedia*, that is associated with the sacred in Africa and the Americas.[366] Here Senior records the indigenous people's use of the cotton tree for canoe building, reminding readers of Columbus' sighting of a huge dugout canoe in Jamaica. Recalling the cotton tree's symbolic history that associated it with "long life and continuity" she notes its centrality in belief and story of the Arawaks of Guyana, the Taino, the Mayas of Guatemala, and the Ashanti of Ghana. Finally, Senior draws our attention to the many events throughout Jamaica to which the cotton tree has been integral, making particular mention of the treaty signed by Cudjoe of the Maroons and Colonel Guthrie on behalf of the English forces, under a large cotton tree growing in the middle of Maroon Town, Kingston. She is told that "the tree was ever after called Cudjoe's tree, and held in great veneration," being the site of negotiated relationship between defeated colonising forces and victorious resistance fighters.[367]

'Hurricane Story, 1903' is a negotiation of past and present, of here and there, between born-ya and blue-foot, between author and audiences. The poem explores the often oppositional and difficult relationship between nature and culture, professional and amateur knowledges, male and female perspectives, indigenous and colonising ways of reading the environment. Something of this difficult relationship can be felt in Senior's poem where Grandfather is likened to a biblical prophet, a man of special talents because he is "the seventh son of the seventh son." The poet's tone is lightly mocking of such (gendered) hubris, but this is also a praise poem in which the passing on of what might be understood as "amateur" or indigenous knowledge from one generation to the next, is accorded value.

Reflecting upon historical attitudes and practices associated with hurricane in the Caribbean, Stuart Schwartz notes how "the great storms were part of the annual cycle of life" and the degree to which the power of storm was respected, often deified; but he also describes how the indigenous peoples of the tropical Americas "sought practical ways to adjust their lives to the storms." He lists "field management and crop selection, urban layout and drainage systems, house construction, forest usage and maintenance;" even warfare, migration and trade. The Calusas of southwest Florida planted rows of trees as windbreak to protect their villages from hurricanes; the Maya of Yucatan avoided building on the coastal strips, recognising the vulnerability of human construction to wind damage and flooding from tidal surge; the Taino who inhabited the islands of Jamaica, Cuba, Hispaniola and Puerto Rico, selected a food staple from root crops like yucca, malanga and yautia because of their resistance to wind-storm damage. Both the Taino and the Carib peoples recognised the seasonality of the great storms, incorporating that knowledge into their cultural practice; they also learned to read "the signs by which their coming could be anticipated." The Caribs, who waged war against the Taino, could navigate "three or four hundred miles by using the shape of clouds, the direction of the wind, the color of the sky, and their knowledge of the stars." Their raids against the Taino were conducted seasonally, soon after the major storms had passed, in order to facilitate safe ocean traverse by canoe, and possibly in anticipation of disarray or preoccupation with storm damage among the Taino settlements. The Caribs' ability to predict bad weather was seen as marvellous by the early European adventurers, among them Frenchman James Bouton, who described their knowledge as "uncanny."[368]

Ritual practices of creolised peoples native to the Caribbean, based upon knowledge both observed and handed down the generations through song and story, are identified in Senior's poem with grandparents – the "born-ya" post-indigenous generation. The tendency to see this ancestral knowledge as mysterious, mythical and possibly supernatural or "uncanny" is reflected in the description given Grandfather by the poet-narrator as "the seventh son of the seventh son." If we read the poet-narrator as synonymous with the blue-foot traveller, the tendency to mythologise and affiliate indigenous knowledge and practice in the tropical Americas with the supernatural can be ascribed to the "stranger" whose perspective is aligned with that of the European or North American anthropologist. But this perspective might also be aligned with a young child who is in awe of her Grandfather, the man capable of "orchestrating disaster" – a child still "too young to be schooled yet on disaster." What does it mean to be "schooled in disaster?" Popular usage of "schooled" suggests that Senior is referring to the school of hard knocks. The child rides out the hurricane on Grandfather's bed, safe in the capable hands of a generation who were schooled in disaster. For the young child, the event of hurricane provides the excitement of adventure, a reinforced sense of belonging, and the comfort of those who have acquired the knowledge of experience to ensure safety. The child's feelings of awe and wonder are a response, not to the hurricane, but to Grandfather's heroic orchestration, to Granny's unexpected nakedness, and to the hoped for birth of an extraordinary bird, born of the very ordinary inhabitants of the domestic fowl coop. All the actions and actors are contained within the bounds of the pinguin fence – that common native demarcation of family plot in Jamaica. The prickly *Bromelia pinguin* not only safeguards animal and plant, human and non-human, it provides fruit for eating and fibre for clothing. Nature sustains culture, so culture must nurture nature – this is both a "joy and an obligation."[369]

When I started writing about hurricane, I didn't expect to be talking of trees; but in the 'Monthly Weather Review' of August 1903, Garriott not only records the barometric readings and the wind force, he records the many losses suffered, noting that:

> The principal sufferers were the owners of banana plantations whose losses were estimated at more than £500,000. The orange, pimento, and coffee crops suffered severely; the towns of Port Antonio and Port Maria were almost destroyed, and throughout the parishes of St. Mary, Portland, St. Andrew, St. Catherine, and St. Thomas the destruction to houses, property, and plantations was appalling.[370]

The loss of plantation crop has a devastating impact on the economic viability of the nation; the impact upon individual lives and communities is enormous. But while plantation crops are destroyed, Senior's poem documents the means by which a poor rural Jamaican family survives – the measures taken to store food underground or in the safety of the tin box, and to take advantage of windfall. Survival is dependent on knowledge of a set of practices, that like story, are told and retold – the core of the tale remaining the same though the embellishments may change with each individual retelling. To talk of trees is not only to give voice to horror, not only to expose and condemn a long history of violence and oppression; to talk of trees is also to give voice to everyday courage, tenacity, heroism and love.

Trees give hurricane voice – they are the natural lyre[371] of the forest. Breath given poetic voice in Percy Bysshe Shelley's 'Ode to the West Wind' is not a gentle breeze that ripples the willows but a ferocious wind that rages through the forest, scouring the land of pestilence – a "Wild Spirit, which art moving everywhere;/Destroyer and Preserver." It is not inappropriate to recall the British colonial education that necessarily informs Senior's poetry. She herself recalls minds yoked to "declensions in Latin/ and the language of Shakespeare" in her poem, 'Colonial Girls School.'[372] But Brathwaite is right: the hurricane does not roar in pentameters. When Anansi is "let out of his bag," the young Jamaican girls are kissed awake by a less than charming prince.[373] The strange and beautiful bird, "fated/to be born out of that great storm," might be a hurricane story poem.

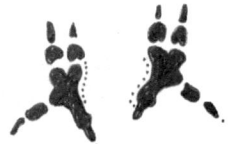

Transcendence

The first birds I noticed were three black cockatoos, floating overhead, as I walked over the highway bridge near North Wollongong station. I was a jumble of worries. Cars clanged and hissed as they passed me. I could see the schoolkids on the platform below: plucking and pinching, snickering and shoving. Doors slammed in the carpark. Underneath the train tracks a stormwater drain, tentacled with graffiti, the remnant of a creek. As I plodded, the cockatoos wafted down, hovered at eye level. I watched them, suspended in the air. Their charcoal wings were fringed against vibrant blue. I could have reached out and touched them. I could see the dirty-yellow smudge on the side of their faces, the glinting beaks, the black eyes ringed with silver. Then, one by one, the cockatoos dropped lower, under the bridge, and flew away. They were bewitching, remote, oblivious.

Much later, Jade tells me, "you know black cockatoos always bring rain with them, bro. And they only travel in pairs."

Life and death

Convivial.

Composition and decomposition.

In Melbourne, as part of a project mapping the 77,000 trees that make up the Urban Forest, the city assigned individual trees ID numbers and email addresses. Clicking on the map of trees (http://melbourneurbanforestvisual.com.au/#mapexplore) brings up the name of the tree, its life expectancy, ID and email address. The idea was that people could report damage, decay or vandalism.

Instead, people wrote letters. The letters recognise how these trees perform multiple tasks across the urban environment.

Some are love letters:

> **To:** Weeping Myrtle, Tree ID 1494392
> *Hello Weeping Myrtle, I'm sitting inside near you and I noticed on the urban tree map you don't have many friends nearby. I think that's sad so I want you to know I'm thinking of you.*
>
> **To:** Algerian Oak, Tree ID 1032705
> *Thank you for giving us oxygen ... Thank you for being so pretty.*

Many are layered with concern:

> **To:** Golden Elm, Tree ID 1037148
> *I'm so sorry you're going to die soon. It makes me sad when trucks damage your branches. Are you as tired of all this construction work as we are?*

To: Variegated Elm, Tree ID 1033102
Dear Elm, I was delighted to find you alive and flourishing, because a lot of your family used to live in the UK, but they all caught a terrible infection and died. Do be very careful, and if you notice any unfamiliar insects e-mail an arboriculturist at once.

A golden elm, living between a busy road and the edge of the Yarra river was the most emailed tree. Over 70 years old, the tree is one of the National Trust's trees of state significance:

Dear Tree, If you are that big round beautiful low hanging tree I think you are my favourite tree. Such beauty on such an ugly road. Keep up the good work.

Hello dearest elm, Do you remember when I used to drive past you and say hello? Why did they ever trim your canopy? Remember how your branches used to spread across the soil? It was glorious.

I used to think you were the Magic Faraway Tree when I was a child. Now that I'm an adult, I still look forward to seeing you as I come around the bend after a tedious crawl down Hoddle Street. A loyal friend always there waiting to say hello.[374]

Virtual

It was the removing of the helmet that I found most disorientating. The room seemed so much smaller, overcrowded with solid objects and staring humans. My hands—which, in the world inside, had glowed—looked pudgy and worn. Ted said: "how did you go?" I closed and opened my fists and the flesh felt like putty. In the inside world, the smallest gesture had manipulated the objects around me: I could swat away floating cargo boxes like they were shuttlecocks, brush aside bullets as if their lines of trajectory were spiderwebs. I pressed into the objective reality of the table top that stood to the left of me. I was disappointed when my hand didn't pass through it. Ted said: "are you all right? The ISS always nauseates me." I did feel light-headed, similar to the feeling I have when a migraine lifts. I tried to take a step forward, but my body didn't want to follow my mind. "How do I drag the world towards me?" I asked.

Wind

stiff breeze blows along miller street

whips the stanchions and lifts your lapels

prods you into the foyer and plays havoc in meetings

a summer shower chatters from chameleon clouds

roiling over the harbour

it will find its way in too, on heels clicking up stairs

a spidery trace left by mute umbrellas

air slides up gleaming towers that were inspired by

none other than nature itself

glides in through cracks in concrete slabs

rises from fresh coffee

outside the sun blisters paint and lips

while you enjoy a square of warm light

in the chill of aircon

small flies buzz around the potted palm

how did they get in?

you inhale one taking a deep patient breath

and cough the world out

another day done, you are again transported on the wind

sucking you through the underground tunnel

spat out in twilight

you watch the planet turn

sun says goodbye, moon says hello

Atomsphere

Thousands of kilometres from the bomb site, and years away, too, there was a discussion:

"When did it change?" someone asked.

"When the atom was split?" This voice was doubtful.

"Yes, that was the moment," came the reply.

"No, no, it was the Trinity explosion, surely," someone else said.

"I agree, that was the marker. It altered everything."

Spinning

Ninety-nine percent of weather occurs in the troposphere. The Earth spins eastwards and its enveloping air spins with it.

Gaspard-Gustave de Coriolis noticed that the things in the air (the *metéōros*) move at a different speed from the planetary surface.[375] The lag produces spinning motion in the atmosphere—clockwise in the northern hemisphere and anti-clockwise in the southern hemisphere—this is known as the Coriolis effect. The speed of spinning columns of air increases the further they travel from the equator, first forming what we classify as a low or depression, a tropical storm, then a cyclone, typhoon or a hurricane. A severe storm system can generate a descending fast-spinning column of air—tornado. Sometimes a thin column of descending air from a thick deck of clouds can generate waterspouts and dust devils.

What matters?

Who matters?

Why matter?

In the air: whipbird/human/koel

Joshua Lobb

Do you remember that day, years and years ago, catching the train to the mountains? A hazy morning, mist in the valleys. Do you remember the songs of the forest and the silences between us?

> Do you remember last night? Or, to be blunt about it, too early this morning? Do you remember what caused me to rumple my body into you, to roll back, to grunt and then to flick the covers away?
>
> It happens every year. The start of summer: an air-ripping cry in the night.
>
> You must have heard it too.

At the cliff tops we were accosted by the grind and hiss of buses and the shouting of school kids. The children slapdashed around us, sucking in the chilled air, puffing out plumes of white. They proclaimed – to us, to the buses, to no one in particular – that there was nothing to see. They were right. The mist had settled in and there was an empty space where the Three Sisters should be. A pipsqueaking ten year-old coo-eed into the void. There was no echo.

We weren't there for the view, you said. You knew the way. You led me past the ruckus and found the track to the stairs into the valley. Well, ladders, really: metal frames bolted into the sandstone. You slivered past crumbling rock and disappeared. The icy-sharp railing blanched my palm. I didn't look down. I breathed in the shrill air and followed. The cliff was smeared with moss, sharp horizontal lines. Ashy sediments marking the millennia. I could hear your boots tinkling against the metal rungs. I breathed in the invisible valley.

Halfway down the cliff – a stratum of silence. Above, the hackling tourists and growling buses. And below –

You were waiting for me in a sandstone alcove. You told me to listen.

I listened.

> You can't have slept through it. At the end of the street, no, three houses down, no, in the tree outside our bedroom window. A discordant plea. Two notes, one sliding into the other: a long rounded tone followed by a sudden higher plosive. Rising in inflection like a question, or a passive-aggressive demand. A pause. The grey air is silent. A chance, I hope, to ruffle back under the covers and into cloudy sleep. I sigh into you. Your body huffs and settles, lost in your own dreamscape. We share a few breaths. Then the call gashes the air again. The second plea at a slightly higher pitch, not-quite desperate, but definitely plaintive, woefully hopeful. Release and whiplash stop. Then silence. A third, up another tone in pitch and intensity. The lash at the end coming quicker, more severe, more expectant.
> I try to snuggle under your warmth, and a puff of objection escapes from your lips. I'm too half-asleep to apologise, too muzzy to recognise your body as anything other than a warm soundproofing shield. I'm trying not to listen for the next lacerating whoop.

I listened.

We were in another world. Or other worlds, really. Our feet had slopped onto the muddy track at the bottom of the ladders, but we weren't at the floor of the valley yet. The path precipiced downward and we followed.

Every layer provided new songs.

I didn't know the names of the songs we heard, nor the names of the birds who sang them. It wasn't like I hadn't heard birds singing before, or even these particular songs. I could have bluffed my way through finches, parrots, cockatoos. I could have made a stab at something and called it sparrow or galah or lapwing. I could have scratched out some easy verbs to manage them in my mind: chirp or warble, screech or whistle. On the misty path at the bottom of the ladder, these were inadequate, thin wisps of breath.

You told me to listen, and I was trying to listen.

> Release and stop. Silence. Release and ripping stop. I groan into the stuffy mattress. My feet get snarled in the blankets. The whooping churls the darkness, irks the air. I kick out. You grumble a few disconcerted, disconnected words. When you twist your torso away from me, you drag the blankets with you. My humming body is floating, anticipatorily, in the stillness of the air, in the gaps between the whoops. These rectangles of silence are irregular, unpredictable. The room expands with expectation.

Many of the calls were barely audible, like a party at the end of the street, or a television left on in the other room. My unformed mind clutched at inadequate analogies. One call sounded like the release of a half-filled balloon, the spittley plastic ends flapping together as it razes around the room. One trebled like a baby giggling; another, a polite cough – short, tentative, as if seeking permission to join in the fun. Another was a melodious metal detector: slow metronomic beeps and then, as it neared its target, increasing in tempo and delight. It was impossible to get the descriptions right. One was R2D2; another was Monkey from the TV show, whistling for his cloud. Another, an off-kilter Mr Whippy van: half a phrase of "Für Elise" and then a sudden dissonant clang.

I couldn't have told you where the sounds were coming from. I couldn't tell if they were clasping the spindly branches above or huddled in the undergrowth or hidden in the petrified grottoes. There was an occasional flustering of leaves. High above us, a flash of yellow among the grey.

The path sidestepped an ancient tree. The bark felt like fur. I smoothed its hide as I passed.

We moved silently through the quivering conversations.

We listened.

> The next whoop is the shrillest of them all. I think, for a moment, that the glass the bedroom window has shattered. Point blank. It breaks the room. But the shards bring revelation. I feel like I've been anointed by an archangel, like a shaft of truth has

pierced my soul. Or maybe it's more biological, like a migraine that was gripping my cheekbones has suddenly detached itself and curled away. The darkness in the room is dazzling. Everything feels jagged and clear.

I know what I need to do.

My body is less eager to follow my new calling. As I stumble out of bed, my knee nicks the corner of the bedside table. You might be muttering something to me now, telling me to get a grip, but I'm on a mission. I blunder out of the room, bumping into the doorframe. I'm clumsily insistent, evangelical, monomaniacal. I fumble through the darkness towards the hallway cupboard. I bang about for the broom and drag it, scrapingly, down the corridor. The screen door yelps as I shove myself outside. I totter over the tiles of the porch. The broom clatters.

The nasty noise is unperturbed. The whoop is a provocation.

I peer into the arms of the tree. A cavernous blackness stares back. I grip the splintery handle and smash the broom into the trunk. My arms tighten as the cut the air. I hack the trunk again, and again, and then again.

The new melody was beautiful. A constellation of calls. A chorus of wind chimes, almost too perfect to be natural. Like sonar. Like white coral tinkling underwater. Two tones – though sometimes it felt like three. The higher note held longer. The lower tone used as a springboard. Sometimes insistent, sometimes ethereal. Sometimes two notes came together, clashing, like children landing

simultaneously on a trampoline. Sometimes three high notes were held in succession. Sometimes a long gap of silence. Then the paired notes would tinkle again.
And, then –

> The broom wheezes through the darkness. The fractured bark muffles the air, like dust.

And then the other call. Or calls, you might have said. Harmonious with the quiet chiming rhythms, working as a counterpoint. A slow softness at first, like a lyrical cicada: increasing intensity, until unwavering and clear. It felt mobile, like it came from nowhere and everywhere, a siren whirring down a city street. It thrummed through our bodies. Then, Doppler-like, the sound changed: a sudden lash, then silence. We waited. A palpable silence. A minute, two minutes later, the siren bent the air from another angle; another slap as the sound cracked off.

We sat on the dewy rocks. The fuzzy moss tousled the hair on my fingers.

This is what I wanted you to hear, you said. Or you might have said. I can't remember.

> I huff, exhausted, against the chiselled bark.

In the deepest part of the forest – the hairpin in the track before it led us back up the cliff – there was a clearing. Mottled picnic tables, remnants of a gazebo from another era. We moved, stealthily, not wanting to interrupt the stillness. There were signs planted at the edges of the space, noting its historical significance or other points of interest. I didn't want words, so I slinked past. But you stopped, tracing the letters with your fingers. Although there was little light down there, the scratchy metal glinted. Then, a whiff of wind created a break in the canopy. A laserbeam of sunshine illuminated the rectangle. The silver spaces around the letters hummed.

The sign declared:
This is Leura Forest. In the bush you may hear the call of the golden whistler, the yellow robin. You might even hear the cockatoos soaring above the valley. In the valley, you'll hear the bell bird and the whipbird.

The whipbird call is a combination of male and female birds. The male calls first and the female with amazing timing answers the male. This is called an 'antiphonal response'. See if you can hear both sides of the conversation.

We didn't say any more about it. We weaved through valley, listening to the call and response.

> The space around the tree feels vacant. The night air feels solid. But it still isn't silent. The whoop returns. More tentative, maybe, but unrelenting, inevitable. I listen. I'm too tired to do anything else but listen. The sequence has looped back to the start: the quiet, slower, dissonant plea. This time, though, now that I'm really listening, it feels listless. Its insistence is provisional. Morose. A pathetic cry. The whoop modulates. Less perfunctory, maybe, but still melancholy.

> I scrape my fingers over the whittled bark, though my dusty hair. The whoop moves up another notch: barefaced, acute, ingenuous.

A shadow forms on the front porch. A body approaches. I feel your warm fingers on my shoulder, the sweaty small of my back. You're whispering to me. Ineptly, I clutch at your dressing gown, gasping out sobs in the night. The air calms around us. You're breathing in and out. I follow your lead.

The whoop starts up again, a wobbly croak in the grey morning light.

Do you remember the journey home? Outside the train, the daylight dimming; inside, the fluoro lights flickering on. Under the quiet light, you let my knee move towards yours. You turned your head and looked at me.

Do you remember the koel last night? Crying into the void, waiting for a response.

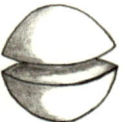

Hemispheres

In the thawing cryosphere

280 million-year-old forests

of lush Permian supercontinent Gondwana

have been found as tree fossils high above

the ice fields on Antarctic mountains.[376]

They thrived through the polar extremes of perpetual light

and total darkness (how?)

and now newly greet the Southern Hemisphere,

already seasoned greenhouse witnesses of mass extinction.

Wondering/wandering

Sorry, I wasn't listening—I wandered off for a moment. I can't keep my thoughts straight. I walk with a friend up the mountain behind the university (Mount Keira, a sibling of Mount Kembla) and our conversation starts with a conversation about climate change, and then jumps to food we ate last night, horror-emails from students and colleagues, an article she's writing, the name of the plant we're passing. I'm here, halfway up the mountain, halfway round the solar system. We're stopped in our tracks by a disturbance in the bush. Among the foliage is a lyrebird, scratching in the dirt. It acknowledges our presence, and then wanders off, deeper into the dark-grey of the mountain.

Portals

Bulgaria. At my great-grandmother's funeral deep in rural Thracia.

She lies in her coffin, head pointing west as a weathervane for the soul, as the village comes to say goodbye.

I watch an old woman bend over the coffin and whisper something, sharp and urgent. She's addressing her long deceased husband, using the body of my great-grandmother as a messenger. She tells her husband, as if he was present in the room, that their son has had another grandson. She tells him that the last winter was bitterly cold and the cow didn't have any calves this time. She asks him to wait for her.

They all come in, one by one, some with messages addressed at relatives who have passed away. The body listens, a portal to the other world, the spirit collecting the messages to be carried across. Waiting.

All who come leave something behind, walnuts, small coins, honey, an embroidered handkerchief.

Singapore. It is early morning and most of Yong Siak Street is still in the shade of the night, slowly retreating from the rising sun. The old lady from the corner house arranges today's offerings for the street spirit. Incense burning over a few oranges. Next to the small altar a cat sleeps on a pile of old phone books.

Ghosts

Adelaide. My mother's funeral. A priest stands over her coffin, chanting. This the same priest she detested. The one she scorned for hypocrisy. How is he here, presiding over her death? What will her spirit be thinking as her body lies still in the soft amber wood? Mourners are saying prayers, but my sister and I cannot utter a word.

A friend tells me that she is reminded of her mother every time a magpie lands on her lawn. She thinks, that is my mother there. What interests me is that I have the same feeling whenever a forest pigeon settles on the branches of the tree next to my verandah. Once, I saw a forest pigeon dead on the concrete. It must have flown into a window and become concussed. I didn't weep at my mother's funeral but on this day I couldn't stop weeping.

Collective

A system is a collection of things. Protons and electron spinning round a nucleus, junctions on a circuit board, nodes in a network. An ecosystem. Humans like to collect things: stones from the beaches we've visited; books we've read (or are yet to read); coins, autographs, memories. The human language likes to collect things, too. As a child, I was obsessed with the concept of the collective noun. A school of fish, a pride of lions, a parliament of owls. Where did they come from? Who decided on the particular term? And what happens to the subjects once they've been collected? John Berger famously asks us to read Van Gogh's *Wheatfield with Crows* (1890) through the lens of "this is the last painting he completed before he died."[377] In my mind, the painting has already been infected with mortality: above the thick waves of yellow wheat hover a *murder* of crows. Why a *murder*?

Why not an *intelligence*? A *collaboration* of crows? Su sends me a YouTube clip about crows in a Japanese city. It's a bit from a David Attenborough documentary.[378] The birds steal walnuts and try to work out a way of opening them. They fly above the busy streets and drop them onto the road below. If the hard surface doesn't break the shell, the crows have learned that the weight of passing cars will. "The problem now," Attenborough explains, "is collecting the bits without getting run over." So the crows drop the walnuts at pedestrian crossings. When the green man blinks and the traffic stops, a crow flies down and retrieves the food. The bird pecks at the broken shell and, when the motorbikes and the cars rev, she flits away. The crow is slicing through a city overstimulated with symbols, light and noise. One moment, part of this busy electric system; another, in a pattern of her own devising. I wonder what the crows think of the red man flashing at the pedestrian crossing, and the loud regular beeps.

Invisible

The atmosphere is thick but invisible. You can sense it but can't see it. You can smell it, feel it, taste it. Have you tasted clouds?

The parrot says: "how do they expect to recognize an alien intelligence if all they can do is eavesdrop from a hundred light years away?"[379]

Road trip

David Carlin

IT'S so easy to blame Americans for arriving at the future first, or for having so much space on the land they conquered, a vast bounty that mixes perfectly with bitumen and rubber, steel and oil and glass, fire inside those rockin' cylinders, and all those gyrating airwaves by which, in the middle of a desert, messages can be beamed into your vehicle from God's own ministers—"are you in pain? Call now!"—or, equally, the SomeSuch Clinic: "are you in pain? Call now!"

It seems a blasphemy that one could have so much highway unto the horizon and still be suffering from pain but this is the capitalist miracle: one can always feel more pain, just as the road will always produce potholes needing to be filled with bitumen and every freeway is only a premonition of a wider freeway, floating higher in the sky.

Drive …

I woke up one morning and I was in America, by which I mean the airspace west of Los Angeles, tragic birthplace of the freeway. I had always sheltered the thought: *one day I'd like to drive across America*. Who hasn't thought that? Now on a short work visit from Australia, I was driving interstate to Arizona, which was at least a start. I could entertain the fantasy of big horizons for a few days. As ethnographer Kathleen Stewart says, "Anything can feel like something you're in."[380] This was my chance to enter the undead nostalgic retro-futuristic atmosphere of the road trip and see where it would go.

After the paperwork and credit cards and automated booths that didn't yet quite work, exiting the hire car place at LAX, a Zen temple of low-wage Taylorist efficiency, car after car ushered out the driveway in a never ending crawl of untipped smiles, a voice pipes up, coolly algorithmic: "In 600 feet turn right onto West Manchester Boulevard."

A jetlagged driver behind the wheel of a lethal metal box should be thankful for any guidance, and he is. The car proceeds in silence. Waiting for the next signal from the heavens.

"Now turn," it says. I do. "Follow the slip road onto San Diego Freeway. Head south," it says. I do.

Entering the freeway: this is the true signal for the movie to begin. Head south. And soon enough: head east. Drive because it is your destiny to drive. You don't need to be told this place only actually makes sense if you are driving.

Intersections. In the classic fantasy of a road-trip there are no intersections; there is only slipping, merging, passing, and driving like flying, far above the earth.

Flyovers. Those are acceptable. A laudable use for concrete.

Leaving the city. But not just any city. Try leaving this one. It's not going to happen all at once. Allow three hours on a Friday afternoon.

The road trip is about private vehicles travelling at speed, surrounded by visible scenery, past billboards advertising FREEDOM and AUTONOMY. The road trip is arguably the limit experience of the automobile (along with the race track, let's say, but that's a more specialist fetish). How many car ads have you seen in which sleek sedans navigate Alpine bends or SUVs leap across flooded roadways like antelopes? In reality cars clog cities with noise and pollution. There, they move in fits and starts. They boil with pent-up fury, their tightly coiled engines spluttering morosely. Cars are surely, emphatically, testosteronic objects, maybe because they've largely been designed and groomed by men in their own phantasmatic self-image, full of thrust and power (ahem).

All of this is old. Similar observations could have been made in the 1950s when cars were still in their dreamy adolescence in the culture. Visions of speed and independence prefigured by the Futurists became the motor of postwar dreams lit by big oil and gas. Burn, baby, burn. The further you drive—the more you live out this particular dream—, the road trip—and the more gasoline your beautiful machine will need to drink. And for all that time you spend frustrated in the city, inching along in traffic, you are at least rehearsing for a road trip theoretically to come.

At home, I don't buy it. I prefer to ride a bicycle or walk wherever possible. In my inner city neighbourhood in Melbourne I have such luxuries available. Or I catch a tram. I like nothing better than riding a bike cheerfully past a traffic jam, willing them with my smug bonhomie to throw off the shackles of their automotive dreams and vote not for more and more roads but for better public transport.

And yet, and yet ... *one day I'd like to drive across America ...*

For most of my long drive among the freeways of Los Angeles, the city itself— the streets where people presumably live in houses and apartments, work, go shopping, love lovers, friends, family and pets—remains hidden beneath the elevated concrete roadways or behind noise protection barriers. Looking around for other things to notice, I see that the freeway, never less than five lanes wide in each direction and sometimes busting out beyond that, often marks one lane apart for carpooling. This civic gesture towards creeping socialism is largely ignored, judging from the lack of traffic over there, even though all you need to become a HOV (High Occupancy Vehicle) is not to be traveling alone. You realise it means that all the other cars in all the other lanes most likely carry just one person, hunched or sprawled at the wheel. Low Occupancy Vehicles Everywhere: this spells LOVE in California. Irony is free.

For a non-American, the dimensions of these heavy metal boxes on wheels are so oversized in every direction—wheelbase so wide, chassis so high, bumper bars so Botox-swelled, pickup trays so voluminous and empty-seeming as if they are carrying small swimming pools along behind their spacious cabs, miraculously slosh-free—they would be ridiculous if not so menacing as they expand to fill the rear vision mirror like monster parodies from an animated movie, growling: GET OUT OF MY WAY! As if the freeways invited the freedom to enact whatever aggressive fantasy you wanted. Occasionally I draw level with a vehicle, sized tall, grandé or Botero, and look across to check out the driver.

Inevitably he or she turns out to be the Wizard of Oz: smaller and less threatening than I expected. A young Asian-American guy, a silver haired white guy wearing a polo shirt, a thirty-something, dark-haired woman: each carrying the same hollowed-out affect of the habitually semi-concentrating driver, expressing *nada* about this most everyday of experiences.

When you travel far enough across the suburbs of Los Angeles they merge seamlessly into more suburbs in a vast landform of malls and bungalows called, fittingly, the Inland Empire. The Inland Empire, a real estate agent's dream, was previously called the Orange Empire after the citrus groves that briefly flourished there. I follow the signs towards a place called Norwalk for the best part of an hour before another freeway merge sends me North and East towards another place I'll never visit. All the time the GPS threatens red, or relents into yellow, as the traffic coagulates into the inevitable Friday peak. Off to the left I glimpse the downtown skyscrapers, and mountains in the distance.

Then, suddenly, darkness and the desert.

Driving in a city is only pretend-driving, like being a dog on a leash, the domain of speed limits ever more restrictive, basically the nanny state. On a road trip you can park wherever the hell you like (it helps if you are a man). You pull over to the side of the road in the middle of nowhere, slam the door shut, stretch your legs and suddenly you are in a Hitchcock movie. Cary Grant. Or maybe it is Fargo. Either way it should make you nervous. It suggests there are things you need to worry about out here, even if or maybe especially because the sky is so enormous, bigger than the proverbial field of corn. You feel again the violence of what is made of men, the nook designated for sweet boys to grow into. You hear an echo of imagined trollish voices: "somewhere else the sky is clogged that's not my problem let's build a wall—." (Cue the crop duster.)

I'm not one of *those* men, I tell myself. *Those* men frighten me. Even if they are straw, I have met real-enough men to frighten me. I'm a sucker for bullies, I'm weak and weedy. A trans-man friend of mine told me recently I dress gay. In practice I'm not gay, although in my twenties I once went to bed with a guy friend, straight too, both of us very drunk. I remember liking it, the curious symmetry of our bodies. And these strange things, penises: like licking paddle pops. Even if I am generally more attracted to women, I would still like *in principle* the freedom to caress a man. Not that in my country, unlike others, I don't have that freedom, but homophobic aggression shadows male-to-male relations. With each other we are supposed to talk and move as characters I've never quite known how to play. My masculine role model is a suicide (my father). I want to say these lines: *why are we so violent, guys? Why do we just love things hotted up, and the fumes of burning, ancient creatures? Is it the fury at what we feel when we are not sure what we feel? When the contradictions snap inside us…?*

Night falls, unfalls. In Victorville the hotel breakfast is a symphony of plastic, corn syrup and cable TV news. Americans are large and friendly. Drive.

I'm driving first to visit my friend Nicole in Flagstaff. Then we'll go in convoy down the long hill to Phoenix on the desert floor, for meetings about a conference. Then we'll split again; I'll take the low road to LA.

A road trip needs a lot of bitumen. You can have gravel road trips and off-road road trips but all roads, apart from some in elite beachside holiday villages, crave, in my opinion, to be bitumenised, the smoother the better. On the modern interstate highway I'm traveling down (the I40), occasional signs tempt with the experience of historic Route 66, the superseded highway that still runs parallel, now revived as a successful tourist attraction. On Route 66 the destination is the road itself, with its promise that you can re-enter a past (mostly, the fifties again) when things were simpler, and (white) people could sleep easy at night. I fall for it, try Route 66 for a while, thinking it might be faster and quieter, a way to avoid the fleets of trucks ferrying containers back and forth. But I find the old road lacerated with rifts and scars, as if it were deeply troubled, as if the desert itself was fed up with the weight of bitumen. I worry about the rental car's suspension. I have to reduce speed; a blight on my Caucasian freedom, right there. Route 66 is quiet as a ghost but bumpy and I need smooth. I want frictionless flow, just like everyone else yesterday in all those other vessels following and passing each other on the LA freeways, like artificially intelligent glowing insects as the afternoon pulsed into dusk. We, all of us, heartbroken, resigned to crawl and stop because sooner or later, as we promised ourselves, a space might open up ahead for flow, endless, endless flow.

At Easter one time, years ago in Adelaide where I lived, my then girlfriend and I set off on an impulse to drive and drive, away from the city towards adventure. When we arrived at adventure (the seaside town of Robe) after an afternoon of squabbling in the car on the theme of driving instruction (she the under-confident learner, I the over-anxious instructor), there were no rooms at the inn, so to speak, certainly no mangers and not even any vacant tent sites at the caravan park. On the Easter long weekend road-trip spontaneity was a currency scorned. We attempted to exercise our freedom to sleep by laying out a mattress on a sand dune under some straggly coastal bushes, our bodies lit up all night by the clockwork swishing of the lighthouse beam, like a prison searchlight. The next day we cut short our trip and drove home again, defeated.

And yet, and yet... To be at the wheel of a heavy metal vehicle engineered to glide across the surface of the earth on a ribbon of compressed rock and semi-solid petroleum made from ancient fossil remnants—the bodies of zooplankton and algae, rotten, sunken, pressurised, preserved for millions of years and finally sucked back to the surface through the ingenuity of drills and nodding pump jacks—this is surely the location nonpareil of the autonomous individual. Who doesn't want to be the one in the driving seat?

Back to Kathleen Stewart. Here she is, trying to describe what is happening to the ordinary human animal—me, for instance—as it travels through its life: "Out there on its own, it seeks out scenes and little worlds to nudge it into being. It wants to be somebody. It tries to lighten up, to free itself, to learn to be itself, to lose itself."[381] If this is what is happening to me all the time, this wanting to be somebody, to learn to be myself but also to lose myself, then maybe it is a heightened version of these lessons and experiences I am seeking on the road trip. Even as I am bombarded with Americana and commerce on all sides, I still believe I might find something out there worth bringing home again.

I drive across the vast majesty of the Mojave Desert and up onto the high desert plateau of northern Arizona. The trees increase in size the more we climb, the clouds gather like a herald. I have lunch in the town where the Unabomber used to live. Deathly quiet.

On the way from Flagstaff down to Phoenix, Nicole drives her car alongside mine so she can easily return home after our meetings. (In Arizona there appears to be almost no such thing, in 2017, as viable public transport.) A road trip in convoy is a variation on a theme. We manage to stay together all the way, weaving in and out of traffic, until, in Phoenix, for which don't imagine a city so much as a vast string of outlying communities across the Sonoran Desert basin tethered together only by their freeways, my GPS starts giving me different instructions to those Nicole's GPS is giving her. Eventually it tells me, in a flat, depressed voice a little like that of the computer Hal in *2001, A Space Odyssey*, "GPS signal lost." At that exact moment Nicole drives through an orange light up ahead and in an instant I am lost. I don't have a phone that works. My GPS is dead. I am alone somewhere in Greater Phoenix. It is night time. Somewhere, on a piece of paper I have the address of the place we are staying written down. I could stop and ask a local citizen for directions, as would have happened in the old days. I could throw myself upon the mercy of a stranger. But this would mean getting out of the car, which at this point, this time and place, would be something weird to do. Remember, generally speaking, it is stranger in some parts of America to walk the streets than to carry a concealed gun. I keep driving for a while. There is no shortage of places I can drive.

Miraculously, as if taking pity on me, the GPS, despite my having tossed it aside so that it has fallen down behind the passenger seat, now bleats in a muffled but distinct voice: "in one mile turn left—." I feel a pang of affection for the little machine and do exactly what it says, hoping it still knows of what it speaks. Next thing Nicole is driving alongside, waving insanely. All is well and eventually we find the rented condominium we are looking for, among the speed-bumped curves of an expansive development named, in direct contradiction to its reality, Mistwood.

Out in the desert west of Phoenix, I pull off the highway at a rest stop to fill my water bottle and empty my bladder. I get out of the car. A sign in front of the landscape, beside the rest stop, warns me against entering. "NO PETS IN THIS AREA: POISONOUS SNAKES AND INSECTS INHABIT THE AREA". Area, stressed twice, appears to mean the desert as a whole; all the visible land stretching north from where I'm standing to a mauve ridge of hills. My place, with or without pets, is on the highway, in my travel capsule. I can stop here and amble between my vehicle and the toilets, as others, mostly middle-aged, are doing alongside me, but then we can only, rationally, start up our separate motors and accelerate away. Only fools would wander out on foot into this dangerous and unknown place of deadly creatures. Needless to say, it feels like we are missing something.

In the car again, a space for daydreams. Wide open road. Time stretches out. The light refracting on the windscreen. At the risk of over-sharing: have you ever driven alone with your lover on a road trip and sometimes the sun is shining with the kind of warmth that makes you feel that stroking each other's bare flesh would create a good sensation and not wearing any pants at all would open up all sorts of possibilities on one or both sides of the vehicle? Sometimes, in these instances, you have to pull over and sometimes you don't and if you're driving you have to be super-attentive to road conditions as well as everything else that's happening. It's not a practice you can widely recommend for obvious reasons and it's rare but very good when it happens. Something about the heat and the vibrations of the engine and the road, the complicity below the eyeline of the window if, say, a car goes by, the tension, the suspense of what you can and cannot do, the way your eyes stay on the road and on the passing landscape as your breath catches, your hand explores its territories, you yourself are undone, taken apart, the windows up. The windows, usually, are up. It keeps the heat in and the world out. Then, after a time you arrive where you were going. All is as it should be. You get out and step onto the ground. You close the door and walk away, the car still warm and humming with its secrets.

And then again you drive …

Now news comes through. I've been trying to find the local frequency for NPR (National Public Radio), the network I overheard a man in a gas station call "the socialist radio station." NPR can form a bubble around the carapace of my vehicle, shielding me from the invasion of Jesus infomercials. There is a story on the radio about animals. Have I seen an animal on this road trip? I've seen birds of prey circling in desert eddies. Surely I've seen horses in a field in the distance? Have I passed trucks loaded with cattle, like I would see in Australia: animals traveling to their slaughter? There's not the road kill by the highway here, the carcasses of kangaroo and wallaby being picked over by crows. It is actually eerily empty. Last time I came to Arizona I saw an elk one morning, standing by an empty carpark near the south rim of the Grand Canyon. The elk stood huge like a statue, and looked at me. What did it see? I've been reading a book about humans and animals—ghosts and monsters, not the imaginary ones but the real ones that we live among, that we create, that create us: that we are. We contain ghosts; we are monsters. So say the many authors of this book, called *Arts of Living on a Damaged Planet*.[382] Across the AUTONOMY billboard they would spraypaint: *SYMBIOSIS*. Despite what we feel like when we embark upon a road trip, strapping ourselves in once more, adjusting the mirrors, turning the key, etcetera, we are not and have never been individuals, explains biologist Scott Gilbert. Not humans or nonhumans, neither Thelma nor Louise —none of us have ever been individuals. This is not a metaphor but material reality.

A revolution in biological knowledge has come about since the late 1970s, I learn by reading zoologist Margaret McFall-Ngai, as new technologies of observation have enabled humans to notice things about the world we couldn't see before. And what McFall-Ngai and other scientists have noticed is that living creatures, of whom the vast majority are microbes, are all of us fundamentally *symbiotic*. We co-evolve and survive only through the intimate co-presence of strangers from companion species, inside and outside our bodies. We are not and never have been individuals. For one thing, "all animals, plants, and fungi have their own unique microbiota—suites of tiny beings with which they live," says McFall-Ngai.[383] More than half of the cells in the human body are nonhuman cells, those of our microbe co-travellers. As for the idea that our DNA makes us unique and individual, "while humans have about twenty-two thousand different genes, the bacteria in us bring approximately 8 million more genes to the scene."[384] What this means is that I'm not alone in the rental car, I'm not even an "I" so much as a co-determined "we." From the driver's seat, I speak now on behalf of or in conjunction with or against the interests of approximately 35 trillion (yes, trillion) other occupants of this vehicle: thousands of different species of bacteria, archaea, fungi and viruses opportunistically hitch-hiking or else snuggled up at home where they belong on what I will persist in calling "my" skin, in my gut, my oral cavity and, if I were a woman inhabiting this most masculine of mythic spaces, my vagina too. This idea, that I am not an individual, is alien to everything I've been cultured into since I emerged from my mother's birth canal, smeared, as I now know I was, with billions of bacteria, and carrying inside me cells not only of my mother but also of each of my elder siblings (does this explain why our handwriting is so similar?).[385] But this is the latest scientific evidence: real-life stories starring characters who are mice, pea aphids, bees and orchids, the Hawaiian bob-tailed squid and a luminescent bacteria called *Vibrio fischeri* that helps the squid disguise itself from predators.[386] If the news is hard to digest, at least none of us are doing it alone.

The fantasy of autonomy is about the freedom to accelerate at will, but maybe the stories we need to inhabit now and the fantasies we need to bring to life in this time of shared fragility and loss are scenes of slowing down: recognising we are not alone, making space for others. And yes, there is no escaping intersections. Bitumen, bodies, fossils, clouds, algorithms, fantasies. Microbes, complicity, thirsty birds. An orange light, refractions. I am not who I think I am. I am multiple. I am all mixed up with others.

And yet, and yet …

On the way back to LA I stop for lunch at Palm Springs, taking Gene Autry Trail past Dinah Shore Drive, avoiding Bob Hope Boulevard. Beyond Palm Springs the road passes through the San Gorgonio Pass where 4000 wind turbines, big, small and in-between, turn in row upon row across the valley. Warm desert air mixes with cooler coastal flows to bring the wind. Things are inexorably shifting.

In LA, finally I find a place to park the car where it makes sense to walk, along the edge of the Pacific. It is early in the morning. Homeless people are packing up their tents and piles of possessions, one or two reading a book in the sunshine. Surfers wait on their boards. The noise of traffic has receded.

The best road trip I ever heard about wasn't in America at all, or even in Australia. In 1982, the writers Julio Cortazar and Carol Dunlop, in a Kombi van they named Fafner the Dragon, set out from Paris on the motorway towards Marseilles. They followed a strict self-imposed rule that they must leave the road to visit every roadside rest-stop on the way, and camp overnight at every second one. Some days they only drove for ten minutes between one rest-stop and the next, so that the overall journey, usually ten hours in duration, lasted 33 days. They played with great solemnity at thinking this was an epic voyage of scientific discovery, like those of Magellan or Marco Polo. In their journals they documented the weather and the timings of each day's journey. They took careful note of meals and occasional showering arrangements. They reported on encounters with strangers in roadhouses and on dodging highway patrols (you weren't supposed to spend thirty-three days living on the motorway between Paris and Marseilles). They sat under trees at fold-out tables and tapped away on typewriters, sipping wine. They made careful observations of the boundaries of their rest-stops, marauding ants, invisible dogs, roadhouse menus, the contours of their daydreams. They talked. They made love in the Kombi. Soon the freeway itself became irrelevant, "a background noise in the distance," as it "seems clearer and clearer, our expedition is first and foremost a navigation of this archipelago of parking lots."[387] It would be their last great adventure together, for they were getting old and she, as it turned out, was dying of cancer. They wrote: "during the course of the expedition [we] identified increasingly with the woods, fields and animals of the freeway's most secret world. It was our fairy-tale side, our innocent ecology, our happiness in full technological clamour, which lovingly obliterated us."[388] Each morning the Dragon roared and they set their controls for wherever they were going. Slowly.

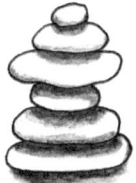

A gathering cloud

In Peru on 9 December 2014, twenty Greenpeace activists set out to defend 'nature' by walking up and over the 2000 year-old Nazca Lines. The area they entered was a giant hummingbird. The message from Greenpeace: "Time for Change! The Future is Renewable."[389] Except they forgot to consider the past. Somehow the traces of the protesters now need to be erased. The lines are more than nature; as a monument, they indicate a human relation to the cosmos. But what is the problem here? What is wrong with a "simple defence of nature"?[390]

Repair

Some damage is forever.

But then, think of the ozone layer.

Think of Hiroshima. The city has been rebuilt from rubble, trolley cars running neat and clean through the centre of town. The trees around Gokoku shrine survive and are still growing. And these days children clamber out from school yards onto the streets at the end of the school day, screaming and laughing, their voices louder than the car horns and bicycle bells.

Care

Nothing comes without its world.[391]

Oscar is in the yard. He is an old dairy steer with one horn. He is a living archive of local weather and climatic change. He is the local lawn mower. We (his collective carers) move him through the community spaces over the year to keep the grass down. He is an expert cutter. This is the driest summer in his fifteen years on earth. We struggle to find him enough to eat and I lose sleep thinking about grass and its absence now. I think more about methane too. I wouldn't if not for Oscar. He makes me smile.

Maria Puig de la Bellacasa writes: "that knowledge is situated means that knowing and thinking are inconceivable without a multitude of relations that also make possible the worlds we think with … relations of thinking and knowing require care."[392]

Oscar ruminates: To ask "who is 'we'?" and "who is *anthropos*?" is a matter of care. 'We' is an open call also, an invitation to respond.

A tweet: "Heading out to the Reef for an interview on the back-to-back bleaching: How do we help a billion surviving corals?"—Terry Hughes, coral reef scientist @ProfTerry Hughes, 1 March 2018.[393]

A memo:
Draw a care cloud
eyes closed
listening
to a ghost bat
back from the dead
read
The
Three
Ecologies.[394]

Heterogeneous

What is material? Coffee cups and tram lines, but also the wondrous encounter with a new toy, or the wondrous revelation of a sacred image. Materiality, like wonder, is relational and performative, just as atoms, accountants, angels and albatrosses. It emerges from the entanglements between entities and scales.

In his appendix* to the *Strange Tales*, Pu Songling provides the following classification of wonders:

1. Local
2. Those buried with the First Emperor
3. Of reddish hue
4. Those that are forgotten
5. Involving foxes
6. Those that initially look ordinary
7. Miraculous ones
8. Guilin Three Flower Wine
9. Those that disappear in the morning
10. The Bianzhong bells of the Marquis Yi of Zeng
11. Others
12. Mermaids
13. Concerning the Imperial Tax Office
14. Those found in a lotus cloud

*Now sadly lost, but one may dream of it when reading Pu Songling and Borges together. [395]

Carbon base

Milliseconds after the Big Bang, there existed three elements: hydrogen, helium and lithium. Carbon had to wait until stars formed. The polyvalent property of the carbon atom allows it to form bonds to other elements: hydrocarbons, carbonate. The carbon cycle of the Planet.

Two places: working and walking with waterways

Kim Williams and Lucas Ihlein

HERE is a map of Australia showing two places: Wollongong and Mackay. Both are coastal regional cities; both have economies built on mining and agriculture. Wollongong is temperate, known for its coal and steel industries, surf beaches and (nowadays less so) for dairy farming. Tropical Mackay is known for sugarcane production and its proximity to coal mines. Both are port cities.

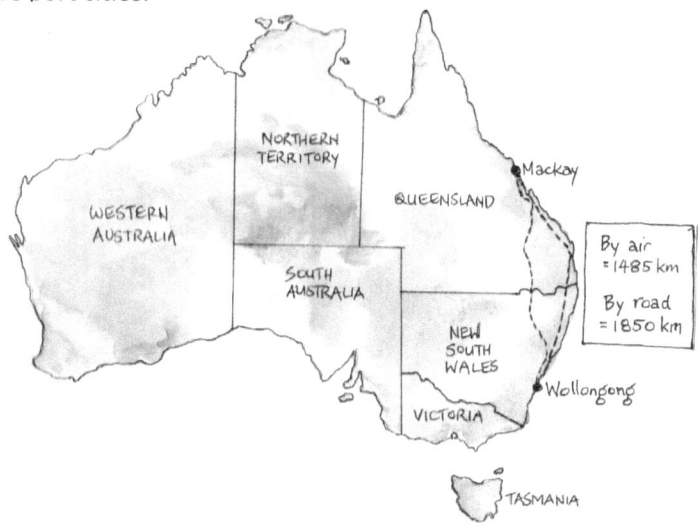

Figure 19: Kim Williams, Map of Australia, showing geographic relationships between Mackay and Wollongong, 2017

We (Kim Williams and Lucas Ihlein) are artists living in Wollongong. This chapter offers a meditation on our experiences working in these two places, near and far. What connects both the places and the artworks is *water*. The cultural and ecological communities in Wollongong and Mackay are deeply shaped by water's inexorable downhill flow. Our text flows back and forth between these two loci, reflecting on our working methods as examples of socially engaged art, and considers how these might enable an ongoing process of embodied learning. Through structured aesthetic experience around waterways in Mackay and Wollongong, our goal is to become more deeply embedded in these places, and to facilitate transformed relationships with land, water and ecology.

~

We begin with two maps showing the relationship between land and sea mediated by waterways in Mackay and Wollongong. The first shows the Pioneer River. This is the major waterway running through the sugarcane fields in the Pioneer Valley of Mackay, Queensland. You can see the railway lines on both sides of the river: small sugar trains transport the freshly cut cane to the mills along these tracks. This map represents an area of roughly fifty kilometres from west to east. It shows the geographic focus of our project entitled *Sugar vs the Reef?*[396]

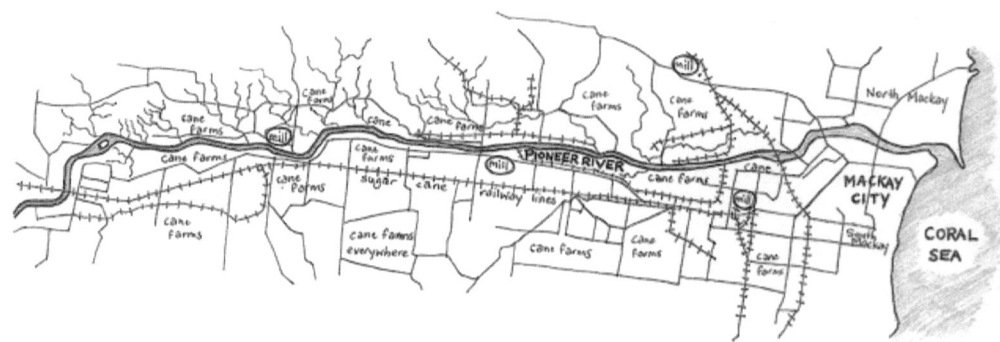

Figure 20: Kim Williams, Map of Pioneer River, Mackay, 2010

The second is a map of Towradgi Creek. This map shows the basic infrastructure surrounding a creek just north of Wollongong: roads, railway line, schools etc. It represents a relatively small geographical area, perhaps three kilometres from west to east. Towradgi Creek is one of the many creeks in our local region which are the focus of the socially-engaged art project *Walking Upstream: Waterways of the Illawarra*[397] produced in collaboration with Brogan Bunt.

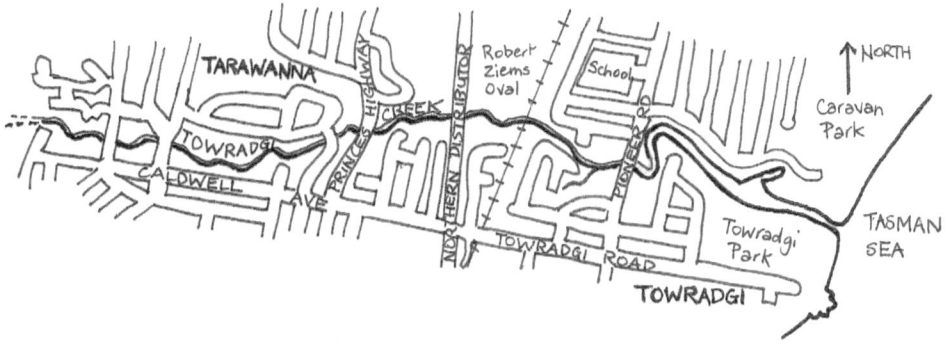

Figure 21: Kim Williams, Map of Towradgi Creek, Wollongong, 2017

While *Sugar vs the Reef?* tackles the cultural, political and environmental tensions of coastal agricultural practices in Mackay, *Walking Upstream* explores the social, cultural and geographic textures of the region in which we live. Before delving into some of the themes emerging from our two projects (themes such as contested land and water use, environmental responsibility, and care), we want to flesh out the cultural and climatic atmospheres of Mackay and Wollongong a little more.

~

In Mackay, solid walls of sugarcane dominate the landscape. Fields of cane flank the airport. The smell of sugar processing during the seasonal "crush" at the local mills hangs sickly sweet over the town. It's hot all year round, very wet in the summer, and sugarcane – a kind of giant perennial grass – flourishes here. Farms spread from the coast right up into the Pioneer Valley. During big rain events, loose soil sediment erodes, and chemical runoff from fertilisers and pesticides that are used on nearly all sugarcane farms leach into dozens of local creeks, flowing down the Pioneer River into the Coral Sea. This run-off from farming exacerbates the conditions for coral bleaching in the Great Barrier Reef. It's this tension between industrial agriculture and an adjacent world heritage site for biodiversity that we're exploring in our work in Queensland.

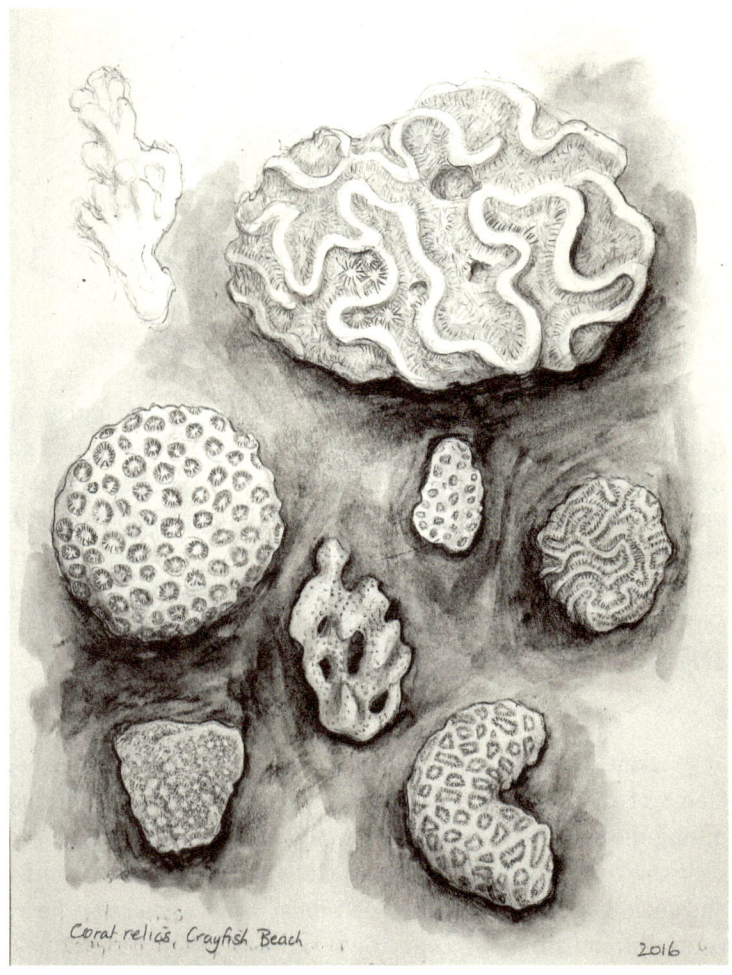

Figure 22: Kim Williams, *Coral Relics, Crayfish Beach, Great Barrier Reef*, drawing, 2016.

Since we began working in Mackay in 2014, a central question has emerged. How can the environmental effects of sugarcane farming be improved? We've begun collaborating with a cohort of sugar cane farmers in Mackay's Pioneer Valley. They are developing and demonstrating methods to build healthy soil and reduce the need for chemical inputs to their crops. These farmers are attempting to generate grassroots cultural change in their own communities. As artists interested in terrestrial and marine environments, we are acting as catalysts to connect these change-maker farmers with the wider public. Our artist-farmer collaboration draws attention to the potential benefits of regenerative agriculture for soil health and water quality in the Coral Sea.

~

Our work in Wollongong is quieter and slower. We are less focused on trying to create discernible transformation "out there". Rather, we walk along creeks in an attempt to develop closer relationships with our local environment – *to know it* more intimately. There are more than fifty creeks in Wollongong. Small and large, they flow down subtropical rainforest gullies from the Illawarra escarpment, which is like a giant green wall squeezing the suburbs towards the coast. At the top of their flow, the waterways of the Illawarra bubble over giant boulders and seep from hidden earthen springs. Further downstream, the creeks bisect housing tracts, industry, farmland and commercial districts, eventually flowing out to the Tasman Sea directly or via Lake Illawarra.

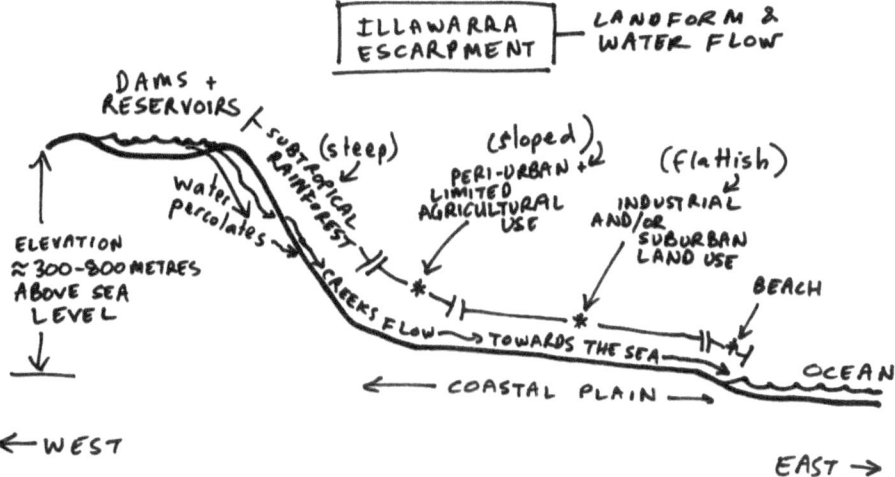

Figure 23: Lucas Ihlein, *Indicative cross-section of Illawarra Escarpment (not to scale)*, drawing, 2018.

Wilfully following a creek line upstream, we cannot help being aware that these waterways were flowing long before Europeans began reshaping the local landscape. The active practice of walking reveals how degraded the waterways of the Illawarra have become since European invasion. Many have been reduced to weed-infested and rubbish-strewn drains. Yet despite the neglect of the waterways (*you wouldn't dare drink the water!*), the riparian areas provide habitat for a diverse range of plant species and creatures: leeches and ticks; bandicoots and feral deer; tree ferns and lantana; noisy miners, frogs, lyrebirds and feral goats.

Land use and its effects

Both projects share our fascination with the ways in which humans have shaped these places through land use. They are both busy places. Many of the Illawarra's waterways are covered over by roads, parklands, railway lines, and concrete; disappearing from view as the utilitarian focus of human activity buries these ancient markers in the landscape. The Pioneer River in Mackay is also surrounded by busy activity: cane farmers pump water out of the river to irrigate their crops, sugar mills draw water for industrial processing, while water skiers buzz up and down the river in their leisure time.

Fundamentally, our projects are about people and landscapes and plants and animals and places of habitation. They are political engagements with environmental policy, agribusiness, farmers and politicians, land ownership and trespass. They are physical engagements with forest, electric fences, rain and heat, blistering sun, cold winds, tropical stingers and subtropical leeches. They are cultural engagements with soil and water, co-option and displacement, indigenous custodianship, and farming practices.

It is impossible to divorce the physical characteristics of these two places from the stories that emerge from working in those landscapes. The things that happen in these places arise not only from the cultural practices of people living (t)here; those cultural practices themselves arise from the landforms, the soils, the weather, and the waters.

~

We began working in Mackay in 2014, when a retired farmer, John Sweet, contacted Lucas to propose an unusual farmer-artist collaboration. John is a devotee of Keyline Design, a farming system invented by PA Yeomans in the 1940s that builds soil and increases the capacity of the land to hold water. He had seen Lucas' previous work with Ian Milliss on *The Yeomans Project*, and saw potential in a new artist-farmer collaboration for North Queensland.[398]

John's ambition is as big as Queensland itself: he argues that in order to save the Great Barrier Reef from agricultural run-off, massive-scale Keyline re-design is needed across the entire catchment, which empties into the Coral Sea. This represents a 2000 kilometre stretch of coastal farmland. A noble proposition! But how can a small group of artists influence change on that vast scale? In reality, the only practical way we know is to start small and local. And so in late 2014 we began visiting Mackay and making friends with sugarcane farmers in the catchment of the Pioneer River. Fairly quickly, we were deeply inhaling the sugar industry's atmosphere, becoming familiar with the local jargon: billets, ratoons, the "crush", bagasse and Best Management Practice. But it's what lies hidden beneath the surface of the soil – friendly nematodes, mycorrhizal fungi, worms – that quickens hearts in the world of regenerative agriculture. According to our farmer friends, healthy soil biology – the tiny things – could make a world of difference for global agriculture and carbon sequestration.[399]

~

Our creek work in Wollongong was more self-initiated. Beginning in 2014, we three friends (Kim Williams, Lucas Ihlein and Brogan Bunt) decided to bring a set of mutual interests (bushwalking, walking-as-art, and dialogical art) together around a clearly identifiable geographical feature in our neighbourhoods. As artists of European descent, our hunch was that focusing on our local creeks might help us to form deeper connections to the places where we live. We often bring along with us a few curious walkers: colleagues, friends or family members. When we can, we try to connect with the traditional Aboriginal custodians of the land through which the creeks flow. Our walks unfold as unspectacular stories of discovery, delight and disappointment. Sometimes we write them up prosaically on our blog as field notes; at other times, playful poems emerge, such as this account of a walk from 2017:

Macquarie Rivulet Creek Walk Poem

>It was a fine day, an AA Milne day,
>
>Smallish clouds puff along in a clear blue sky,
>
>Four adults and child meet at Shearwater Drive:
>
>Let's find the mouth! – and off stump the five.
>
>But the Big Metal Fence and the Very Big Dogs
>
>Put a stop to the start of our journey:
>
>No go.   NO TRESPASS!
>
>… so perhaps
>
>take a roundabout way to the mouth?
>
>Instead
>
>a new house up for sale (Come in! Come on in!)
>
>Three beds, two baths and a double garage,
>
>Our decoys talk mortgage and offers and rates
>
>while the rest fill our pockets with free chocolates
>
>Slyly checking: Will the backyard let out on the mouth?
>
>No luck. No access. No way to squeeze through.
>
>And so back to our creek, its path to pursue.

Alongside the banks, eating a sanga, in Darcy Dunster Park,

Under the freeway and aircraft hangar

– not (how can I put it?) "Textbook Romantic"

We spy a discarded franger.

Press on! Time to go! Follow that creek!

But a sign says

No go. NO TRESPASS!

Do we comply? Or turn a blind eye?

We turn it, crawl under the wire.

To help out a friend (who cannot quite bend)

Kim lifts up the fencewire (a live one)

Watch her dance! (or convulse) - señorita possessed,

And the wire on the rebound hits Joshua's back,

With two thousand volts going clickety clack

He lies face down and shocked in the mud.

Through lush green paddock alongside the creek

with a herd in the distance mooing

We're stopped by an impasse in very long grass –

a creek branch too deep to be crossed.

So we head for the Herd with barely a word

the fine milk machines of our region,

We commit minor offence: "Crawling Under a Fence

And Consorting with Holstein and Friesians."

As we make muddy way through the muck and the hay

past the milking shed's earthy aroma

to the road leading back to our creek-walking track:

Time to be heading off home, huh?

Whose land? Whose water?

From our account of these two projects so far, it's clear that physically inhabiting and moving our bodies about in these places is essential to our work. We are constantly traversing land, whether on foot, or by car, and sometimes crossing water by kayak or boat. These experiences create a shift in our awareness of the territory we inhabit at any given moment, and our behaviour shifts with the territory.

Walking along creeks in our home region, we are aware we are breaching the legal boundaries of territory. What is public space and what is private space? What is recreational or functional or abandoned or untouched land? It's not always clear. When we travel to Mackay, the movement between territories is similar, though the edges of the urban and rural rub more closely against each other.

Land divisions clearly define both the Illawarra and Mackay regions. Roads and fences range across the underlying topographies of places. Landscapes that have long been cared for by the Dharawal (Illawarra) and the Yuwibara (Mackay) peoples become fragmented by infrastructure.

~

Land ownership comes into sharp focus in the world of industrial sugarcane farming in Queensland. Indigenous people were dispossessed of their lands prior to the establishment of sugarcane farms up and down the Queensland coast in the mid-1800s. Locking up these lands as farms was a way of establishing British dominance and warding off perceived threats from Asian colonisation. To provide cheap labour for the farms, 'blackbirding' was commonly practised. Men (and some women and children) from Pacific Islands such as the Solomon Islands, Vanuatu and New Caledonia were forcibly removed and taken by ship to the canefields of Queensland, where they worked in slave-like conditions.[400]

When the White Australia Policy came into effect in 1901, many of the Islander workers, even those born in Australia, were deported to their countries of origin. Most of the Australian

South Sea Island population in Mackay today are descendants of the 'blackbirded' workers who were allowed to remain in Australia – or who were permitted to return during the labour shortages of the First World War.

Despite this complex multicultural history, we are struck by the disconnection between the contemporary cane-farming community of Mackay, and the Aboriginal and South Sea Islander communities.

These days, cane-farmers don't often discuss the pre-history of their paddocks. It is as if the walls of sugarcane are walls of silence.[401] While our work in Mackay began with an environmental focus (regenerative agriculture and its positive impacts on soil and water quality), inevitably cane farming's cultural background would emerge and demand attention. Since 2016, we have made an effort to meet and develop connections with the local Aboriginal and Australian South Sea Islander people: the Mackay and District Australian South Sea Islander Association (MADASSIA) and the Yuwibara traditional descendants. We attempt to create situations where the Aboriginal, South Sea Islander and farming communities may begin to talk and work together. We take advice on social protocols from members of these communities, and our intention is to honour the place of Aboriginal and South Sea Islander people in an industry that historically exploited their labour and lands.

~

In Wollongong, our walks happen on the lands and waters of Dharawal Country. Dividing, fencing and 'owning' land and water – these are legal constructs, which are very new in Australia. The dominant property ownership system imported from Europe 230 years ago does not align with the human-land systems developed over many thousands of years by Aboriginal peoples prior to invasion. In NSW, even creeks are subject to colonial property law. If a creek runs through a suburban backyard, the creek bed and banks (*but not the water flowing through it!*) are legally the property of the homeowner.

In 2017, we published a book called *12 Creek Walks*, which attempts to codify some of our experiences into a sort of user's manual. Some of the creeks are harder to walk than others – and this is generally due to human-made impediments. If we wish to proceed, we are forced to trespass. In the introduction to the book, we write:

> While we cannot simply do away with the current legal system, that does not mean we have to agree with the idea that it is "right" for a creek to be privately owned. We believe that fences, except where sensitive ecosystem repair is being conducted, should not obstruct access to creeks. We believe that private property owners should leave a riparian corridor alongside creeks, and should definitely not run fence-lines right down to the water's edge. We believe that creeks belong to everyone, but most of all, creeks belong to themselves.[402]

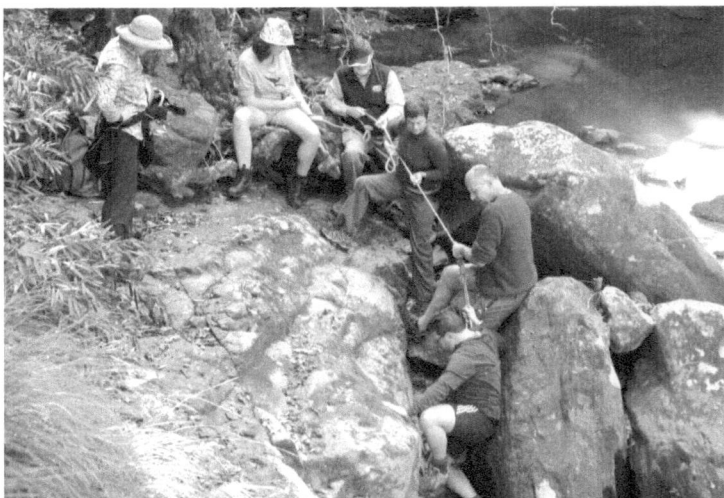

Figure 24: Vincent Bicego, *Walking (and climbing) in the upper reaches of Byarong Creek*, photography, 2017.

Dialogical aesthetics: the art of reframing problems

We now turn to a closer reflection on the methods we use for our engagement with Mackay and Wollongong. One important process – ever-present in our work – is conversation. In his book *Conversation Pieces: Community and Communication in Modern Art*, art historian Grant Kester identifies a tendency in contemporary art he calls "dialogical aesthetics", in which talking is not just a means of establishing the conditions for the production of an artwork, or a way of critiquing t after the fact. Rather, Kester argues, the act of talking (or more broadly, "the creative facilitation of dialogue and exchange") can itself be the work of art.[403] Conversation without the pressure of outcomes, listening without judgement, and in-situ dialogue occurring outside of our normal social circles, are all part of our artmaking repertoire in Wollongong and Mackay.

While the most obvious 'method' used in *Walking Upstream* is walking, an important aspect of this project is *talking* – making connections, forming a loose community of people who share an interest in walking creeks. When walking, we are invariably talking – getting to know each other better, talking about our immediate experience and our observations, sharing knowledge about plants and animals, voicing opinions about current events both local and global, forging new friendships, learning from each other, making jokes and laughing.

Talking is also a central method in *Sugar vs the Reef?* The project has evolved through engagement with the farming community, attending farm field days, talking to sugar industry representatives and reef scientists, building connections with natural resource management and community organisations, getting to know the Indigenous and the Australian South Sea Islander communities, making overtures to politicians, pitching ideas to funding bodies—in short, learning the territory of industrial sugarcane farming and Great Barrier Reef advocacy and inserting ourselves into this territory. Our talks in Queensland generally don't happen while walking, but while sitting down. We 'sit down' with local experts, we put ourselves in front of them for a time, usually with a cup of tea, talk and listen and slowly build trust.

In making ourselves available for public conversations along creeks and in canefields, we become witness to myriad problems – environmental degradation, erosion, questions about farming profitability, land use regulations – faced by local people. We have a dual role, both insiders (in Wollongong) and outsiders (in Mackay) and this sometimes allows us the opportunity and insight to see a problem situation from an unusual angle. In this, we are guided by the tradition of eco-social art established by the Harrison Studio in California – a tradition that attempts to mobilise seemingly "stuck" circumstances by reframing them as opportunities to bring forth "a new state of mind."[404]

For example, as we walk the creeks in Wollongong, here and there we notice tracts of native plant regeneration, nurtured by bushcare groups who are working to improve and care for their neighbourhood riparian corridors. It is always admirable seeing these efforts to restore native habitat and clear creeks of weed and rubbish. A woman from a local bushcare group attended a talk we gave at the Wollongong Art Gallery during our 2017 exhibition.

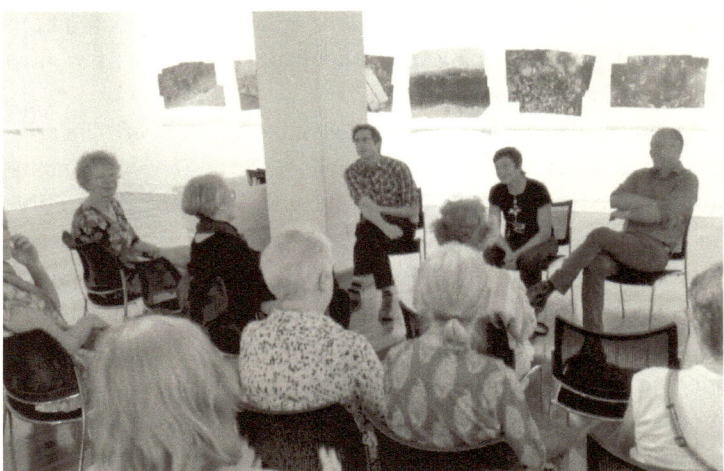

Figure 25: Lucas Ihlein, Kim Williams and Brogan Bunt - artists' talk at Wollongong Art Gallery for *Walking Upstream: Waterways of the Illawarra* exhibition, December 2017. Photo: WayWard Films

She, who knew far more about plants than we ever will, was passionate but also despondent about her bushcare group's efforts. She felt as though they were fighting a losing battle. She asked us, *"What can we do? How can we carry on?"* It was an existential question. How to best care for creeks while caring for one's own mental health?

In response, we tried to reframe the problem. Rather than thinking of this as a battle, why not look upon the situation as an opportunity to craft relationships? The creek is a natural corridor uncared for by the state: it is a grey zone. Creek land backs onto private housing. It is *not-quite-public-enough*. Apart from a few sections that are zoned 'recreational', most creek corridors are left to fend for themselves. Similarly, the duty of care shown by private homeowners usually extends only to the limits of their own back fence. So creek-care is an opportunity for self-organised community building. And as long as the challenge of garbage and weeds continues, there is an incentive for neighbours to emerge from behind the picket fence and care for something they don't 'own': forging relationships with non-human entities (place, water, soil, plants, animals, etc.) as well as with other people.

Sometimes in our work, problems emerge without warning. In late 2016, together with sugarcane farmer Simon Mattsson, we made a proposal for the *Watershed Land Art Project* to the Mackay Regional Botanic Gardens. Stage One of the project involved planting a dual crop of sugarcane and sunflowers in the Gardens. Our goal was that the crop would be a demonstration of regenerative agriculture over an 18-month period, grown in a horticultural setting popular with locals and visitors to the region. The idea was to create a public platform for discussions, workshops and events that could amplify the potential of regenerative agricultural methods.

The Botanic Gardens agreed in principle to the proposal and there was some local media coverage. A period of silence followed, after which a scathing letter arrived from the chair of a community group which cultivates native plants, runs guided tours and generally supports the Gardens. They opposed our plan, holding the view that sugarcane is an entirely inappropriate species to grow in a Botanic Garden.

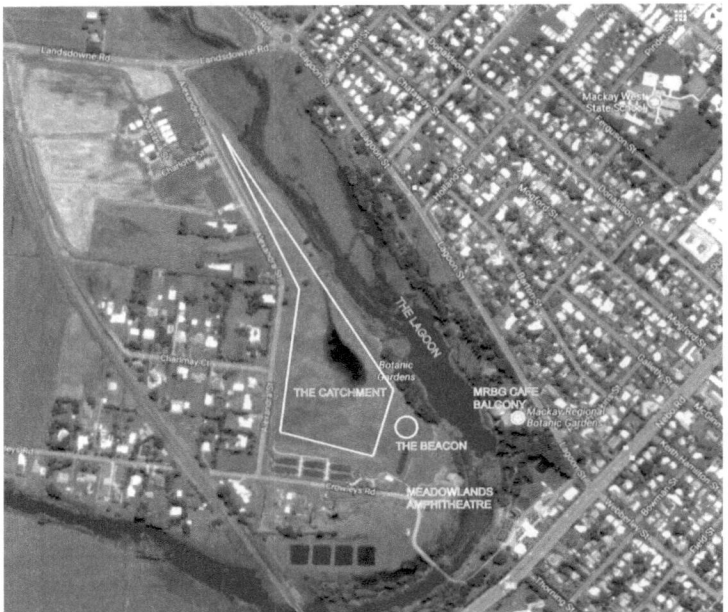

Figure 26: Kim Williams and Lucas Ihlein, *Plan of proposed planting zones, Watershed Land Art Project, Mackay Regional Botanic Gardens*, 2017–19

The irony of the situation wasn't lost on us. We are attempting to reframe the problem of industrial sugarcane production and its impact on the Great Barrier Reef. Promoting regenerative agriculture is an acknowledgment that conventional sugarcane cultivation methods are problematic for soil health, with negative impacts on terrestrial and marine habitats. Growing a multispecies crop of sugarcane and sunflowers in the Botanic Gardens is an opportunity to open up dialogue about co-habitation of species: native, horticultural and agricultural. It is potentially a means of bringing these non-human 'communities' together to explore ways to disrupt monoculture cropping conventions, using techniques to improve both soil and habitat on farms.

While we're trying to draw together incongruous communities of plants, we are attempting something similar with humans. These encounters are not easy (and this one in particular remains unresolved). Before the *Watershed Land Art Project* had even begun, simply circulating the proposal brought to the surface seemingly opposing worldviews about the purpose and function of botanic gardens, and the role of native versus agricultural species. The discomfort involved in pursuing these conversations is precisely the material of our work as artists engaging with the social characteristics of complex environmental management situations.

Overlapping Methods in Socially Engaged Art

Our working methods sit within the field of socially engaged art (SEA), a set of practices that evolved through the late twentieth century from a diverse lineage: avant-garde art, feminism, community arts and political activism. SEA has been energised in the early twenty-first century through the growth of grass-roots political activism using cultural forms such as performative gatherings, visual and tactile arts, public events, design and media production. These forms are further mediated through digital technologies and social media. New York curator Nato Thompson speaks of "the inevitable tide of cultural producers who are frustrated with art's impotence and who are eager to make a tangible change in the world."[405] Thompson distinguishes SEA from its avant-garde predecessors, which could be defined as *movements*: Dada, Situationism, Fluxus and Happenings for example. Instead, he describes SEA as an indicator of a new social order which models "ways of life that emphasize participation, challenge power, and span disciplines ranging from urban planning and community work to theater and visual arts."[406]

Socially engaged art employs a diverse set of practices ranging between "art and non-art."[407] For Grant Kester, SEA expands beyond the studio-gallery relationship, "in which the artist deposits an expressive content into a physical object, to be withdrawn later by the viewer."[408] It is, rather, a relationship of reciprocity, where the artwork emerges through the interaction of diverse participants or collaborators. In the context of socially engaged art, the ethical process of relational engagement is

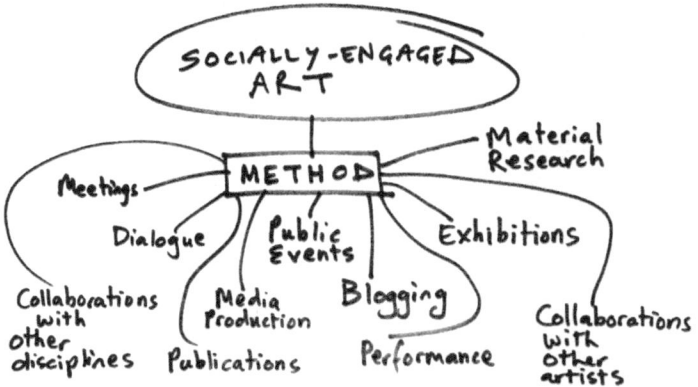

Figure 27: Lucas Ihlein, *Diagram of methods and materials in Socially Engaged Art with a particular focus on* Sugar vs the Reef? *and* Walking Upstream: Waterways of the Illawarra. 2017.

front and centre, through which creative responses to complex situations may emerge. To work in this field means questioning the standard focus on outcome over method. We negotiate the ambiguous territory between means and ends.

In our own projects, we frequently find ourselves wearing three hats as we shuttle between diverse communities. Our role is ambiguous and mobile. When we articulate our methodology and insights using the language of research, we behave as academics within the university system; when we work on encouraging regenerative agriculture practices, or team up with creek regeneration groups, we operate in an activist mode; and when our activities generate discernible objects, artefacts and actions to be presented within an artworld context, we are identifiable as artists.

Different social milieux call for shifts in our identity, but it may not always be clear to our collaborators exactly who we are. For example, since 2016 we have been meeting with politicians in Mackay, lobbying alongside farmers and community activists for government support to establish a farmer-led demonstration farm for the sugarcane industry. We introduce ourselves wearing *all three* of our hats at the same time: as artists, university

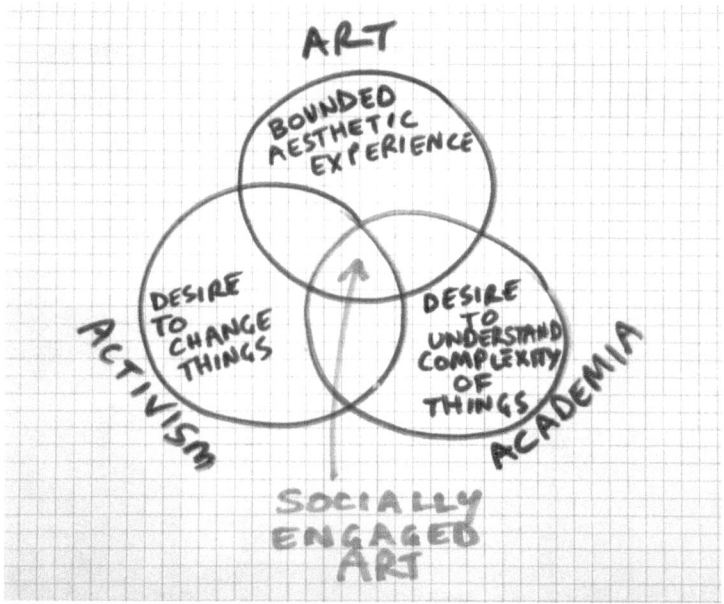

Figure 28: Lucas Ihlein, *Socially Engaged Art in a Venn diagram*, 2014.

researchers (the "Dr" before Lucas' name on his business card is frequently useful); and members of the farmer group Central Queensland Soil Health Systems. The ambiguous role played by socially engaged artists at these meetings can help to shift the conversational atmosphere beyond the standard 'script' – as it is not immediately clear to the politicians what we stand for. Artist and educator Pablo Helguera has also noticed the value of ambiguity in such situations. In fact, in his analysis, this virtuous lack of clarity may be the defining contribution of SEA. Helguera writes:

> Socially engaged art functions by attaching itself to subjects and problems that normally belong to other disciplines, moving them temporarily into a space of ambiguity. It is this temporary snatching away of subjects into the realm of art making that brings new insights to a particular problem or condition, and in turn makes it visible to other disciplines.[409]

By shuttling back and forth between academic, artistic and activist contexts, we risk being not quite 'legitimate' in any of them. Being prepared to embrace the ambiguity of our role is a social experiment in its own right – and if it works, one of the rewards is the opportunity to cross-pollinate ideas from one realm to another, and potentially allow new solutions to scale up from the local to the regional or the global.

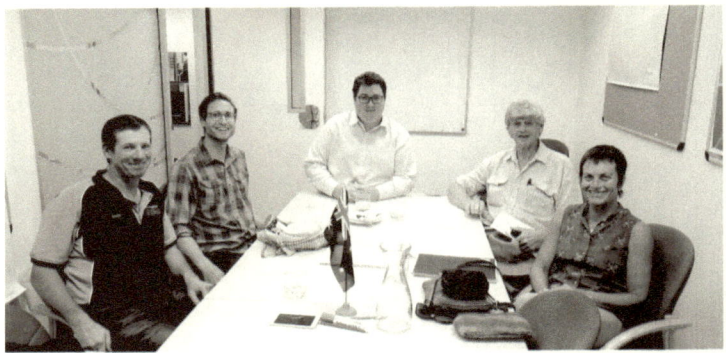

Figure 29: Artists-activists-academics-farmers meeting with conservative federal MP George Christensen to propose a large-scale demonstration farm for the sugarcane industry, March 2017.

Worldscapes: working at multiple scales

While the spatial scales that we operate within (creek, catchment, paddock, watershed, reef) operate at the level of landscape, the veteran practitioners from the Harrison Studio urge a wider view. They use the term "Worldscape" to describe the intricate interconnectedness of ecological and social processes. The Harrisons' definition is dense:

> Worldscapes are problems with global reach that have three properties: They refer to complex systems for which single cause and effect solutions are ineffectual. The problem itself reveals the disciplines required for resolution as well as determining how deeply the people involved must engage these disciplines. Multiple feedback loops are inherently part of the process. Any resolution both ennobles the place in question and the people at work.[410]

What this notion of worldscapes offers is a way to consider the intricate connections between social processes (everyday life practices, scientific research, policy making and implementation) and environmental processes (watersheds, atmospheric cycles, biological functioning). Our human methods for managing environments (and even the paternalistic notion of "management") can be limiting, in that they chop up problems into disciplinary boxes – and yet the functioning of worldscapes pays no attention to the boundaries of human systems. An important challenge at the conclusion of the Harrison's definition is that any resolution to a problem should "ennoble the place in question and the people at work." Would this rule out sweeping large-scale top-down governance (such as the wholesale displacement of populations to build mega-dams, or mass-retreat from rising sea levels)? How can small-scale communities contribute to decision-making about worldscape-scale problems?

~

In Wollongong, we skip across rocks from one side of Byarong Creek to the other, ducking overhanging branches, passing backyards with dogs. Some of us take photos, some draw pictures, some make maps. Others just talk. A botanist plucks a delicate stalk of grass from the creekside and inspects its seeds through thick glasses.

In a clearing we come across a lounge-setting, its stuffing hanging out. Bongs are stashed nearby. A cosy place for a Saturday night.

A helicopter flies overhead and we wave from below. The video camera on board sees the creek system. It sees the Pacific Ocean and Tom Thumb Lagoon. It sees the steelworks guarding the mouth of Allans Creek, poisoned by industry. It sees the confluences of the waterways that flow into Allans Creek: Charcoal Creek, American Creek, Byarong Creek. It follows Byarong Creek up Mount Keira until the creek disappears, then it floats over the top of the mountain and spies Cordeaux Dam nestling in the forest up above the escarpment.[411]

Government bodies publish flood mitigation plans, flood studies, hydrological graphs and catchment management plans for the Illawarra. In flood, creeks that are usually benign trickles become raging torrents, funnelling down the gullies of the steep escarpment. In flood, creeks become capable of carrying away backyards, capable of moving cars and shipping containers out to sea.

At the start of this project in late 2014 a question immediately arose for us: could these creeks ever be drinkable again? It seemed far-fetched and overly ambitious at the time, but now, having built a small community of interest in local creeks, perhaps it is possible. By focusing our energy on a single creek, a local waterway could become a site of care, where people could go to "take the waters" and appreciate what is special about the Illawarra.

~

In Mackay, as we sit around farmhouse kitchen tables or ramble through rows of sugarcane keeping an eye out for snakes, we keep thinking about scales, small and large.

The paddock you can walk across with your own feet; the broadacre scale you need a tractor to manage; the river-valley you can see from the window of an aeroplane as it comes in to land at Mackay airport; and the scale of the entire reef catchment system, visible only by satellite.

These *geographical* scales map loosely onto *social* scales. The discussions that take place within the boundaries of a single farming family; two farmers having a yarn over a shared fence; what goes on at a farmer-led soil health meeting; the sugarcane mills and their rules and regulations; and the fickle nature of state and federal environment policy. The Great Barrier Reef 'belongs' to Queensland, but at the same time, it is a registered World Heritage Site, and in this way, it belongs to everyone on the planet. But does 'everyone' have a right to tell farmers what to practise on their land? Increasingly, farmers need to earn their "social license to farm."[412] The vast social scales of the Great Barrier Reef's catchment always come back to the local.

Temporal scales, too. Thousands of years for forests to establish, for the reef to grow; decades for the Aboriginal custodians to be displaced or to resist; years, for the trees to be cleared by South Sea Islanders working under slavery conditions; the annual cycle of planting and harvesting shaped by seasonal variations; the time it takes for soil to be depleted of nutrients and organic matter; the catastrophic moment when a cyclone devastates a year's hard farm work; the dawning awareness of warming oceans killing coral at the end of a hot summer.

~

Where freshwater flows into saltwater, life proliferates. Human settlements grow abundantly in these transitional zones—so it is not surprising that some of the world's largest population centres locate themselves around the mouths of rivers. At our peril, we disregard our responsibility to maintain healthy waterways.

Our work as socially engaged artists in these two places – near and far – is a mode of learning about the functioning of their geographical features. The cultural, economic and environmental meanings of creeks, rivers and catchments are inextricably enmeshed and complex. Through collaboration, our goal is to create the conditions for deepened awareness and preparedness to change. Walking, talking, planting and proposing, telling stories, and demonstrating possibility: our work aspires to an ethical engagement with lands, waters and peoples.

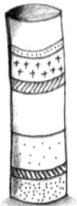

Compost

Leaf mould is a compost made using fallen leaves. The finished product has a soft and loose structure. It has a high water-holding capacity and makes excellent humus.

To make leaf mould:

1. Choose a suitable site to build the compost.
2. Make a containment area using stakes and chicken wire.
3. After wetting the ground, collect and place leaves into the bin. The heap should be moist but not soaking wet.
4. Leaf mould can be built over an 8-week period.
5. The heap does not require turning but an occasional check on moisture level would be helpful.
6. Leaf mould is ready when the materials become homogeneous. The process can take from 12 months to 2 years.

On a smaller scale, to compost daily vegetable and food scraps:

1. Find a compost bin with a lid, from a recycling centre attached to the local rubbish tip.
2. Or use a plastic 75-litre rubbish bin with clip-on lid. Cut a wide circle out of the base. Upend the bin, with the cut hole uppermost. Pick a patch of ground where the bin will live. Two bins are best.
3. Start with a layer of brown stuff (dry leaves, cuttings or straw) at the base. Add the day's vegie scraps (no dairy, no meat; egg shells are fine).

4. As the green layer builds, add another layer of brown stuff. A ratio close to 1 green (nitrogen-rich): 4 brown (carbon-rich) by volume works best.

5. Poke several deep holes down through the layers to aerate the pile. A broom handle works well.

6. The last layer will be brown stuff. When the bin is full, leave it, lid secure, to break down further. Do not add fresh material to this batch. Use the second compost bin.

7. Turn the compost after two weeks. Tend, and turn occasionally after that. Welcome the earthworms that enter and aid breakdown. The first bin will be ready with sweet-smelling compost by the time the second is full.

My friend lost his keys and could not find them anywhere. Locks had to be changed everywhere. Later, one day, he was turning over his compost and a bunch of metal objects were dangling at the end of his compost stirrer. This is a ficto-factual account.

I lost my keys and could not find them anywhere. Locks had to be changed everywhere. Six months later I was walking down Burelli St at lunchtime and a sudden shower of rain caused me to open my umbrella. The keys hit me on the head. This is a factual account with minor embellishments.

Blanket

Someone at the conference said: "But doesn't the atmosphere keep us safe?" Without it, we're faced with the biting cold of the universe, the suffocation of open space.

The sleeping figure stirs, unsettled. The figure's foot is poking out of the covers, the toes exposed to the iciness of the night. A half-conscious rearrangement of blankets. The foot retreats; the head settles under the covers, only the nose poking out so the body can breathe.

My daughter says that without the trees the planet will lose all its gravity and we will float away.

The body dreams, and wonders. A poet whispers to the dreamer, wandering in the darkness: "you cannot stand on sky, but you can be in it as you can in water or in sleep … this will do, this walking with only one's head in the clouds."[413]

Acknowledging Country ...

... You can acknowledge Country ... It's what we should be doing all the time ... where a Welcome and Acknowledgment is the call and response protocol for entering another's Country ... *Acknowledging* Country is something that we should be consistently doing ... In our everything ... It's like having your daily prayer or daily moment of gratitude ... taking that moment to be grateful ... *Acknowledging* Country is paying respect, to the provisions that have been given from Country.

Practice

What does practice *do*? How does practice *act*?

The conference of the birds

Their feet dusty with dirt, their brows thick with sweat, they clambered over the quartz boulders to the crest of the hill. They'd been walking for what seemed like millennia, but it could have been years or just a long summer afternoon. The spindly bushes had scratched their arms and legs, some of them had tripped and grazed their shins on gravel, or stepped in wombat poo. Their journey had taken them through bushland and swamps, over slippery ice lakes, into ancient crumbling valleys, across radioactive deserts, under the humming concrete of motorways; they'd felt their way in the dark, listening to the calls of birds and bats, beneath the branches of a glowing ghost gum, through paddocks of sunflowers and sugar cane, children's playing fields, neat municipal parks, along the beach, across land Country and sea Country. They'd struggled through swirling storms and fog and blistering 50-degree days. They'd collected more travellers along the way, and ideas, and objects: a set of keys, a splintery broom, an almanac and a collection of postcards, VR goggles, a piece of chalk.

They'd been looking for something. Or someone—no one could quite remember. A mythical creature. It was said that she had the body of a parrot with the head of a cat, and, in her tail, a sting sharper than a bee's. Sometimes, however, she had a human face, human hands. Or maybe she was made of granite. A figure so old that she had seen the destruction of the world five times over. Someone said she was a ghost, or a street spirit, a practitioner of juju. "Of what?" asked another.

As they'd walked, they'd told stories. They'd wondered and wandered off the path, they'd complained and laughed and cried tears of stone. They'd flicked the flies away from their faces. They'd felt the air heavy and comforting and cool against the heat of their skin.

At the crest of the hill they stopped. One or two of them gasped. There, down in the valley, was the river, glinting, arcing its way round the bend of the hill. They looked into its depths. They all saw the same thing, but they each saw it differently. A silvery snail trail, the spiralling leaves of a palm tree, the meandering patterns on brain coral, animal tracks, computer cords, isobars, ocean currents, a line of a bird's flight.

They saw themselves looking back.

They heard each other's breath.

Someone said: "What do we do now?"

All mixed up

Still, the blu tack doesn't always work. They don't make blu tack like they used to. Atmospheres are liable to flutter about, set sail into the air when somebody opens a window. This book is something not yet fully made. Even at this point it falls apart and is subject to repair. Luckily, as Su said, things are numbered. But what happens when 36 becomes 24 and later 57? So much striking out. Things remain, as ever, messy, all mixed up, contaminated, intertwined—

Notes

1. Deborah Bird Rose, *Wild Dog Dreaming*, (Charlottesville and London: University of Virginia Press, 2011): 5.
2. Alfred North Whitehead, *The Concept of Nature*, (Cambridge: Cambridge University Press, 1920): 29.
3. David Carlin, "The Essay in the Anthropocene: Towards Entangled Nonfiction", *TEXT Journal: The Essay*, Special Issue No. 39 (April 2017).
4. Gayatri Chakravorty Spivak, "World Systems and the Creole", *Narrative* 14, no. 6, (January 2006): 102–12.
5. Kamau Brathwaite, "Negus (Islands)", in *The Arrivants: A New World Trilogy*, (Oxford: Oxford University Press, 1973): 224.
6. Anna Lowenhaupt Tsing, *The Mushroom at the End of the World: On the Possibility of Life in Capitalist Ruins*, (Princeton and Oxford: Princeton University Press, 2015): vii.
7. Elizabeth Millan, "The Quest for the Seeds of Eternal Growth: Goethe and Humboldt's Presentation of Nature", *Goethe Yearbook XVIII* (2011): 97.
8. Johann Wolfgang von Goethe, "The works of J.W. von Goethe volume 12, letters from Italy, Part 111 'From Verona to Venice'; 'Padua, Sept. 27 [1786]'", https://en.wikisource.org/wiki/The_Works_of_J._W._von_Goethe/Volume_12/Letters_from_Italy/Part_III
9. Millan, "The Quest for the Seeds of Eternal Growth": 98.
10. Cited in Millan, "The Quest for the Seeds of Eternal Growth": 98.
11. Johann Wolfgang von Goethe, *The Metamorphosis of Plants* introduction and photography by Gordon L. Miller, (Cambridge, Massachusetts and London, England: MIT Press, 2009): 16.
12. The Padua (Padova) botanical gardens features in numerous histories of medicine, see: Università Degli Studi Di Padova, "Botanical Garden," 2018, http://www.unipd.it/en/university/cultural-heritage-0/botanical-garden and Manning, Gideon, and Klestinec, Cynthia, eds., *Professors, Physicians and Practices in the History of Medicine : Essays in Honor of Nancy Siraisi*, (Cham: Springer International Publishing, 2017).

13 "Botanical Garden (Orto Botanico) Padua" United Nations, UNESCO, World Heritage List, December 1997, http://whc.unesco.org/en/list/824

14 Kate Fowle, "Survival of the Fittest", in Aliza Watters, ed., *Taryn Simon: Paperwork and the Will of Capital*, (Ostfildern and New York: Hatje Cantz, Gagosian, 2016): 7.

15 These days such arrangements are at the entrance of every supermarket chain, usually positioned somewhere near the only checkout that sells cigarettes.

16 Aliza Watters, ed., *Taryn Simon: Paperwork and the Will of Capital*, (Ostfildern and New York: Hatje Cantz, Gagosian, 2016): 109

17 Watters, *Taryn Simon: Paperwork and the Will of Capital*: 109.

18 Tim Entwisle, "Old Fan Palms inspire Johanns", *Talking Plants*, September 2012, http://talkingplants.blogspot.com.au/2012/09/old-fan-palms-inspire-johanns.html

19 Alessandro Minelli, ed., *The Botanical Garden of Padua 1545–1995*, (Marsilio: Venice, 1995.)

20 Stephen Mosley "Environmental History of Air Pollution and Protection" in *The Basic Environmental History*, ed. M Agnoletti and S Neri Serneri, *Environmental History*, vol 4. (Switzerland: Springer, 2014). See also C MacFarling Meure, et al. "Law Dome CO_2, CH_4 and N_2O ice core records extended to 2000 years BP", *Geophysical Research Letters* 33, no. 14 (21 July 2006): https://doi.org/10.1029/2006GL026152

21 William Ruddiman, *Earth's Climate: Past and Future*, 3rd ed., (New York: Macmillan Learning, 2014): 126.

22 Ruddiman, *Earth's Climate: Past and Future*: 336.

23 Ruddiman, *Earth's Climate: Past and Future*: 3.

24 Ruddiman, *Earth's Climate: Past and Future*: 375. For the authoritative data see also Intergovernmental Panel on Climate Change, *Climate Change 2014: Synthesis Report, Contribution of Working Groups I, II and III to the Fifth Assessment Report of the Intergovernmental Panel on Climate Change*, eds. Core Writing Team, Rajendra K. Pachauri and Leo A Meyer (Geneva: IPCC, 2014): 1–151, http://ar5-syr.ipcc.ch/ipcc/ipcc/resources/pdf/IPCC_SynthesisReport.pdf

25 Ruddiman, *Earth's Climate: Past and Future*: 338.

26 Michele Brunetti, Maurizio Maugeri Fabio Monti and Teresa Nanni, "Temperature and precipitation variability in Italy in the last two centuries from homogenised instrumental time series", *International Journal of Climatology* 26, no. 3, (January 2006): 345–381.

27 NASA "Climate Change: How do we know?" *Global Climate Change: Vital Signs of the Planet*, 16 May 2018, https://climate.nasa.gov/evidence/

28 Ruddiman, *Earth's Climate: Past and Future*: 341.

29 Ruddiman, *Earth's Climate: Past and Future*: 65.

30 Ruddiman, *Earth's Climate: Past and Future*: 59.

31 Ruddiman, *Earth's Climate: Past and Future*: 65.

32 Millan, "The Quest for the Seeds of Eternal Growth": 100.

33 Ruddiman, *Earth's Climate: Past and Future*: 8.

34 Walter Benjamin, "To the Planetarium" [written 1923–1926, published 1928] in *One-Way Street* ed. Michael W Jennings, trans. EFN.Jephcott, (Cambridge, Massachusetts: The Belknap Press, 2016): 95–96.

35 Millan, "The Quest for the Seeds of Eternal Growth": 101.

36 Walter Benjamin, "To the Planetarium": 95–96.

37 US Department of Energy, "The Manhattan Project: an interactive history," *Office of History and Heritage Resources*, 2013, https://www.osti.gov/opennet/manhattan-project-history/

38 US Department of Energy, "The Manhattan Project."

39 Colin N Waters, Jan Zalasiewicz et al. "The Anthropocene is Functionally and Stratigraphically distinct from the Holocene", *Science* 351, no. 6269, (8 January 2016) http://science.sciencemag.org/content/351/6269/aad2622

40 Chris SM Turney, Jonathan Palmer et al. "Global Peak in Atmospheric Radiocarbon Provides a Potential definition for the Onset of the Anthropocene Epoch in 1965", *Nature* 8, no. 3293, (19 February 2018) https://www.nature.com/articles/s41598-018-20970-5#article-info https://doi.org/10.1038/s41598-018-20970-5

41 IPCC, *Climate Change 2014: Synthesis Report*.

42 Tsing, *The Mushroom at the End of the World*: 111.

43 Gregory Bateson, *Mind and Nature: a Necessary Unity,* (New York: EP Dutton, 1979): 24.

44 Bateson, *Mind and Nature*: 16-17.

45 Bateson, *Mind and Nature*: 69.

46 Brian Kahn "The world passes 400PPM Threshold. Permanently," *Climate Central* (27 September 2016): http://www.climatecentral.org/news/world-passes-400-ppm-threshold-permanently-20738

47 See Charles D. Keeling, "Rewards and Penalties of Monitoring the Earth," *Annual Review of Energy and the Environment* 23 (November 1998): 25–82.

48 Ruddiman, *Earth's Climate: Past and Future*: 343.

49 Elena Paoletti, "Ozone and Urban Forests in Italy" *Environmental Pollution* 157, no.5, (May 2009): 1506–1512 and also Elena Paoletti, Tommaso Bardelli, Gianluca Giovannini et al. "Air Quality impact of an urban park over time" *Procedia Environmental Sciences* 4, 2011, http://www.sciencedirect.com/science/article/pii/S1878029611000284

50 Gayatri Chakravorty Spivak, *Death of a Discipline* (Columbia: Columbia University Press, 2005): 102.

51 Bruno Latour, in conversation with Heather Davis, "Diplomacy in the Face of Gaia" in *Art in the Anthropocene: Encounters Among Aesthetics, Politics, Environments and Epistemologies* ed. Heather Davis and Etienne Turpin, (London: Open Humanities Press, 2015): 44.

52 Latour, "Diplomacy in the Face of Gaia": 44.

53 Graeme I Pearman, Paul J Fraser and John R Garratt, "CSIRO High-precision Measurement of Atmospheric CO_2 Concentration in Australia. Part 2: Cape Grim, Surface CO_2 Measurements and Carbon Cycle Modelling", *Historical Records of Australian Science*, 28 no. 2, (October 19, 2017): 126–139. https://doi.org/10.1071/HR17015

54 Ruddiman, *Earth's Climate: Past and Future*: 126.

55 A daily reading can be found at the Scripps Institution of Oceanography: https://scripps.ucsd.edu/programs/keelingcurve/

56 Iris Murdoch, *Metaphysics as a Guide to Morals*, (London: Random House, 2003): 3.

57 Christine Eriksen et al. "Children Aren't Liabilities in Disasters; they can help if we let them", *The Conversation*, 5 April 2018, https://theconversation.com/children-arent-liabilities-in-disasters-they-can-help-if-we-let-them-93794

58 Millan, "The Quest For the Seeds of Eternal Growth": 103.

59 Millan, "The Quest For the Seeds of Eternal Growth": 106.

60 Isabelle Stengers, "Introductory Notes on an Ecology of Practices," *Cultural Studies Review* 11, no.1 (2005): 195.

61 Anna Lowenhaupt Tsing, *The Mushroom at the End of the World: On the Possibility of Life in Capitalist Ruins* (Princeton and Oxford: Princeton University Press, 2015): 293.

62 Sirocco Kākāpō (@siroccokakapo) "BOOM! Guess who's back..." Facebook, 8 February 2018. https://www.facebook.com/siroccokakapo/

63 Richard Sennett, *The Craftsman* (New Haven: Yale University Press, 2008).

64 Fernand Braudel, *Civilization and Capitalism 15th–18th Century, Vol. II: The Wheels of Commerce*, trans. Sian Reynolds (London: Collins, 1982): 30.

65 Percy Bysshe Shelley, "Ode to the West Wind," [1820] *Selected Poetry and Prose: Shelley*, (New York: Signet, New American Library, 1966): 212–215.

66 Kamau Brathwaite, "Veve (Islands)", in *The Arrivants*, (Oxford: Oxford University Press, 1973): 266.

67 Lorraine Daston, *Things That Talk: object lessons from art and science* (New York: Zone Books, 2004): 11.

68 Bruno Latour, "Agency at the time of the Anthropocene," *New Literary History* 45, no. 1 (2014): 14.

69 Lorraine Daston and Peter Galison, *Objectivity* (New York: Zone Books, 2007): 67.

70 Teodor Mitew, "Do Objects Dream of an Internet of Things?" *Fibreculture Journal* 23, (2014): https://web.archive.org/web/20180501045637/http://twentythree.fibreculturejournal.org/fcj-168-do-objects-dream-of-an-internet-of-things/

71 Ian Bogost, *Alien Phenomenology, or What It's Like to Be a Thing* (Minneapolis, MN: University of Minnesota Press, 2012).

72 Bruno Latour, "What is iconoclash? Or is there a world beyond the image wars?" in *Iconoclash: Beyond the Image Wars in Science, Religion, and Art*, ed. Bruno Latour and Peter Weibel (Cambridge, MA: MIT Press, 2002): 37.

73 Latour, "Agency at the time of the Anthropocene": 8.

74 Lorraine Daston and Katharine Park, *Wonders and the Order of Nature, 1150 – 1750* (New York: Zone Books, 1998): 26.

75 Latour, "Agency at the time of the Anthropocene": 14.

76 Erik Bordeleau, "Bruno Latour and the Miraculous Present of Enunciation," in *Breaking the Spell: Contemporary Realism Under Discussion*, ed. Anna Longo and Sarah de Sanctis (Milan: Mimesis International, 2015): 157.

77 Peter Sloterdijk, "Atmospheric Politics," in *Making Things Public: atmospheres of democracy*, ed. Bruno Latour and Peter Weibel (Karlsruhe and Cambridge, MA: ZKM and The MIT Press, 2005): 944–951.

78 Latour, "Agency at the time of the Anthropocene": 15.

79 Adam Miller, *Speculative Grace: Bruno Latour and Object-Oriented Theology* (New York: Fordham University Press, 2013): 49.

80 Bogost, *Alien Phenomenology*: 64.

81 Jane Bennett, *Vibrant Matter: A Political Ecology of Things* (Durham: Duke University Press, 2010): 120.

82 Mircea Eliade, *Cosmos and History: The Myth of the Eternal Return*, trans. Willard Trask (New York: Harper Torchbooks, 1959); and Mircea Eliade, *The Sacred and the Profane: the nature of religion*, trans. Willard Trask (New York: Harcourt, Brace & World, 1959).

83 Eliade, *Cosmos and History*: 4.

84 Eliade, *Cosmos and History*: 4.

85 "Press release: Amazon.com Announces Third Quarter Sales up 34% to $43.7 Billion" Amazon, 26 October 2017, https://archive.fo/UJ7GB

86 Bennett, *Vibrant Matter*: 34.

87 Shaun Nichols, "TV anchor says live on-air 'Alexa, order me a dollhouse' – guess what happens next," *The Register*, 7 January 2017, https://web.archive.org/web/20180501045959/http://www.theregister.co.uk/2017/01/07/

tv_anchor_says_alexa_buy_me_a_dollhouse_and_she_ does/?mt=1483795705927

88 Will Oremus, "Terrifyingly Convenient," *Slate*, 3 April 2016, https://web.archive.org/web/20180501050123/http://www.slate.com/articles/technology/cover_story/2016/04/alexa_cortana_and_siri_aren_t_novelties_anymore_they_re_our_terrifyingly.html

89 Alex Hern, "Amazon gadget hijacks owner's heating after hearing radio report," *The Guardian*, March 11, 2016, https://web.archive.org/web/20180501050230/https://www.theguardian.com/technology/2016/mar/11/amazon-gadget-echo-hijacks-owner-heating-radio-report

90 Annie Palmer, "'There's a good chance I get murdered tonight': Terrified Amazon Echo users reveal Alexa has been emitting 'bone chilling' laughs at random and is ignoring their commands," *Daily Mail*, March 7, 2018, https://archive.fo/E78ls

91 Vanessa Wong, "Amazon Knows Alexa Devices Are Laughing Spontaneously And It's 'Working To Fix It,'" *Buzzfeed*, 8 March 2018, https://web.archive.org/web/20180519060442/https://www.buzzfeed.com/venessawong/amazon-alexa-devices-are-laughing-creepy?utm_term=.ea9jj-v3WkW#.rtnMMeKQNQ

92 Sally Applin and Michael Fischer, "Pervasive Computing in Time and Space: The Culture and Context of 'Place' Integration," in *International Conference on Intelligent Environments (IE'11)* (Nottingham Trent University, UK: IE, 2011): https://doi.org/10.1109/IE.2011.65

93 Sally Applin and Michael Fischer, "Thing Theory: Connecting Humans to Location-Aware Smart Environments," in *Third International Workshop on Location Awareness for Mixed and Dual Reality LAMDa'13* (Santa Monica, CA: LAMDa, 2013): https://web.archive.org/web/20180519063009/http://www.dfki.de/LAMDa/2013/accepted/13_ApplinFischer.pdf

94 Robert Maniura, *Pilgrimage to Images in the Fifteenth Century: The Origins of the Cult of Our Lady of Czestochowa* (Suffolk: Boydell Press, 2004).

95 Anna Niedźwiedź, *The Image and the Figure: Our Lady of Czestochowa in Polish Culture and Popular Religion* (Kraków: Jagiellonian University Press, 2010).

96 Elżbieta Bilska and Jan Nalaskowski, "The Cult of the Virgin Mary outside Poland," *Peregrinus Cracoviensis*, no. 3 (1996): 191–201.

97 Małgorzata Oleszkiewicz-Peralba, *The Black Madonna in Latin America and Europe: Tradition and Transformation* (Albuquerque: University of New Mexico Press, 2007).

98 Latour, "What is iconoclash? Or is there a world beyond the image wars?": 33.

99 Latour, "What is iconoclash? Or is there a world beyond the image wars?": 32.

100 "Wide Infra-red Survey Explorer," WISE, posted 27 July 2011: https://web.archive.org/web/20180501051703/http://www.astro.ucla.edu/~wright/WISE/

101 Martin Connors, Paul Wiegert, and Christian Veillet. "Earth's Trojan asteroid," *Nature*, no. 475 (July 2011): 481–483.

102 Charles Choi, "First Asteroid Companion of Earth Discovered at Last," Scientific American, July 27, 2011, https://archive.fo/6EBGd

103 Richard Miles, "Earth's first 'Trojan' asteroid discovered," *Journal of the British Astronomical Association* 121, no. 5 (2011): 264.

104 Choi, "First Asteroid Companion of Earth Discovered at Last."

105 Choi, "First Asteroid Companion of Earth Discovered at Last."

106 Connors et al, "Earth's Trojan asteroid."

107 Choi, "First Asteroid Companion of Earth Discovered at Last."

108 Jorge Luis Borges, *The Book of Imaginary Beings*, trans. Andrew Hurley (London: Penguin Books, 2005): 90.

109 Gustav Meyrink, *The Golem*, trans. Madge Pemberton (Boston: Houghton Mifflin, 1928): 41.

110 Daston, *Things That Talk*: 39.

111 Letter John Keats to Percy Bysshe Shelley, August 16th, 1820. "To Percy Shelley", http://www.john-keats.com/briefe/160820.htm

112 Matthew Flinders, *Matthew Flinders' Narrative of Tom Thumb's Cruise to Canoe Rivulet,* ed. Keith Bowden (Brighton, Victoria: South Eastern Historical Association, 1952): 27.

113 Matthew Flinders, *Matthew Flinders: Personal letters from an extraordinary life,* ed. Paul Brunton (Sydney: Hordern House, 2002): 4.

114 Jade Kennedy, qtd. in Catherine McKinnon, "Writing white, writing black, and events at Canoe Rivulet," *TEXT: Journal of Writing and Writing Programs* 16, no. 2 (2012): 8.

115 Michael Organ and Carol Speechley, "Illawarra Aborigines," *A History of Wollongong* eds. Jim Hagan and Andrew Wells (University of Wollongong Press: Wollongong,1997): 7.

116 Jade Kennedy, qtd. in Catherine McKinnon, "Writing white, writing black, and events at Canoe Rivulet," *TEXT: Journal of Writing and Writing Programs* 16, no. 2 (2012): 8.

117 William Blake, "Auguries of Innocence," in *The Selected Poems of William Blake,* ed. Bruce Woodcock (Ware, Hertfordshire: Wordsworth Editions, 1994): 135.

118 Agnieszka Golda, "Feeling: sensing the affectivity of emotional politics through textiles," in *The Handbook of Textile Culture,* ed. H. Clark, J. Jefferies & D. Wood Conroy. (London: Bloomsbury Publishing, 2016): 401–415.

119 Donna Haraway, "Tentacular Thinking: Anthropocene, Capitalocene, Chthulucene," *e-flux,* no. 75 (September 2016) http://www.e-flux.com/journal/75/67125/tentacular-thinking-anthropocene-capitalocene-chthulucene/

120 The Dark Mountain Project, *Walking on Lava: Selected Works for Uncivilised Times* (White River Junction VT: Chelsea Green Publishing, 2017): 2.

121 "The Atmosphere of the Solar System," Compound Interest, accessed November 1, 2017, http://www.compoundchem.com/2014/07/25/planetatmospheres/; David R. Williams, "Earth Fact Sheet," NASA Space Science Data Coordinated Archive, accessed May 2, 2018, https://nssdc.gsfc.nasa.gov/planetary/factsheet/earthfact.html

122 Rebecca Solnit, *A Field Guide to Getting Lost* (London: Penguin, 2006): 4–5.

123 Teodor Mitew, 2017, notes for this publication.

124 Isabelle Stengers, "Wondering About Materialism," in *The Speculative Turn: Continental Materialism and Realism,*

edited by Levi Bryant, Nick Srnicek, and Graham Harman (Melbourne, Australia: re.press, 2011): 368–380.

125 Stengers, *Wondering About Materialism*, 371.

126 Levi Bryant, Nick Srnicek, and Graham Harman, "Towards a Speculative Philosophy," in *The Speculative Turn: Continental Materialism and Realism*, ed. Levi Bryant, Nick Srnicek and Graham Harman (Melbourne, Australia: re.press, 2011): 15.

127 Victor Turner, "Betwixt and Between: The Liminal Period in Rites of Passage," in *The Forest of Symbols: Aspects of Ndembu Ritual*, ed. Victor Turner (Ithaca and London: Cornell University Press, 1967): 27.

128 Brian Massumi, "The Autonomy of Affect", in *Deleuze: A Critical Reader*, ed. Paul Patton (Oxford, UK, and Cambridge, Massachusetts: Blackwell Publishers, 1996): 221–222.

129 Andrea Eckersley, "The Event of Painting", in *Deleuze and the Schizoanalysis of Visual Art*, ed. Ian Buchanan and Lorna Collins (London, New York: Bloomsbury Publishing, PLC, 2014): 205.

130 Harriet Hawkins and Anja Kanngieser, "Artful Climate Change Communication: Overcoming Abstractions, Insensibilities and Distances," *WIREs Climate Change* 8, no. 5 (2017), https://doi.org/10.1002/wcc.472. See also: Linda Williams, "Affective Poetics and Public Access: The Critical Challenges of Environmental Art," *Australasian Journal of Ecocriticism and Cultural Ecology* 3 (2013–2014).

131 Elisabeth Grosz, *Chaos, Territory, Art: Deleuze and the Framing of the Earth*, (New York and Chichester: Columbia University Press, 2008): 23.

132 Diana Coole, "From Within the Midst of Things: New Sensibility, New Alchemy, and the Renewal of Critical Theory" in *Realism, Materialism, Art*, edited by Christophe Cox, Jenny Jaskey, and Suhail Malik (New York, Berlin: Sternberg Press, 2015): 41.

133 Holli Riebeek, *Paleoclimatology: The Ice Core Record*, NASA Earth Observatory, December 19, 2005, Accessed May 15, 2018. https://earthobservatory.nasa.gov/Features/Paleoclimatology_IceCores/

134 Hans Ulrich Obrist, *Olafur Eliasson* (Köln: Verlag der Buchhandlung Walther König 2008): 15–16.

135 Obrist, *Olafur Eliasson*: 16.

136 Obrist, *Olafur Eliasson*: 22.

137 Alexander Wilson, "Pragmatics of Raw Art," in *Deleuze and the Schizoanalysis of Visual Art*, ed. Ian Buchanan and Lorna Collins, (Bloomsbury Publishing, London, New York, 2014): 5; 57–76.

138 Olafur Eliasson, *Playing with Space and Light* TED Talk 2009, Accessed May 17, 2018. https://www.ted.com/talks/olafur_eliasson_playing_with_space_and_light

139 Eliasson, *Playing with Space and Light*.

140 Simon O'Sullivan, *Art Encounters Deleuze and Guattari* (Basingstoke, Hampshire and New York: Palgrave Macmillan, 2006): 19.

141 O'Sullivan, *Art Encounters Deleuze and Guattari*, 21.

142 Brian Massumi, *A User's Guide to Capitalism and Schizophrenia: Deviations from Deleuze and Guattari* (Cambridge, Massachusetts: MIT Press, 1992): 17–18.

143 Juliana Engberg, "Tempest: A Journey Log," in *Exhibition catalogue* (Tasmanian Museum and Art Gallery, 2016): 22–24.

144 O'Sullivan, *Art Encounters Deleuze and Guattari*: 17.

145 Adrian Searle, "Age and Beauty," *Guardian UK*, Tuesday 20 February 2001.

146 Jean-Christophe Royoux, Marina Warner, Germaine Greer, *Tacita Dean*, ed. Garrett C. Williams G., Contemporary Artists (London and New York: Phaidon Press Ltd, 2013): 17.

147 Royoux, Warner, Greer, *Tacita Dean*: 25.

148 Royoux, Warner, Greer, *Tacita Dean*: 15–16.

149 O'Sullivan, *Art Encounters Deleuze and Guattari*, 18.

150 Royoux, Warner, Greer, *Tacita Dean*: 17.

151 Royoux, Warner, Greer, *Tacita Dean*: 17.

152 O'Sullivan, *Art Encounters Deleuze and Guattari*: 26.

153 O'Sullivan, *Art Encounters Deleuze and Guattari*: 17.

154 Coole, *From within the Midst of Things*: 41.

155 O'Sullivan, *Art Encounters Deleuze and Guattari*: 17–18.

156 Gilles Deleuze, *Difference and Repetition*, trans. Paul Patton (London: The Athlone Press, 1994): 139–140.

157 Solnit, *A Field Guide to Getting Lost*: 4–5.

158 O'Sullivan, *Art Encounters Deleuze and Guattari*: 20–21.

159 Michel Serres, "Revisiting the Natural Contract": 6.

160 Massumi, "The Autonomy of Affect": 235.

161 Italo Calvino, *Six Memos for the Next Millennium* (London: Vintage Press, 1996): 124.

162 Anna Lowenhaupt Tsing, *The Mushroom at the End of the World: On the Possibility of Life in Capitalist Ruins* (Princeton: Princeton University Press, 2015): 37.

163 David Attenborough, "Climate Change is the Major Challenge Facing the World," *The Independent*, 23 May 2006, http://www.independent.co.uk/environment/attenborough-climate-change-is-the-major-challenge-facing-the-world-479459.html

164 John Beck, "The Call of the Anthropocene," *Cultural Politics* 10, no. 3 (2014): 9.

165 Damian Carrington, "Ozone Layer Not Recovering Over Populated Areas, Scientists Warn," *The Guardian*, 6 February 2018, https://www.theguardian.com/environment/2018/feb/06/ozone-layer-not-recovering-over-populated-areas-scientists-warn

166 2015 Paris Agreement, quoted in "Asia Faces Climate Change Disaster: Report," *SBS World News*, 14 July 2017, https://www.sbs.com.au/news/asia-faces-climate-change-disaster-report

167 Amitav Ghosh, *The Great Derangement*, (Chicago and London, University of Chicago Press, 2016): 24.

168 Greg Garrard, Gary Handwer, and Sabine Wilke, "Imagining Anew: Challenges of Representing the Anthropocene," *Environmental Humanities* 5, no. 1 (2014): 150.

169 Bill McKibben, "Introduction," in *I'm with the Bears: Short Stories from a Damaged Planet*, ed. Mark Martin (London: Verso, 2011): 4.

170 Fiona Probyn-Rapsey, "Review Article: Multispecies Mourning: Thom van Dooren's *Flight Ways: Life and Loss at the Edge of Extinction*,." *Animal Studies Journal* 3, no. 2 (2014): 7.

171 Bernard Stiegler, "Escaping the Anthropocene," in *The Crisis Conundrum: How to Reconcile Economy and Society*, ed. Mauro Magatti (Cham: Palgrave Macmillan, 2017): 151.

172 Roy Scranton, "Learning How to Die in the Anthropocene," *New York Times*, 10 November 2013, https://opinionator.blogs.nytimes.com/2013/11/10/learning-how-to-die-in-the-anthropocene/

173 Deborah Bird Rose, "In the Shadow of All This Death," in *Animal Death*, ed. Jay Johnson and Fiona Probyn-Rapsey (Sydney: Sydney University Press, 2013): 1.

174 "Royal Cam: Live Stream and Highlights," Department of Conservation Te Papa Atawhai, http://www.doc.govt.nz/royalcam

175 Jane Davidson, "Fish Tales: Attributing the First Illustration of a Fossil Shark's Tooth to Richard Verstegan (1605) and Nicolas Steno (1667)," *Proceedings of the Academy of Natural Sciences of Philadelphia*, 150, no. 14, (April 2000): 329–44.

176 Martin J. S. Rudwick, *Georges Cuvier, Fossil Bones, and Geological Catastrophes: New Translations and Interpretations of the Primary Texts*, translated from 'Espèces des elephants', [1796] (Chicago and London: University of Chicago Press, 2008): 24.

177 David Raup quoted in Elizabeth Kolbert, *The Sixth Extinction: An Unnatural History*, (London: Bloomsbury 2014): 16.

178 Trevor Paglen, "Geographies of Time (The Last Pictures)" in *In the Holocene*, ed. João Ribas (Cambridge Massachusetts and Berlin: MIT List Visual Arts Centre and Sternberg Press, 2014): 25–33.

179 Roger Hooke, "On the Efficacy of Humans as Geomorphic Agents," *GSA Today (Publication of the Geological Society of America)* 4, no.9 (September 1994): 217.

180 There is no definitive list of extinct birds, but the following sources provide detail of the lives and deaths of birds since the dodo; Avibase: The World Bird Database, accessed September 10, 2017, https://avibase.bsc-eoc.org/avibase.jsp?lang=EN&pg=home; The IUCN Red List of Threatened Species, http://www.iucnredlist.org/; "Extinct Birds," Ornithology: The Science of Birds, https://ornithology.com/extinct-birds/

181 Gilles Deleuze, quoted in translation by Maria Puig de la Bellacasa, "'Nothing Comes without Its World': Thinking with Care," The Sociological Review 60, no. 2 (2012): 211, https://doi.org/10.1111/j.1467-954X.2012.02070.x

182 Judith Wright, "Sanctuary," in *Collected Poems* (Sydney: Angus and Robertson, 1994): 139.

183 Paul Parsons and Gail Dixon, *The Periodic Table: A Visual Guide to the Elements*, (London: Quercus, 2014): 26–29.

184 Roy Scranton, *Learning to Die in the Anthropocene: Reflections on the End of a Civilization*, (San Francisco: City Lights Books, 2015): 19.

185 Jane Bennett, *Vibrant Matter: A Political Ecology of Things*, (Durham and London: Duke University Press, 2010): xv;10, paraphrased by Diana Coole, *From Within the Midst of Things: New Sensibility, New Alchemy, and the Renewal of Critical Theory*, in Cox, Jaskey and Malik (eds) *Realism, Materialism, Art*, (New York and Berlin: Bard College and Sternberg Press, 2015): 44.

186 Liza Dalby, *East Wind Melts the Ice: A Memoir through the Seasons* (London: Chatto & Windus, 2007).

187 Alexandra Harris, *Weatherland: Writers and Artists under the English Skies* (London: Thames & Hudson, 2015).

188 Harris, *Weatherland*: 166.

189 Harris, *Weatherland*: 166.

190 Alva Noë, *Strange Tools: Art and Human Nature* (New York: Hill and Wang, 2015): 206.

191 Noë, *Strange Tools*: 152.

192 Esther Leslie, "Traces of Craft," *Journal of Design History*, no. 1 (1998): 11. The meaning of the German word *Kraft* is power. Kraftwerk can also be translated to 'power plant'.

193 Leslie, "Traces of Craft": 38.

194 Leslie, "Traces of Craft": 48.

195 Harris, *Weatherland*: 166.

196 Aldo Leopold, *A Sand County Almanac* (New York: Ballantine, 1966).

197 Leopold, *A Sand County Almanac*: 239–240.

198 Levi Bryant, "Wilderness Ontology," in *Preternatural* (Brooklyn: Punctum Books, 2011): 26.

199 Sei Shonogon, *The Pillow Book*, trans. Meredith McKinney (London: Penguin, 2006).

200 Kyo Maclear, *Bird Art Life and Death: A Field Guide to the Small and Significant* (London: 4th Estate, 2017).

201 Maclear, *Bird Art Life and Death*: 5.

202 Rachel DiNitto, "Return of the 'Zuihitsu': Print Culture, Modern Life, and Heterogeneous Narrative in Prewar Japan," Harvard Journal of Asiatic Studies 64, no. 2 (2004): 70.

203 DiNitto, "Return of the 'Zuihitsu'": 75

204 DiNitto, "Return of the 'Zuihitsu'": 77.

205 DiNitto, "Return of the 'Zuihitsu'": 79.

206 Dalby, *East Wind Melts the Ice*: xvii.

207 Maclear, *Bird Art Life and Death*: 119.

208 Harris, *Weatherland*: 165.

209 Harris, *Weatherland*: 207.

210 Maclear, *Bird Art Life and Death*: 247.

211 Tim Ingold, *Lines: A Brief History* (London & New York: Routledge, 2007): 2.

212 Alfred Wainwright, *Pictorial Guides to the Lakeland Fells: Being an Illustrated Account of a Study and Exploration of the Mountains in the English Lake District* (London: Frances Lincoln, 2008).

213 Amanda Thomson, "Making a Place: Art, Writing, and a More-than-Textual Approach," *The Geographical Review* 103, no. 2 (2013): 245.

214 Thomson, "Making a Place": 246.

215 Thomson, "Making a Place": 245.

216 Martin: 19.

217 Leon Van Schaik, "Spatial Intelligence" in *Kowloon Cultural District: An Investigation into Spatial Capabilities in Hong Kong*, ed. Esther Lorenz and Li Shiqiao (Hong Kong: MCCM Creations, 2015): 249.

218 Van Schaik, "Spatial Intelligence": 244–5.

219 American Association for the Advancement of Science, "Did Mars's Magnetic Field Die With a Whimper or a Bang?", *Science,* last modified 20 April 2009, https://www.sciencemag.org/news/2009/04/did-marss-magnetic-field-die-whimper-or-bang

220 Kaylee Lewis, "30 Years on, Norway's radioactive reindeer are a stark reminder of Chernobyl legacy," *Independent,* 1 March 2016, https://www.independent.co.uk/news/world/europe/chernobyl-radioactive-reindeer-norway-a6903571.html; Göran Bostedt, "Reindeer Husbandry, the Swedish market for Reindeer meat, and the Chernobyl effects," *Agricultural Economics* 26, no. 3 (December 2001): 217–226, http://ageconsearch.umn.edu/bitstream/181437/2/agec2001v026i003a003.pdf

221 Jon Moen, "Climate Change: Effects on the Ecological Basis for Reindeer Husbandry in Sweden," *AMBIO: A Journal of the Human Environment* (Royal Swedish Academy of Sciences 37, no. 4 (2008): 304–311, http://www.bioone.org/doi/abs/10.1579/0044-7447%282008%2937%5B304%3ACCEOTE%5D2.0.CO%3B2

222 Hannibal Rhoades, Tero Mustonen, "Arctic indigenous Peoples Leading the Way in Ecological Restoration and Climate Resilience," *Intercontinental Cry,* 3 April 2017, https://intercontinentalcry.org/arctic-indigenous-peoples-leading-way-ecological-restoration-climate-resilience-says-major-new-study/

223 Justin Worland, "More than 700 North American Bee Species Are Headed Toward Extinction," *Time Science,* March 2, 2017, http://time.com/4688417/north-american-bee-population-extinction/

224 Don Bradshaw and Jess Reid, "Bees Give up searching for food when we degrade their land" (University of Western Australia's Centre for Integrative Bee Research): *University News,* 8 February 2017, http://www.news.uwa.edu.au/201702089380/international/bees-give-searching-food-when-we-degrade-their-land

225 WB Yeats, "The Stare's Nest By My Window", in *The Collected Poems of WB Yeats: A New Edition,* ed. Richard J. Finneran (New York: Collier Books): 211. A 'stare' is known as a starling in Australia.

226 Ted Chiang, "The Great Silence", in *The Best American Short Stories 2016,* ed. Junot Diaz (New York: Houghton Mifflin Harcourt, 2016): 69–72.

227 "Feeding Sugar to Honey Bees," NSW Government Department of Primary Industries, http://www.dpi.nsw.gov.au/__data/assets/pdf_file/0018/532260/Feeding-sugar-to-honey-bees.pdf

228 Ruth Gates, quoted in Alex Riley, "The Women with a Controversial Plan to Save Corals," *BBC Earth*, 22 March 2016, http://www.bbc.com/earth/story/20160322-the-women-with-a-controversial-plan-to-save-corals

229 "Wolf Reintroduction Changes Ecosystem: June 22, 2011," My Yellowstone Park.com, https://www.yellowstonepark.com/things-to-do/wolf-reintroduction-changes-ecosystem

230 Melinda A Norton, Kris French, and Andrew W Claridge, "Habitat associations of the long-nosed potoroo (*Potorous tridactylus*) at multiple spatial scales," *Australian Journal of Zoology* 58, no. 5 (2011): 303, https://doi.org/10.1071/ZO10042

231 John CZ Woinarski, Andrew A Burbidge, and Peter L Harrison, "Ongoing unraveling of a continental fauna: Decline and extinction of Australian mammals since European settlement", *Proceedings of the National Academy of Sciences of the United States* 112, no. 15 (2015): 4531, https://doi.org/10.1073/pnas.1417301112

232 Dana Nucitelli, "'The atmosphere is being radicalized' by climate change," *The Guardian*, 24 October 2016, https://www.theguardian.com/environment/climate-consensus-97-per-cent/2016/oct/24/the-atmosphere-is-being-radicalized-by-climate-change.

233 Anna Tsing, *The Mushroom at the End of the World: On the Possibility of Life in Capitalist Ruins* (Princeton, NJ: Princeton University Press, 2015).

234 Rachel Carson, *Silent Spring* (London: Penguin Classics, 1962 (2000)). On the Great Acceleration, see: Steffen et al., *The Anthropocene: conceptual and historical perspectives*, Phil. Trans. R. Soc. A, 369 (2011): 849, https://doi.org/10.1098/rsta.2010.0327.

235 Rob Nixon, *Slow Violence and the Environmentalism of the Poor* (Cambridge Mass.: Harvard Press, 2013): 2.The phrase "unequal relations of destruction": Kirsti Robertson, "Plastiglomerate," *e-flux Journal* 78 (December 2016): http://www.e-flux.com/journal/78/82878/plastiglomerate/.

236 Cecilia Åsberg, "A thousand tiny anthropocenes: Worlding troubles from Swedish feminist environmental humanities

perspectives," Keynote Lecture, *Feminist, Queer, Anticolonial Propositions for Hacking the Anthropocene* (Sydney: Sydney University, April 8, 2016).

237 Donna Haraway, "Tentacular Thinking: Anthropocene, Capitalocene, Chthulucene," *e-flux Journal* 75 (September 2016): http://www.eflux.com/journal/75/67125/tentacular-thinking-anthropocene-capitalocene-chthulucene/.

238 Carson, *Silent Spring*, 179.

239 Val Plumwood, "Nature in the Active Voice," *Australian Humanities Review* 46 (2009): 121.The phrase "earth others": Val Plumwood, *Feminism and the Mastery of Nature* (London: Routledge, 1993): 137.

240 "Thick time" is a transcorporeal stretching of present-past-future in the archive that is a body, as Astrida Neimanis and Rachel Walker conceive. See: Astrida Neimanis and Rachel L Walker, "Weathering: Climate Change and the "Thick Time" of Transcorporeality," *Hypatia* 29 (2014): 558, https://doi.org/10.1111/hypa.12064.

241 Commonwealth of Australia Bureau of Meteorology, "Indigenous Weather knowledge," http://www.bom.gov.au/iwk/dharawal/.

242 Franco Berardi, *The Soul at Work: From Alienation to Autonomy*, trans. Francesca Cadel and Giuseppina Mecchia (Los Angeles: Semiotext(e): 2009): 130.

243 Avoca Bi-Centenary Committee, *Echoes Through the Mist: A History of the Avoca District* (Avoca: Avoca Bi-Centenary Committee, 1988): v. "Warreeah" is the Dharawal name for the messmate stringybark, *Eucalyptus oblique*. See: Sue Wesson, *Murni Dhungang Jirrar: Living in the Illawarra, Murni Dhungang Jirrar: Living in the Illawarra* (Sydney: Office of Environment & Heritage, 2009): 92, http://www.environment.nsw.gov.au/resources/cultureheritage/illawarraAboriginal-ResourceUse.pdf.

244 Geoscience Australia, "Astronomical Definitions," http://www.ga.gov.au/scientific-topics/astronomical/astronomical-definitions#heading-2.

245 I use *synsensorial* to articulate the synthetic and synergistic effect of multiple senses in play—at *synwork*—in an affective provocation, with a shift in focus to the proximal and interoperative modes of touch, hearing smell, proprioception and kinesis (the moving body) *as well as* vision.

I propose this is more than polysensorial; more than the sum of senses. A *synsensorium* is the immersive chamber or intersectional encounter space in which a powerful, heightened affectivity is experienced (Louise Boscacci, "The Trace of an Affective Object Encounter" (PhD diss., University of Wollongong, 2016): 185–86.

246 Patricia Clough and Jean Halley, eds, *The Affective Turn: Theorizing the Social* (Durham: Duke University Press, 2007): 2.

247 *A-bodied,* in preference to *embodied,* is a neologistic retuning to actively entwine the somatic and the cognitive—the sensing-feeling-thinking body—in encountering. See: Louise Boscacci, "Wit(h)nessing," 345. The word is adapted from Brian Massumi's expression, *a-bodying:* "if everything is alive, it is because the expressive gestures of nature go a-bodying" (Brian Massumi, *What Animals Teach Us About Politics* (Durham and London: Duke University Press, 2014): 97.

248 Elizabeth Grosz, *Chaos, Territory, Art* (New York: Columbia University Press, 2008): 2.

249 Boscacci, "The Trace": 155.

250 Biologists such as Gerardo Ceballos and colleagues now write of the "biological annihilation" of the anthropogenic Sixth Mass Extinction. See: Gerardo Ceballos et al., "Accelerated modern human-induced species losses: Entering the sixth mass extinction," *Science Advances* 1, no. 5 (2015) e1400253, https://doi.org/10.1126/sciadv.1400253.

251 Andreas Huyssen, *Twilight Memories: Marking Time in a Culture of Amnesia* (New York: Routledge, 1995).

252 Craig Martin, "The Invention of Atmosphere," *Studies in the History and Philosophy of Science,* 52 (August (2015): 44, https://doi.org/10.1016/j.shpsa.2015.05.007.

253 Martin, "The Invention of Atmosphere": 46.

254 Timothy Chandler, "Reading Atmospheres: The Ecocritical Potential of Gernot Böhme's Aesthetic Theory of Nature," *Interdisciplinary Studies in Literature and Environment* 18, no. 3 (2011): 558, https://doi.org/10.1093/isle/isr079.

255 Gernot Böhme, "Atmosphere as the fundamental concept of a new aesthetics," *Eleven* 36, no. 1 (1993): 113.

256 Böhme, "Atmosphere": 114.

257 Gernot Böhme, *The Aesthetics of Atmospheres*, ed. Jean-Paul Thibaud (London: Routledge, 2017): 2; Böhme, "Atmosphere": 113–114.

258 Ben Anderson, "Affective Atmospheres," *Emotion, Space and Society* 2, no. 2 (2009): 80.

259 NOAA/ESRL, "Global Greenhouse Gas Reference Network, Trends in Atmospheric Carbon Dioxide", https://www.esrl.noaa.gov/gmd/ccgg/trends/data.html. Data from the Mauna Loa Observatory Hawaii; representative of air at mid-altitudes over the Pacific Oceans. Keeling et al., "Atmospheric CO_2 and 13 CO_2 exchange with the terrestrial biosphere and oceans from 1978 to 2000: observations and carbon cycle implications," in *A History of Atmospheric CO2 and its effects on Plants and Animals and Ecosystems*, ed. JR Ehleringer, TE Cerlinbg, and MD Dearing (New York: Springer Verlag, 2005): 83–113.

260 Brian Kahn, "We Just Breached the 410 Parts Per Million Threshold." *Climate Central*, 20 April 2017, http://www.climatecentral.org/news/we-just-breached-the-410-parts-per-million-threshold-21372; Robert Monroe, "What Does 400 ppm Look Like?" *Scripps Institution of Oceanography*, 3 December 2013, https://scripps.ucsd.edu/programs/keelingcurve/2013/12/03/what-does-400-ppm-look-like/

261 Louise Boscacci, "Wit(h)nessing, "*Environmental Humanities* 10, no. 1 (2018): 343, https://doi.org/10.1215/22011919-4385617.

262 Val Plumwood, "Nature in the Active Voice," *Australian Humanities Review* 46 (2009): 125–126.

263 Haraway, *Staying with the Trouble:* 1.

264 Anna Tsing et al., eds, *Arts of Living on a Damaged Planet* (Minneapolis: University of Minnesota Press, 2017): 1.

265 Solastalgia describes the lived experience of loss or destruction of a home place through anthropocenic activities and forces: it is "the homesickness you have when you are still at home" (Glenn Albrecht, "The age of solastalgia," *The Conversation*, 7 August 2012, https://theconversation.com/the-age-of-solastalgia-8337.).

266 The Sun Metals Zinc Refinery (Korea Zinc Company Limited). Zinc Road, Townsville: Latitude 19°33'66"S, Longitude 146°86'61"E.

267 Susan Schuppli, "Dirty Pictures," in *Living Earth: Field Notes from the Dark Ecology Project 2014–2016*, ed. Mirna Belina (Amsterdam: Sonic Acts Press, 2016): 190.

268 Val Plumwood, "Shadow Places and the Politics of Dwelling," *Australian Humanities Review* 44 (2008): 139.

269 Plumwood, "Shadow Places": 139–147.

270 Over a two-year tracking study, 122 shadow port places in 25 countries spread across the planet connected to the Port of Townsville through shipping movement. The *shadows trace* actualises Plumwood's concept of the shadow places (Boscacci, "The Trace": 140).

271 Jane Bardon, "McArthur River mine's burning waste rock pile sparks health, environmental concerns among Gulf of Carpentaria Aboriginal groups," *The Guardian*, 27 July 2014, http://www.abc.net.au/news/2014-07-27/mcarthur-river-mine-gulf-of-carpentaria-anger-smoke-plume/5625484. Jane Bardon, "The race to avert disaster at the NT's McArthur River Mine Friday," *Background Briefing*, ABC Radio National, 12 February 2016, http://www.abc.net.au/radio-national/programs/backgroundbriefing/the-race-to-avert-disaster-at-the-nts-mcarthur-river-mine/7159504.

272 Helen Davidson, "Adam Giles: 'emotional' mine protesters need to have its benefits explained," *The Guardian*, 4 December 2014, https://www.theguardian.com/australia-news/2014/dec/04/adam-giles-emotional-mine-protesters-need-to-have-its-benefits-explained.

273 Davidson, "Adam Giles."

274 Helen Davidson, "'They'll get rich and go': Glencore's McArthur River mine may take 300 years to clean up," *The Guardian*, 15 May 2017, https://www.theguardian.com/australia-news/2017/may/15/theyll-get-rich-and-go-glencores-mcarthur-river-mine-could-take-300-years-to-clean-up.

275 Bardon, "Darwin Festival: The power and politics of Indigenous anti-mine art," *ABC News*, 16 August 2017, http://www.abc.net.au/news/2017-08-16/darwin-festival-power-and-politics-of-indigenous-anti-mine-art/8810290.

276 *Open Cut: Jacky Green, Sean Kerins, Therese Ritchie*. The Cross Arts Project, 24 February to 31 March 2018. Exhibition Floor Talk, 24 February 2018. See: http://www.crossart.com.au/current-show/329-open-cut.

277 Jason Moore, "Introduction: Anthropocene or Capitalocene? Nature, History, and the Crisis of Capitalism," in *Anthropocene or Capitalocene? Nature, History, and the Crisis of Capitalism*, ed. Jason W. Moore (Oakland CA: PM Press, 2016): 5–6.

278 TJ Demos, *Against the Anthropocene: Visual Culture and Environment Today* (Berlin: Sternberg Press, 2017): 86.

279 Haraway, *Staying with the Trouble*: 102.

280 *Ethico-aesthetics* is a contraction of *ethico-political aesthetics* in the ethico-aesthetic paradigm of Félix Guattari. See: Simon O' Sullivan, "From Aesthetics to the Abstract Machine: Deleuze, Guattari and Contemporary Art Practice," in *Deleuze and Contemporary Art*, ed. Stephen Zepke and Simon O'Sullivan (Edinburgh: Edinburgh University Press, 2010): 206.

281 Boscacci, "The Trace": 150. Resonance is heard with the World of Matter group of artists and theorists in the northern hemisphere who investigate flow lines of commodities and capital as 'planetary aesthetics'. See: Krista Lynes and World of Matter, "World of Matter," in *Elemental: An Arts and Ecology Reader*, ed. James Brady (Manchester: Gaia, 2016): 109.

282 Jan Zalasiewicz et al., "The Working Group on the Anthropocene: Summary of evidence and interim recommendations," *Anthropocene* 19 (2017): 57, https://doi.org/10.1016/j.ancene.2017.09.001.

283 The iceberg separated from the Larsen C ice shelf between July 10 and 12, 2017. "Larsen C: Giant iceberg breaks away from ice shelf in Antarctica," *ABC News*, 13 July 2017, http://www.abc.net.au/news/2017-07-12/huge-iceberg-breaks-away-from-antarctica-larsen-c-shelf/8703238; On the geological distinction between the Holocene and the Anthropocene: Waters et al., "The Anthropocene is functionally and stratigraphically distinct from the Holocene," *Science* 351, no. 6269 (2016) aad2622: 1–10, https://doi.org/10.1126/science.aad2622.

284 Carson, *Silent Spring*: 32.

285 Carson, *Silent Spring*: 25, 224.

286 Linda Lear, *Lost Woods: The Discovered Writing of Rachel Carson* (Boston: Beacon Press, 1999): 89. Carson called

the postwar time she was living in as "this atomic age" as early as 1951.

287 Rachael Carson, *The Sense of Wonder* (New York: HarperCollins, 1998 (1965)).

288 Carson, *The Sense of Wonder*: 98.

289 Lear, *Lost Woods*: 164.

290 Carson identified publicly as an ecologist in her last speech in 1963. Lear, *The Lost Woods*, 231.

291 Carson, *Silent Spring*, 21.

292 Lear, *The Lost Woods*, 176. From a television script on clouds, "Something about the Sky" (1957).

293 Linda Lear notes the book was published without any augmentation. See: Carson, *Sense of Wonder*: 11.

294 Lear, *The Lost Woods:* 9.

295 Carson, *Sense of Wonder*: 59.

296 Carson, *Sense of Wonder*: 59.

297 Carson, *Sense of Wonder*: 98.

298 Carson, *Silent Spring*: 225.

299 Carson, *Silent Spring*: 226.

300 Carson, *Silent Spring*: 121.

301 Carson, *Silent Spring*: 217.

302 Lear, *The Lost Woods*: 203

303 Lear, *The Lost Woods*: 94.

304 Carson, *Silent Spring*: 214.

305 Scripps Institution of Oceanography, *Scripps CO2 Program, Atmospheric CO2 Data*, http://scrippsco2.ucsd.edu/data/atmospheric_co2/primary_mlo_co2_record.

306 Benedict de Spinoza, *Ethics*, ed. and trans. Edwin Curley (London: Penguin, 1996 (1677)). Wonder is considered in Part III (Prop LII): p.97 and "Definition of the Emotions", IV: 105.

307 Michael Rosenthal, "Miracles, Wonder, and the State in Spinoza's *Theological-Political Treatise*," in *Cambridge Critical Guide to Spinoza's Theological-Political Treatise*, ed. Yitzhak Melamed and Michael A. Rosenthal (Cambridge: Cambridge University Press, 2010): 231–49. Michael

A Rosenthal, email communication with the author, 7 March 2018.

308 "Response-ability" is referred to as the "capacity to respond" in: Donna Haraway, "Symbiogenesis, Sympoiesis, and Art Activisms for staying with the Trouble," in *Arts of Living on a Damaged Planet*, ed. Anna Tsing et al. (Minneapolis: University of Minnesota Press, 2017): 38.

309 Félix Guattari, *Three Ecologies*, trans. Ian Pindar and Paul Sutton (London: Bloomsbury, 2014 (2000)): 40. Franco Berardi refers to the three ecologies as "atmosphere, infosphere and psychosphere" (Berardi, *The Soul at Work*, 31).

310 Linda Lear, *Rachel Carson: Witness for Nature* (New York: Mariner Books, 1997): 312.

311 Berardi, *After the Future*: 165.

312 Scott Gilbert, "Holobiont By Birth: Multilineage Individuals as the Concretion of Cooperative Processes," in *Arts of Living on a Damaged Planet*, ed. Anna Tsing et al. (Minneapolis: University of Minnesota Press, 2017): 73–89.

313 James Heppner, "A study of relationships between the aurora borealis and the geomagnetic disturbances caused by electric currents in the ionosphere" (PhD diss., California Institute of Technology, 1954): http://resolver.caltech.edu/CaltechETD:etd-12152003-111801

314 JR Carpenter, *The Gathering Cloud* (Axminster: Uniform Books, 2017): 59.

315 Jerzy Kosinski, *Painted Bird* (New York: Modern Library,1970 [1965]): 51.

316 Deborah Bird Rose, "Judas Work: Four Modes of Sorrow," *Environmental Philosophy* 5 no.2 (2008): 65; 66.

317 Donna Haraway, "Situated Knowledges: The Science Question in Feminism and the Privilege of Partial Perspective," *Feminist Studies* 14, no. 3, Autumn (1988): 575–99.

318 "Slow Flow – Te Ia Kōrero," The Greenbench Ltd., http://www.greenbench.org/project/slowflow/

319 Roland Barthes, *Camera Lucida: Reflections on Photography*, (New York: Hill and Wang, 1981).

320 Eleanor Ainge Roy, "New Zealand River Granted Same Legal Rights as Human Being," *The Guardian*, 16 March 2017,

https://www.theguardian.com/world/2017/mar/16/new-zealand-river-granted-same-legal-rights-as-human-being

321 Barbara Maria Stafford, "Revealing Technologies/Magical Domains," in *Devices of Wonder: From the World in a Box to Images on a Screen*, Barbara Maria Stafford and Frances Terpak (Los Angeles: Getty Research Institute, 2001): 6.

322 Amitav Ghosh, *The Great Derangement*, (Chicago and London, University of Chicago Press: 2016): 72–73.

323 Damian Carrington, "Plastic fibres found in tap water around the world, study reveals," *The Guardian*, 6 September 2017, https://www.theguardian.com/environment/2017/sep/06/plastic-fibres-found-tap-water-around-world-study-reveals

324 Jessica Glenza, "Sea salt around the world is contaminated by plastic, studies show," *The Guardian*, 9 September 2017, https://amp.theguardian.com/environment/2017/sep/08/sea-salt-around-world-contaminated-by-plastic-studies

325 Richard C. Thompson, "Plastics, environment and health," in *Accumulation: The Material Politics of Plastics*, ed. Jennifer Gabrys, Gay Hawkins, and Mike Michael (New York: Routledge, 2013): 150–169.

326 "Current projects," Oceanlinx, https://web.archive.org/web/20080610110251/http://www.oceanlinx.com:80/Currentprojects.asp; "Oceanlinx wave generator", NSW Government: Transport Roads and Maritime Services, http://www.rms.nsw.gov.au/projects/illawarra/oceanlinx/index.html

327 "A note from the new developers of the Oceanlinx technology," Oceanlinx, http://www.oceanlinx.com/

328 David Priddel et al., "Establishment of a new breeding colony of Gould's petrel (*Pterodroma leucoptera leucoptera*) through the creation of artificial nesting habitats and the translocation of nestlings," *Biological Conservation* 128, (2015): 560.

329 Jimmy Carter, quoted in John Beck, "The Call of the Anthropocene," *Cultural Politics* 10, no. 3, (2014): 409.

330 Anna Lowenhaupt Tsing, *The Mushroom at the End of the World: On the Possibility of Life in Capitalist Ruins*, (Princeton: Princeton University Press, 2015): 159.

331 Olive Senior, "Hurricane Story, 1903," in *Gardening in the Tropics* (Toronto: McClelland & Stewart, 1994): 19–20.

332 Olive Senior, "Embroidery", in *over the roofs of the world* (Toronto: Insomniac Press, 2005): 79.

333 Olive Senior, "Here and There", *over the roofs*, 57.

334 Kamau Brathwaite, "Negus", in *The Arrivants* (Oxford: Oxford University Press, 1973): 223–4.

335 Kamau Brathwaite, "Preface", in *Mother Poem* (Oxford: Oxford University Press, 1977): np. "kumina" is an Afro-Caribbean religious practice derived from the Congo region of West Central Africa.

336 Kamau Brathwaite, "Driftword", *Mother Poem*, 116–117.

337 Olive Senior, "Cockpit Country Dreams", in *Talking of Trees* (Kingston: Calabash, 1985): 3.

338 Bertolt Brecht quoted by Senior in *Talking of Trees*: 45.

339 Senior herself makes this association in many of the poems in *Gardening in the Tropics*. Although English language convention refers to vernacular plant names in lower case, I have retained Senior's use of capitalisation throughout this essay. This also includes the capitalisation of the names of Caribbean and African divinities. Capitalisation is a means of alerting readers to the importance she and I attach to vernacular and indigenous naming rights.

340 Olive Senior, 'Talking of Trees," *Talking of Trees*: 80. 'su-su" is gossip.

341 Olive Senior, "Notes," *Talking of Trees*: 86.

342 Senior explains: In Jamaica the word "yard defines one's dwelling and the space around it ... 'yard' is a powerfully emotive word that defines one's spatial as well as social relationships and is used by expatriate Jamaicans in reference to the homeland, Jamaica. 'Back a yard' means back home." *Encyclopedia of Jamaican Heritage* (St. Andrews: Twin Guinep Publishers, 2003): 528.

343 Olive Senior, Entry for "Woman's Tongue," *Encyclopedia of Jamaican Heritage*: 518.

344 Olive Senior, "Talking of Trees," *Talking of Trees*: 80–81. Lignum Vitae is the national flower of Jamaica; a native of continental tropical America and the Caribbean; used by the indigenous peoples of tropical America for medicinal

and sacred purposes and still in use as a "folk medicine" throughout the Caribbean. See Senior's entry on "Lignum Vitae" in *Encyclopedia of Jamaican Heritage*: 282–3.

345 Olive Senior, "Plants," *Gardening*: 62.

346 Olive Senior, "Osanyin: God of Herbalism", *Gardening*: 117.

347 See "Ode to Pablo Neruda," in *over the roofs* (92–104) in which Senior rediscovers the joy to be found in a poet's obligation to "call out" those responsible for violence, darkness, misery and "call in" those who have suffered, those who are lost. The thunder of calling out and the healing rain of calling in are central to the work of the poet.

348 Edward Said, "Speaking Truth to Power," in *Representations of the Intellectual* (New York: Vintage, 1994): 85–102.

349 Olive Senior, "Ode to Pablo Neruda," *over the roofs*: 100.

350 Olive Senior, "Ode to Pablo Neruda," *over the roofs*: 101.

351 Olive Senior, "Ode to Pablo Neruda," *over the roofs*: 101.

352 Olive Senior, "Oya: Goddess of the Wind," *Gardening*: 127.

353 This also recalls Brathwaite's phrase "tongued with the wind" (Kamau Brathwaite 1973, "Vèvè," in *Arrivants*: 265) and Guyanese-born black British poet John Agard's poem "Listen Mr Oxford don" in which he declaims "I only armed wit mih human breath/but human breath/is a dangerous weapon", (*Alternative Anthem*, Tarset: Bloodaxe Books, 2009: 16.) In recitation, Agard "breathes" the word "breath".

354 See my discussion of hurricane (in particular Hurricane Gilbert, 1988) in *Tracking the Literature of Tropical Weather* (New York & UK: Palgrave Macmillan, 2017): 251–269.

355 Kamau Brathwaite, *History of the Voice: The Development of Nation Language in Anglophone Caribbean Poetry* (London: New Beacon Books, 1984): 9–10.

356 Edouard Glissant, "Voices," in *Caribbean Discourse: Selected Essays*, trans. Michael Dash (Charlottesville: University Press of Virginia, 1999): 237.

357 Edouard Glissant, "Voices,": 237.

358 EB Garriott, "Forecasts and Warnings," in *Monthly Weather Review* (August, 1903): XXXI.8: 365.

359 Olive Senior, "Hurricane Watch," *Kunapipi* 34.2 (2012): 181.

360 Martha Beckwith [1929]. *Black Roadways: A Study of Jamaican Folk Life* (New York: Negro Universities Press, 1969).

361 BW Higman, *Jamaica Food: History Biology Culture* (Jamaica: University of the West Indies Press, 2008): 75.

362 Quoted by Michel de Certeau, "Annals of Everyday Life" in Michel de Certeau, Luce Giard & Pierre Mayol, *The Practice of Everyday Life*, Vol 2, trans Timothy Tomasik (Minneapolis: University of Minnesota Press, 1998): 3.

363 Michel de Certeau, Luce Giard & Pierre Mayol, *The Practice of Everyday Life*, Vol 2, trans Timothy Tomasik (Minneapolis: University of Minnesota Press, 1998): 3.

364 BW Higman, *Jamaica Food: History Biology Culture*. Jamaica: University of the West Indies Press, 2008, xvii–xviii.

365 Olive Senior, "Ode to Pablo Neruda," *over the roofs*: 102.

366 Olive Senior, *Encyclopedia of Jamaican Heritage*. St. Andrews: Twin Ginep Publishers, 2003: 134.

367 Olive Senior, *Encyclopedia of Jamaican Heritage*: 134.

368 Stuart Schwartz, *Sea of Storms: A History of Hurricanes in the Greater Caribbean* (Princeton: Princeton University Press, 2015): 5–9.

369 The words are Pablo Neruda's taken from one of the final stanzas in Senior's "Ode to Pablo Neruda": "And so, my trickster powers evolving, I'm leaning like you,/Pablo Neruda veteran tightrope walker, to swing more easily/*between joy and obligation*" (*over the roofs*: 103).

370 EB Garriott, "Forecasts and Warnings," in *Monthly Weather Review* (August, 1903): XXXI.8: 365.

371 "Percy Bysshe Shelley asks the wind to "Make me thy lyre, even as the forest is" in "Ode to the West Wind," (1820) in *Selected Poetry and Prose* (New York: Signet, New American Library, 1966): 212–215.

372 Olive Senior, "Colonial Girls School", *Talking of Trees*: 26-7.

373 See Olive Senior, "Colonial Girls School".

374 Sally Cameron, "Melbourne's CBD Trees Receive Thousands of Love Letters", citygreen: Urban Landscape Solutions, August 16, 2015, http://citygreen.com/blog/melbournes-cbd-trees-receive-thousands-of-love-letters/; James Rothwell, "Melbourne Inundated with Thousands of Love

Letters Addressed to the City's Trees," *The Telegraph*, 15 July 2015, https://www.telegraph.co.uk/news/worldnews/australiaandthepacific/australia/11740957/Melbourne-inundated-with-thousands-of-love-letters-addressed-to-the-citys-trees.html
Matthew Dunn, "People around the World have been Emailing Trees in Melbourne to Confess their Love," News.com.au, 17 July 2015, http://www.news.com.au/technology/environment/conservation/people-around-the-world-have-been-emailing-trees-in-melbourne-to-confess-their-love/news-story/e271b76b4524a998fee3b27d6d4b9bb3

375 Roger Graham Barry and Richard J Chorley, *Atmosphere, Weather and Climate* (London: Routledge, 2003).

376 Stephanie Pappas, "280-Million-Year-Old Fossil Forest Discovered in ... Antarctica," *Live Science*, 15 November 2017, https://www.livescience.com/60944-ancient-fossil-forest-discovered-in-antarctica.html

377 John Berger, *Ways of Seeing* (London: British Broadcasting Corporation and Penguin): 28.

378 David Attenborough, "Wild Crows Inhabiting the City Use it to their Advantage," YouTube, 12 February 2007, https://www.youtube.com/watch?v=BGPGknpq3e0

379 Ted Chiang, "The Great Silence" in *The Best American Short Stories 2016*, ed. Junot Diaz (New York: Houghton Mifflin Harcourt, 2016): 69–72.

380 Kathleen Stewart, "Atmospheric attunements," *Environment and Planning D: Society and Space*, vol. 29 (2011): 449.

381 Kathleen Stewart, *Ordinary Affects*, (Durham and London: Duke University Press, 2007): 59.

382 Anna Tsing, Swanson, H, Gan E & Bubandt, N (eds): *Arts of Living on a Damaged Planet*, (Minneapolis: University of Minnesota Press, 2017)

383 Margaret McFall-Ngai, "Noticing Microbial Worlds," in Tsing et al, *Arts of Living*: 66.

384 Scott Gilbert, "Holobiont by Birth", in Tsing et al, *Arts of Living*: 76.

385 See McFall-Ngai, "Noticing": 52.

386 See McFall-Ngai, "Noticing".

387 Julio Cortazar and Carol Dunlop, *Autonauts of the Cosmoroute*, (New York: Archipelago Books, 1983): 126.

388 Cortazar and Dunlop, *Autonauts:* 19.

389 Associated Press, "Peru to Take Legal Action over Greenpeace Stunt at Ancient Nazca Lines," *The Guardian*, 10 December 2014, https://www.theguardian.com/world/2014/dec/10/peru-legal-action-greenpeace-stunt-nazca-lines

390 Felix Guattari, *The Three Ecologies*, trans. Ian Pindar and Paul Sutton (London and New Brunswick: The Athlone Press, 2000): 66–67.

391 Maria Puig de la Bellacasa, "'Nothing Comes without Its World': Thinking with Care," *The Sociological Review* 60, no. 2 (2012): 197–216.

392 Puig de la Bellacasa, "Nothing Comes": 198.

393 Terry P Hughes et al., "Global warming transforms coral reef assemblages," *Nature*, vol. 556, (2018): 492–496, https://doi.org/10.1038/s41586-018-0041-2

394 Félix Guattari, *The Three Ecologies*, trans. Ian Pindar and Paul Sutton (London: Bloomsbury, 2014 [2000]), 17–47.

395 Pu Songling, *Strange Tales from a Chinese Studio*, trans. John Minford. (London: Penguin, 2006).

396 *Sugar vs the Reef?* (2014–19) is a collaboration between the authors. See Lucas Ihlein and Kim Williams, "About the Project," *Sugar vs the Reef?* Blog, http://www.sugar-vs-the-reef.net/about/.

397 *Walking Upstream: Waterways of the Illawarra* (2015–18) is a project by the authors in collaboration with Brogan Bunt. See Brogan Bunt, Lucas Ihlein and Kim Williams, *Walking Upstream: Waterways of the Illawarra* blog, http://walking-upstream.net.

398 Lucas Ihlein and Ian Milliss, "About this project," *The Yeomans Project*, http://yeomansproject.com/about-this-project/.

399 Graham Stirling and Simon Mattsson, "Intercropping sugarcane with sunflower and mixtures of plant species: effects on the soil biological community," *Proceedings of the Australian Society of Sugar Cane Technologists*, 40 (2018): 86–96.

400 Stephanie Affeldt, *Consuming Whiteness: Australian Racism and the 'White Sugar' campaign* (Berlin: Lit Verlag, 2014): 5.

401 Ross Gibson, *Seven Versions of an Australian Badland* (Brisbane: University of Queensland Press, 2008).

402 Brogan Bunt, Lucas Ihlein, and Kim Williams, *12 Creek Walks* (Wollongong: Leech Press, 2017): 6–7.

403 Grant Kester, *Conversation Pieces: Community and Communication in Modern Art* (Berkeley and Los Angeles: University of California Press, 2004): 8.

404 Anne Whiston Spirn, "Helen and Newton Harrison: The Art of Inquiry, Manifestation, and Enactment," in Harrison Studio, *The Time of the Force Majeure: After 45 Years Counterforce is on the Horizon*, (Munich: Prestel Verlag, 2016): 436.

405 Nato Thompson, *Living as Form: Socially Engaged Art from 1991-2011* (New York: Creative Time Books, 2012): 86.

406 Thompson, *Living as Form:* 19.

407 Kester, *Conversation Pieces*: 8.

408 Kester, *Conversation Pieces*: 10.

409 Pablo Helguera, *Education for Socially Engaged Art Practice: A Materials and Techniques Handbook*, (New York: Jorge Pinto Books, 2011): 5.

410 Harrison Studio, *Center for the Study of the Force Majeure*, (Santa Cruz: University of California, 2018): 6.

411 This passage refers to an actual helicopter journey we commissioned in collaboration with Hayden Griffiths of Phoenix Media, to produce an aerial video of the entire Allans Creek system. See Brogan Bunt, Lucas Ihlein and Kim Williams, "Wollongong Exhibition 2017–18," *Walking Upstream: Waterways of the Illawarra* blog, http://walking-upstream.net/wollongong-exhibition-2017-18/

412 Paul Martin and Mark Shepheard, "What is meant by the social licence?" in *Defending the Social Licence of Farming: Issues, Challenges and New Directions for Agriculture*, ed. Jacqueline Williams and Paul Martin (Collingwood: CSIRO Publishing, 2011): 3–12. Mark Tredinnick, "Days in the Plateau," *Kunapipi* 29, no. 2, (2007): 137.

References

ABC News. "Larsen C: Giant iceberg breaks away from ice shelf in Antarctica." 13 July 2017. http://www.abc.net.au/news/2017-07-12/huge-iceberg-breaks-away-from-antarctica-larsen-c-shelf/8703238.

Affeldt, Stefanie. *Consuming Whiteness: Australian Racism and the 'White Sugar' campaign*. Berlin, Munster, London, Vienna and Zurich: Lit Verlag, 2014.

Agard, John. *Alternative Anthem: Selected Poems*. Tarset: Bloodaxe Books, 2009.

Ahmed, Sara. "Happy Objects." In *The Affect Theory Reader*, edited by Melissa Gregg and Greg Seigworth, 29–51. Durham NC: Duke University Press, 2010.

Albrecht, Glenn. "The age of solastalgia." *The Conversation*, 7 August 2012. https://theconversation.com/the-age-of-solastalgia-8337.

Amazon. "Press release: Amazon.com Announces Third Quarter Sales up 34% to $43.7 Billion", 26 October 2017. https://archive.fo/UJ7GB

American Association for the Advancement of Science. "Did Mars' Magnetic Field Die with a Whimper or a Bang?" *Science*, 30 April 2009. https://www.sciencemag.org/news/2009/04/did-marss-magnetic-field-die-whimper-or-bang

Anderson, Ben. "Affective Atmospheres." *Emotion, Space and Society* 2, no. 2 (2009): 77–81.

Applin, Sally, and Michael Fischer. "Pervasive Computing in Time and Space: The Culture and Context of 'Place' Integration." In *International Conference on Intelligent Environments (IE'11)*, Nottingham Trent University, UK: IE, 2011. https://doi.org/10.1109/IE.2011.65

Applin, Sally, and Michael Fischer. "Thing Theory: Connecting Humans to Location-Aware Smart Environments." In *Third International Workshop on Location Awareness for Mixed and Dual Reality LAMDa'13*, Santa Monica, CA: LAMDa, 2013. https://web.archive.org/web/20180519063009/http://www.dfki.de/LAMDa/2013/accepted/13_ApplinFischer.pdf

Åsberg, Cecilia. "A Thousand Tiny Anthropocenes: Worlding Troubles from Swedish Feminist Environmental Humanities Perspectives." Keynote Lecture presented at *Feminist, Queer, Anticolonial Propositions for Hacking the Anthropocene*, Sydney University, Sydney, 8 April 2016.

Associated Press. "Peru to Take Legal Action over Greenpeace Stunt at Ancient Nazca Lines." *The Guardian*, 10 December 2014. https://www.theguardian.com/world/2014/dec/10/peru-legal-action-greenpeace-stunt-nazca-lines

Attenborough, David. "Wild Crows Inhabiting the City Use it to their Advantage." YouTube, 12 February 2007. https://www.youtube.com/watch?v=BGPGknpq3e0

Attenborough, David. "Climate Change is the Major Challenge Facing the World." *The Independent*, 23 May 2006. http://www.independent.co.uk/environment/attenborough-climate-change-is-the-major-challenge-facing-the-world-479459.html

Avibase: The World Bird Database. "Welcome to Avibase." https://avibase.bsc-eoc.org/avibase.jsp?lang=ENandpg=home

Avoca Bi-Centenary Committee. *Echoes Through the Mist: A History of the Avoca District*. Avoca NSW: Avoca Bi-Centenary Committee, 1988.

Ballard, Susan. "New Ecological Sympathies: Contemporary Art and Species Extinction" *Environmental Humanities* 9 no.2 (November 2017): 255–279. https://doi.org/10.1215/22011919-4215229

Ballard, Susan. "Stretching Out: Species Extinction and Planetary Aesthetics in Contemporary Art." *ANZJA Australia and New Zealand Journal of Art* 17 no.1 (August 2017): 2–16.

Bardon, Jane. "McArthur River mine's burning waste rock pile sparks health, environmental concerns among Gulf of Carpentaria Aboriginal groups." *The Guardian*, 27 July 2014. http://www.abc.net.au/news/2014-07-27/mcarthur-river-mine-gulf-of-carpentaria-anger-smoke-plume/5625484.

Bardon, Jane. "The race to avert disaster at the NT's McArthur River Mine Friday." *Background Briefing, ABC Radio National*, 12 February 2016. http://www.abc.net.au/radionational/programs/backgroundbriefing/the-race-to-avert-disaster-at-the-nts-mcarthur-river-mine/7159504.

Bardon, Jane. "Darwin Festival: The power and politics of Indigenous anti-mine art." *ABC News* 16 August 2017. http://www.abc.net.au/news/2017-08-16/darwin-festival-power-and-politics-of-indigenous-anti-mine-art/8810290.

Barry, Roger Graham, and Richard J. Chorley. *Atmosphere, Weather and Climate*. London: Routledge, 2003.

Barthes, Roland. *Camera Lucida: Reflections on Photography*. New York: Hill and Wang, 1981.

Bateson, Gregory. *Mind and Nature: a Necessary Unity*. New York: EP Dutton, 1979.

Beck, John. "The Call of the Anthropocene." *Cultural Politics* 10, no. 3 (2014): 404–414.

Beckwith, Martha. *Black Roadways: A Study of Jamaican Folk Life*. New York: Negro Universities Press, 1969 [1929].

Benjamin, Walter. "To the Planetarium" [1928]. In *One-Way Street*, edited by Michael W. Jennings, 58–59. Translated by E.F.N. Jephcott. Cambridge, Massachusetts: The Belknap Press, 2016.

Bennett, Jane. *Vibrant Matter: A Political Ecology of Things*. Durham and London: Duke University Press, 2010.

Berardi, Franco. *The Soul at Work: From Alienation to Autonomy*. Translated by Francesca Cadel and Giuseppina Mecchia. Los Angeles: Semiotext(e), 2009.

Berardi, Franco. *After the Future*. Edited by Gary Genosko and Nicholas Thorburn. Edinburgh: AK Press, 2011.

Berger, John. *Ways of Seeing*. London: British Broadcasting Corporation and Penguin.

Bilska, Elżbieta, Jan Nalaskowski. "The Cult of the Virgin Mary outside Poland." *Peregrinus Cracoviensis*, no. 3 (1996): 191–201.

Blake, William. *The Selected Poems of William Blake*, edited by Bruce Woodcock. Ware, Hertfordshire: Wordsworth Editions, 1994.

Bogost, Ian. *Alien Phenomenology, or What It's Like to Be a Thing*. Minneapolis: University of Minnesota Press, 2012.

Bogue, Ronald. "Gilles Deleuze: The Aesthetics of Force." In *Deleuze: A Critical Reader*, edited by Paul Patton, 257-269. Oxford and Cambridge: Blackwell Publishers, 2003.

Böhme, Gernot. "Atmosphere as the fundamental concept of a new aesthetics." *Thesis Eleven* 36, no. 1 (1993): 113–126.

Böhme, Gernot. *The Aesthetics of Atmospheres*. Edited by Jean-Paul Thibaud. London: Routledge, 2017.

Bordeleau, Erik. "Bruno Latour and the Miraculous Present of Enunciation." In *Breaking the Spell: Contemporary Realism Under Discussion*, edited by Anna Longo and Sarah de Sanctis, 155–167. Milan: Mimesis International, 2015.

Borges, Jorge Luis. *The Book of Imaginary Beings*. Translated by Andrew Hurley, London: Penguin Books, 2005.

Boscacci, Louise. "Wit(h)nessing." *Environmental Humanities* 10, no. 1 (2018): 343–347. https://doi.org/10.1215/22011919-4385617.

Boscacci, Louise. "The Trace of An Affective Object Encounter: A picture postcard, its provocations, and processual becomings." PhD diss., University of Wollongong, 2016. http://ro.uow.edu.au/theses/4725.

Bostedt, Göran. "Reindeer Husbandry, the Swedish market for Reindeer meat, and the Chernobyl effects." *Agricultural Economics* 26, no. 3 (December 2001): 217–226.

Bradshaw, Don, and Jess Reid, "Bees Give up searching for food when we degrade their land." *University News*, 8 February 2017. http://www.news.uwa.edu.au/201702089380/international/bees-give-searching-food-when-we-degrade-their-land

Brathwaite, Kamau. *History of the Voice: The Development of Nation Language in Anglophone Caribbean Poetry*. London: New Beacon Books, 1984.

Brathwaite, Kamau. *Mother Poem*. Oxford: Oxford University Press, 1977.

Brathwaite, Kamau. *The Arrivants: A New World Trilogy*. Oxford: Oxford University Press, 1973.

Braudel, Fernand. *Civilization and Capitalism 15th–18th Century, Vol. II: The Wheels of Commerce*. Translated by Sian Reynolds. London: Collins, 1982.

Brunetti, Michele, Maurizio Maugeri Fabio Monti and Teresa Nanni. "Temperature and precipitation variability in Italy in the last two centuries from homogenised instrumental time series." *International Journal of Climatology* 26, no. 3 (January 2006): 345–381.

Bryant, Levi. "Wilderness Ontology." In *Preternatural*, edited by Celina Jeffery, 19–26. Brooklyn: Punctum Books, 2011.

Bryant, Levi, Nick Srnicek, and Graham Harman. "Towards a Speculative Philosophy." In *The Speculative Turn: Continental Materialism and Realism*, edited by Levi Bryant, Nick Srnicek and Graham Harman, 1–18. Melbourne: re.press, 2011.

Buchanan, Ian, and Lorna Collins, eds. *Deleuze and the Schizoanalysis of Visual Art*. London and New York: Bloomsbury Publishing, 2014.

Calvino, Italo. *Six Memos for the Next Millennium*. London: Vintage Press, 1996.

Cameron, Sally. "Melbourne's CBD Trees Receive Thousands of Love Letters." citygreen: Urban Landscape Solutions, August 16, 2015. http://citygreen.com/blog/melbournes-cbd-trees-receive-thousands-of-love-letters/

Carlin, David. "The Essay in the Anthropocene: Towards Entangled Nonfiction." *TEXT Journal* Special Issue No. 39, *The Essay* (April 2017). http://www.textjournal.com.au/speciss/issue39/Carlin.pdf

Carpenter, J. R. *The Gathering Cloud*. Axminster: Uniform Books, 2017.

Carrington, Damian. "Ozone Layer Not Recovering Over Populated Areas, Scientists Warn." *The Guardian*, 6 February 2018. https://www.theguardian.com/environment/2018/feb/06/ozone-layer-not-recovering-over-populated-areas-scientists-warn

Carrington, Damian. "Plastic fibres found in tap water around the world, study reveals." *The Guardian*, 6 September 2017. https://www.theguardian.com/environment/2017/sep/06/plastic-fibres-found-tap-water-around-world-study-reveals

Carson, Rachel. *Silent Spring*. London: Penguin Classics, 2000 [1962].

Carson, Rachel. *The Sense of Wonder*. New York: HarperCollins, 1998 [1965].

Ceballos, Gerardo, Paul R. Ehrlich, Anthony D. Barnosky, Andrés García, Robert M. Pringle, and Todd M. Palmer. "Accelerated modern human-induced species losses: Entering the sixth mass extinction." *Science Advances* 1, no. 5 (2015) e1400253. https://doi.org/10.1126/sciadv.1400253

Chandler, Timothy. "Reading Atmospheres: The Ecocritical Potential of Gernot Böhme's Aesthetic Theory of Nature." *Interdisciplinary Studies in Literature and Environment* 18, no. 3 (2011): 553–568. https://doi.org/10.1093/isle/isr079

Chiang, Ted. "The Great Silence." In *The Best American Short Stories 2016*, edited by Junot Diaz, 69-72. New York: Houghton Mifflin Harcourt, 2016.

Choi, Charles. "First Asteroid Companion of Earth Discovered at Last." *Scientific American*, July 27, 2011. https://archive.fo/6EBGd

Clough, Patricia Ticineto, and Jean Halley, eds. *The Affective Turn: Theorizing the Social*. Durham NC: Duke University Press, 2007.

Collett, Anne, Russell McDougall, and Sue Thomas. *Tracking the Literature of Tropical Weather: Typhoons, Hurricanes, and Cyclones*. New York and London: Palgrave Macmillan, 2017.

Commonwealth of Australia Bureau of Meteorology. "Indigenous Weather knowledge." http://www.bom.gov.au/iwk/dharawal/.

Compound Interest. "The Atmosphere of the Solar System." http://www.compoundchem.com/2014/07/25/planetatmospheres/

Connors, Martin, Paul Wiegert, and Christian Veillet. "Earth's Trojan asteroid." *Nature*, no. 475 (July 2011): 481–483.

Coole, Diana. "From Within the Midst of Things: New Sensibility, New Alchemy, and the Renewal of Critical Theory." In *Realism, Materialism, Art*, edited by Christophe Cox, Jenny Jaskey, and Suhail Malik, 41-46. New York and Berlin: Bard College and Sternberg Press, 2015.

Cortazar, Julio, and Carol Dunlop. *Autonauts of the Cosmoroute*. New York: Archipelago Books, 1983.

Cox, Christophe, Jenny Jaskey, and Suhail Malik, eds. *Realism, Materialism, Art*. New York and Berlin: Center for Curatorial Studies, Bard College, Sternberg Press, 2015.

Dalby, Liza. *East Wind Melts the Ice: A Memoir through the Seasons*. London: Chatto and Windus, 2007.

The Dark Mountain Project. *Walking on Lava: Selected Works for Uncivilised Times*. White River Junction VT: Chelsea Green Publishing, 2017.

Daston, Lorraine. *Things That Talk: object lessons from art and science*. New York: Zone Books, 2004.

Daston, Lorraine, and Peter Galison. *Objectivity*. New York: Zone Books, 2007.

Daston, Lorraine, and Katharine Park. *Wonders and the Order of Nature, 1150 - 1750*. New York: Zone Books, 1998.

Davidson, Helen. "'They'll get rich and go': Glencore's McArthur River mine may take 300 years to clean up," *The Guardian*, May 15, 2017.

https://www.theguardian.com/australia-news/2017/may/15/theyll-get-rich-and-go-glencores-mcarthur-river-mine-could-take-300-years-to-clean-up.

Davidson, Helen. "Adam Giles: 'emotional' mine protesters need to have its benefits explained." *The Guardian*, December 4, 2014. https://www.theguardian.com/australia-news/2014/dec/04/adam-giles-emotional-mine-protesters-need-to-have-its-benefits-explained.

Davidson, Jane. "Fish Tales: Attributing the First Illustration of a Fossil Shark's Tooth to Richard Verstegan (1605) and Nicolas Steno (1667)." *Proceedings of the Academy of Natural Sciences of Philadelphia* 150, no. 14, (April 2000): 329–44.

de Certeau, Michel de, Luce Giard and Pierre Mayol. *The Practice of Everyday Life*, Vol 2. Translated by Timothy Tomasik. Minneapolis: University of Minnesota Press, 1998.

Deleuze, Gilles. *Difference and Repetition*. Translated by Paul Patton. London: The Athlone Press, 1994 [1968].

Demos, TJ. *Against the Anthropocene: Visual Culture and Environment Today*. Berlin: Sternberg Press, 2017.

Department of Conservation Te Papa Atawhai. "Royal Cam: Live Stream and Highlights." http://www.doc.govt.nz/royalcam

DiNitto, Rachel. "Return of the 'Zuihitsu': Print Culture, Modern Life, and Heterogeneous Narrative in Prewar Japan." *Harvard Journal of Asiatic Studies* 64, no. 2 (2004): 251-290.

Dunn, Matthew. "People around the World have been Emailing Trees in Melbourne to Confess their Love." News.com.au, 17 July 2015. http://www.news.com.au/technology/environment/conservation/people-around-the-world-have-been-emailing-trees-in-melbourne-to-confess-their-love/news-story/e271b76b4524a998fee3b27d6d4b9bb3

Eckersley, Andrea. "The Event of Painting." In *Deleuze and the Schizoanalysis of Visual Art*, edited by Ian Buchanan and Lorna Collins: 205–225. London and New York: Bloomsbury Publishing, 2014.

Eliade, Mircea. *Cosmos and History: The Myth of the Eternal Return*. Translated by Willard Trask, New York: Harper Torchbooks, 1959.

Eliade, Mircea. *The Sacred and the Profane: the nature of religion*. Translated by Willard Trask, New York: Harcourt, Brace and World, 1959.

Eliasson, Olafur. "Playing with Space and Light." TED Talk 2009. https://www.ted.com/talks/olafur_eliasson_playing_with_space_and_light.

Engberg, Juliana. "Everything Starts With A Storm." In *Exhibition catalogue*, Hobart: Tasmanian Museum and Art Gallery, 2016.

Entwisle, Tim. "Old Fan Palms inspire Johanns." *Talking Plants* September, 2012. http://talkingplants.blogspot.com.au/2012/09/old-fan-palms-inspire-johanns.html

Eriksen, Christine et al. "Children Aren't Liabilities in Disasters; they can help if we let them." *The Conversation*, April 5, 2018. https://theconversation.com/children-arent-liabilities-in-disasters-they-can-help-if-we-let-them-93794

Flinders, Matthew. *Matthew Flinders' Narrative of Tom Thumb's Cruise to Canoe Rivulet*. Edited by Keith Bowden. Brighton, Victoria: South Eastern Historical Association, 1952.

Flinders, Matthew. *Matthew Flinders: Personal letters from an extraordinary* life. Edited by Paul Brunton. Sydney: Hordern House, 2002.

Garrard, Greg, Gary Handwer, and Sabine Wilke "Imagining Anew: Challenges of Representing the Anthropocene." *Environmental Humanities* 5, no. 1 (2014): 149–153.

Garriott, E.B. "Forecasts and Warnings." *Monthly Weather Review* XXXI.8 (August, 1903): 365–6. http://www.aoml.noaa.gov/hrd/hurdat/mwr_pdf/1903.pdf

Ghosh, Amitav. *The Great Derangement: Climate Change and the Unthinkable*. Chicago and London: University of Chicago Press, 2016.

Gibson, Ross. *Seven Versions of an Australian Badland*, Brisbane: University of Queensland Press, 2008.

Gideon, Manning and Cynthia Klestinec, eds. *Professors, Physicians and Practices in the History of Medicine : Essays in Honor of Nancy Siraisi*. Cham: Springer International Publishing, 2017.

Gilbert, Scott. "Holobiont by Birth: Multilineage Individuals as the Concretion of Cooperative Processes." In *Arts of Living on a Damaged Planet*, edited by Anna Tsing, Heather Swanson, Elaine Gan, and Nils Bubandt, 73–89. Minneapolis: University of Minnesota Press, 2017.

Glenza, Jessica. "Sea salt around the world is contaminated by plastic, studies show." *The Guardian*, 9 September 2017. https://amp.theguardian.com/environment/2017/sep/08/sea-salt-around-world-contaminated-by-plastic-studies

Glissant, Edouard. *Caribbean Discourse: Selected Essays*. Translated by Michael Dash. Charlottesville: University Press of Virginia, 1999.

Goethe, Johann Wolfgang von. "The works of J.W. von Goethe volume 12, letters from Italy, Part 111 'From Verona to Venice'; 'Padua, Sept. 27 [1786]'", https://en.wikisource.org/wiki/The_Works_of_J._W._von_Goethe/Volume_12/Letters_from_Italy/Part_III

Goethe, Johann Wolfgang von. *The Metamorphosis of Plants*. Introduction and photography by Gordon L. Miller. Cambridge, Massachusetts and London, England: MIT Press, 2009.

Golda, Agnieszka. "Feeling: sensing the affectivity of emotional politics through textiles." In *The Handbook of Textile Culture*, edited by H. Clark, J. Jefferies and D. Wood Conroy, 401–415. London: Bloomsbury Publishing, 2016.

The Greenbench Ltd. "Slow Flow – Te Ia Kōrero." http://www.greenbench.org/project/slowflow/

Grosz, Elizabeth. *Chaos, Territory, Art: Deleuze and the Framing of the Earth*. New York and Chichester: Columbia University Press, 2008.

Grynsztejn, Madeleine, Daniel Birnbaum, and Michael Speaks. *Olafur Eliasson*. London: Phaidon Press International, 2002.

Guattari, Félix. *The Three Ecologies*. Translated by Ian Pindar and Paul Sutton. London: Bloomsbury, 2014 [2000].

Haraway, Donna. "Symbiogenesis, Sympoiesis, and Art Activisms for staying with the Trouble." In *Arts of Living on a Damaged Planet*, edited by Anna Tsing, Heather Swanson, Elaine Gan, and Nils Bubandt, 25–50. Minneapolis: University of Minnesota Press, 2017.

Haraway, Donna. *Staying with the Trouble: Making Kin in the Chthulucene*. Durham: Duke University Press, 2016.

Haraway, Donna. "Tentacular Thinking: Anthropocene, Capitalocene, Chthulucene." *e-flux*, no. 75 (September 2016): http://www.e-flux.com/journal/75/67125/tentacular-thinking-anthropocene-capitalocene-chthulucene/

Haraway, Donna. *The Companion Species Manifesto: Dogs, People and Significant Otherness*. Chicago: University of Chicago Press, 2003.

Haraway, Donna. "Situated Knowledges: The Science Question in Feminism and the Privilege of Partial Perspective." *Feminist Studies* 14, no. 3, Autumn (1988): 575–99.

Harris, Alexandra. *Weatherland: Writers and Artists under the English Skies*. London: Thames and Hudson, 2015.

Harrison, Helen Mayer. and Harrison, Newton. *The Time of the Force Majeure*, Munich, London and New York: Prestel, 2016.

Harrison Studio. *Centre for the Study of the Force Majeure*. Santa Cruz: University of California, 2018.

Hawkins, Harriet, and Kanngieser, Anja. "Artful Climate Change Communication: Overcoming Abstractions, Insensibilities and Distances." *WIREs Climate Change* 8, no. 5 (September/October 2017). http://dx.doi.org/10.1002/wcc.472

Helguera, Pablo. *Education for Socially Engaged Art Practice: A Materials and Techniques Handbook*. New York: Jorge Pinto Books, 2011.

Heppner, James. "A study of relationships between the aurora borealis and the geomagnetic disturbances caused by electric currents in the ionosphere." PhD diss., California Institute of Technology, 1954.

Hern, Alex. "Amazon gadget hijacks owner's heating after hearing radio report." *The Guardian*, 11 March 2016. https://web.archive.org/web/20180501050230/https://www.theguardian.com/technology/2016/mar/11/amazon-gadget-echo-hijacks-owner-heating-radio-report

Higman, B.W. *Jamaica Food: History Biology Culture*. Jamaica: University of the West Indies Press, 2008.

Hooke, Roger. "On the Efficacy of Humans as Geomorphic Agents." *GSA Today (Publication of the Geological Society of America)* 4, no.9 (September 1994): 217; 224–225.

Hughes, Terry P. et al., "Global warming transforms coral reef assemblages." *Nature* 556 (2018): 492–496, https://doi.org/10.1038/s41586-018-0041-2

Huyssen, Andreas. *Twilight Memories: Marking Time in a Culture of Amnesia*. New York: Routledge, 1995.

Ihlein, Lucas, and Kim Williams. "Sugar vs the Reef?" http://www.sugar-vs-the-reef.net/

Ihlein, Lucas and Ian Milliss. "About this project." http://yeomansproject.com/about-this-project/

Ingold, Tim. *Lines: A Brief History*. London and New York: Routledge, 2007.

Intergovernmental Panel on Climate Change (IPCC). *Climate Change 2014: Synthesis Report, Contribution of Working Groups I, II and III to the Fifth Assessment Report of the Intergovernmental Panel on Climate Change*, edited by Core Writing Team, Rajendra K. Pachauri and Leo A. Meyer. Geneva: IPCC, 2014. http://ar5-syr.ipcc.ch/ipcc/ipcc/resources/pdf/IPCC_SynthesisReport.pdf.

The IUCN Red List of Threatened Species. http://www.iucnredlist.org/

Kahn, Brian. "The world passes 400PPM Threshold. Permanently." *Climate Central* (27 September 2016). http://www.climatecentral.org/news/world-passes-400-ppm-threshold-permanently-20738

Kahn, Brian. "We Just Breached the 410 Parts Per Million Threshold." *Climate Central*, (20 April 2017). http://www.climatecentral.org/news/we-just-breached-the-410-parts-per-million-threshold-21372.

Keats, John. "To Percy Shelley." http://www.john-keats.com/briefe/160820.htm

Keeling, Charles D, SC Piper, RB Bacastow, M Whalen, TP Whorf, M Heimann and HA Meijer. "Atmospheric CO_2 and 13 CO_2 exchange with the terrestrial biosphere and oceans from 1978 to 2000: observations and carbon cycle implications." In *A History of Atmospheric CO2 and its effects on Plants and Animals and Ecosystems*, edited by JR Ehleringer, TE Cerlinbg, and MD Dearing, 83–113. New York: Springer Verlag, 2005.

Keeling, Charles D. "Rewards and Penalties of Monitoring the Earth." *Annual Review of Energy and the Environment* 23 (November 1998): 25–82.

Kester, Grant. *Conversation Pieces: Community and Communication in Modern Art*. Berkeley and Los Angeles: University of California Press, 2004.

Kolbert, Elizabeth. *The Sixth Extinction: An Unnatural History*. London: Bloomsbury, 2014.

Kosinski, Jerzy. *Painted Bird*. New York: Modern Library, 1970 [1965].

Latour, Bruno. "Agency at the time of the Anthropocene." *New Literary History* 45, no. 1 (2014): 1–18.

Latour, Bruno. "What is iconoclash? Or is there a world beyond the image wars?" In *Iconoclash: Beyond the Image Wars in Science, Religion, and Art*, edited by Bruno Latour and Peter Weibel, 14–37. Cambridge, MA: MIT Press, 2002.

Latour, Bruno. In conversation with Heather Davis. "Diplomacy in the Face of Gaia." In *Art in the Anthropocene: Encounters Among Aesthetics, Politics, Environments and Epistemologies* edited by Heather Davis and Etienne Turpin, 43–56. London: Open Humanities Press, 2015.

Lear, Linda. *Rachel Carson: Witness for Nature*. New York: Mariner Books, 1997.

Lear, Linda. *Lost Woods: The Discovered Writing of Rachel Carson*. Boston: Beacon Press, 1999.

Leopold, Aldo. *A Sand County Almanac*. New York: Ballantine, 1966.

Leslie, Esther. "Walter Benjamin: Traces of Craft." *Journal of Design History* no. 1 (1998): 5–13.

Lewis, Kaylee. "30 Years on, Norway's radioactive reindeer are a stark reminder of Chernobyl legacy." *Independent*, 1 March 2016. https://www.independent.co.uk/news/world/europe/chernobyl-radioactive-reindeer-norway-a6903571.html

Lynes, Krista Geneviève and World of Matter. "World of Matter." In *Elemental: An Arts and Ecology Reader*, edited by James Brady, 109–131. Manchester: Gaia, 2016.

Maclear, Kyo. *Bird Art Life and Death: A Field Guide to the Small and Significant*. London: 4th Estate, 2017.

MacFarling Meure, C. et al. "Law Dome CO_2, CH_4 and N_2O ice core records extended to 2000 years BP." *Geophysical Research Letters* 33, no. 14 (21 July 2006). https://doi.org/10.1029/2006GL026152

Maniura, Robert. *Pilgrimage to Images in the Fifteenth Century: The Origins of the Cult of Our Lady of Czestochowa*. Suffolk: Boydell Press, 2004.

Martin, Craig. "The Invention of Atmosphere." *Studies in History and Philosophy of Science*. 52 (August 2015): 44–54. https://doi.org/10.1016/j.shpsa.2015.05.007.

Martin, Paul, and Mark Shepheard. "What is meant by the social licence?" In *Defending the Social Licence of Farming: Issues, Challenges and New Directions for Agriculture*, edited by Jacqueline Williams and Paul Martin, 3–12. Collingwood: CSIRO Publishing, 2011.

Martin, Mark, ed. *I'm with the Bears: Short Stories from a Damaged Planet*. London: Verso, 2011.

Massumi, Brian. *What Animals Teach Us About Politics*. Durham and London: Duke University Press, 2014.

Massumi, Brian. "The Autonomy of Affect." In *Deleuze: A Critical Reader*, edited by Paul Patton, 217–239. Oxford, UK and Cambridge, Massachusetts: Blackwell Publishers, 1996.

Massumi, Brian. *A User's Guide to Capitalism and Schizophrenia: Deviations from Deleuze and Guattari*. Cambridge: MIT Press, 1992.

McFall-Ngai, Margaret, "Noticing Microbial Worlds: The Postmodern Synthesis in Biology" In *Arts of Living on a Damaged Planet*, edited by Anna Tsing, Heather Swanson, Elaine Gan, and Nils Bubandt, 51–69. Minneapolis: University of Minnesota Press, 2017.

McKinnon, Catherine. "Writing white, writing black, and events at Canoe Rivulet." *TEXT: Journal of Writing and Writing Programs* 16, no. 2 (2012): 1–17.

Meyrink, Gustav. *The Golem*. Translated by Madge Pemberton, Boston: Houghton Mifflin, 1928.

Miles, Richard. "Earth's first 'Trojan' asteroid discovered." *Journal of the British Astronomical Association* 121, no. 5 (2011): 264.

Millan, Elizabeth. "The Quest for the Seeds of Eternal Growth: Goethe and Humboldt's Presentation of Nature." *Goethe Yearbook XVIII* (2011): 97.

Miller, Adam. *Speculative Grace: Bruno Latour and Object-Oriented Theology*. New York: Fordham University Press, 2013.

Minelli, Alessandro. ed., *The Botanical Garden of Padua 1545–1995*. Marsilio: Venice, 1995.

Mitew, Teodor. "Do Objects Dream of an Internet of Things?" *Fibreculture Journal* 23, (2014): https://web.archive.org/web/20180501045637/http://twentythree.fibreculturejournal.org/fcj-168-do-objects-dream-of-an-internet-of-things/

Moen, Jon. "Climate Change: Effects on the Ecological Basis for Reindeer Husbandry in Sweden." *AMBIO: A Journal of the Human Environment* 37, no. 4 (2008): 304–311.

Monroe, Robert. "What Does 400 ppm Look Like?" *Scripps Institution of Oceanography*, December 3, 2013. https://scripps.ucsd.edu/programs/keelingcurve/2013/12/03/what-does-400-ppm-look-like/.

Moore, Jason W. "Introduction: Anthropocene or Capitalocene? Nature, History, and the Crisis of Capitalism." In *Anthropocene or Capitalocene? Nature, History, and the Crisis of Capitalism*, edited by Jason W. Moore, 1–13. Oakland CA: PM Press, 2016.

Mosley, Stephen. "Environmental History of Air Pollution and Protection." In *The Basic Environmental History*, edited by M. Agnoletti and S. Neri Serneri, 149–169. Basel: Springer, 2014.

Murdoch, Iris. *Metaphysics as a Guide to Morals*. London: Random House, 2003.

My Yellowstone Park.com. "Wolf Reintroduction Changes Ecosystem: June 22, 2011." https://www.yellowstonepark.com/things-to-do/wolf-reintroduction-changes-ecosystem

NASA. "Climate Change: How do we know?." *Global Climate Change: Vital Signs of the Planet* 16 May 2018. https://climate.nasa.gov/evidence/

Neimanis, Astrida, and Rachel L. Walker. "Weathering: Climate Change and the "Thick Time" of Transcorporeality." *Hypatia* 29 (2014): 558–575. https://doi.org/10.1111/hypa.12064.

Niedźwiedź, Anna. *The Image and the Figure: Our Lady of Czestochowa in Polish Culture and Popular Religion*. Kraków: Jagiellonian University Press, 2010.

Nichols, Shaun. "TV anchor says live on-air 'Alexa, order me a dollhouse' – guess what happens next." *The Register*, 7 January 2017. https://web.archive.org/web/20180501045959/http://www.theregister.co.uk/2017/01/07/tv_anchor_says_alexa_buy_me_a_dollhouse_and_she_does/?mt=1483795705927

Nixon, Rob. *Slow Violence and the Environmentalism of the Poor*. Cambridge Mass.: Harvard Press, 2013.

Noë, Alva. *Strange Tools: Art and Human Nature*. New York: Hill and Wang, 2015.

Norton, Melinda A., Kris French, and Andrew W. Claridge. "Habitat associations of the long-nosed potoroo (*Potorous tridactylus*) at multiple spatial scales." *Australian Journal of Zoology* 58, no. 5 (2011): 303–316. https://doi.org/10.1071/ZO10042

NSW Government Department of Primary Industries. "Feeding Sugar to Honey Bees." http://www.dpi.nsw.gov.au/__data/assets/pdf_file/0018/532260/Feeding-sugar-to-honey-bees.pdf

NSW Government: Transport Roads and Maritime Services. "Oceanlinx wave generator." http://www.rms.nsw.gov.au/projects/illawarra/oceanlinx/index.html

Nuccitelli, Dana. "'The atmosphere is being radicalized' by climate change." *The Guardian*, 24 October 2016. https://www.theguardian.com/environmentclimate- consensus-97-per-cent/2016/oct/24/the-atmosphere-is-being-radicalized-by-climate-change.

Obrist, Hans Ulrich. *Olafur Eliasson*. The Conversation Series. Köln: Verlag der Buchhandlung Walther König, 2008.

Oceanlinx. "Current projects." https://web.archive.org/web/20080610110251/http://www.oceanlinx.com:80/Currentprojects.asp

Oceanlinx. "A note from the new developers of the Oceanlinx technology." http://www.oceanlinx.com/

Oleszkiewicz-Peralba, Małgorzata. *The Black Madonna in Latin America and Europe: Tradition and Transformation*. Albuquerque: University of New Mexico Press, 2007.

Oremus, Will. "Terrifyingly Convenient." *Slate*, 3 April 2016. https://web.archive.org/web/20180501050123/http://www.slate.com/articles/technology/cover_story/2016/04/alexa_cortana_and_siri_aren_t_novelties_anymore_they_re_our_terrifyingly.html

Organ, Michael, and Carol Speechley. "Illawarra Aborigines." In *A History of Wollongong*, edited by Jim Hagan and Andrew Wells: 7–22. University of Wollongong Press: Wollongong, 1997.

Ornithology: The Science of Birds. "Extinct Birds." https://ornithology.com/extinct-birds/

O'Sullivan, Simon. "From Aesthetics to the Abstract Machine: Deleuze, Guattari and Contemporary Art Practice." In *Deleuze and Contemporary Art*, edited by Stephen Zepke and Simon O'Sullivan, 189–207. Edinburgh: Edinburgh University Press, 2010.

O'Sullivan, Simon. *Art Encounters: Deleuze and Guattari*. Basingstoke and New York: Palgrave Macmillan, 2006.

Paglen, Trevor. "Geographies of Time (The Last Pictures)." In *In the Holocene*, edited by João Ribas, 25–33. Cambridge Massachusetts and Berlin: MIT List Visual Arts Centre and Sternberg Press, 2014.

Palmer, Annie. "'There's a good chance I get murdered tonight': Terrified Amazon Echo users reveal Alexa has been emitting 'bone chilling' laughs at random and is ignoring their commands." *Daily Mail*, 7 March 2018. https://archive.fo/E78ls

Paoletti, Elena, Tommaso Bardelli, Gianluca Giovannini et al. "Air Quality impact of an urban park over time." *Procedia Environmental Sciences* 4 (2011). http://www.sciencedirect.com/science/article/pii/S1878029611000284

Paoletti, Elena. "Ozone and Urban Forests in Italy." *Environmental Pollution* 157, no.5 (May 2009): 1506–1512.

Pappas, Stephanie. "280-Million-Year-Old Fossil Forest Discovered in ... Antarctica." *Live Science*, 15 November 2017. https://www.livescience.com/60944-ancient-fossil-forest-discovered-in-antarctica.html

Parsons, Paul, and Gail Dixon. *The Periodic Table: A Visual Guide to the Elements*. London: Quercus, 2014.

Patton, Paul, ed. *Deleuze: A Critical Reader*. Oxford and Cambridge: Blackwell Publishers, 1996.

Pearman, Graeme I., Paul J. Fraser and John R. Garratt "CSIRO High-precision Measurement of Atmospheric CO_2 Concentration in Australia. Part 2: Cape Grim, Surface CO_2 Measurements and Carbon Cycle Modelling." *Historical Records of Australian Science* 28, no. 2 (October 19, 2017): 126–139. https://doi.org/10.1071/HR17015

Plumwood, Val. "Nature in the Active Voice." *Australian Humanities Review* 46 (2009): 113–129.

Plumwood, Val. "Shadow Places and the Politics of Dwelling." *Australian Humanities Review* 44 (2008): 139–50.

Plumwood, Val. *Feminism and the Mastery of Nature*. London: Routledge, 1993.

Priddel, David, Nicholas Carlile, and Robert Wheeler. "Establishment of a new breeding colony of Gould's petrel (*Pterodroma leucoptera leucoptera*) through the creation of artificial nesting habitats and the translocation of nestlings." *Biological Conservation* 128, (2015): 553–563.

Probyn-Rapsey, Fiona. "Review Article: Multispecies Mourning: Thom van Dooren's *Flight Ways: Life and Loss at the Edge of Extinction*." *Animal Studies Journal* 3, no. 2 (2014): 4–16.

Pu, Songling. *Strange Tales from a Chinese Studio*. Translated by John Minford. London: Penguin, 2006.

Puig de la Bellacasa, Maria. "'Nothing Comes without Its World': Thinking with Care." *The Sociological Review* 60, no. 2 (2012): 197–216. https://doi.org/10.1111/j.1467-954X.2012.02070.x

Rhoades, Hannibal, and Tero Mustonen. "Arctic indigenous Peoples Leading the Way in Ecological Restoration and Climate Resilience." *Intercontinental Cry*, 3 April 2017. https://intercontinentalcry.org/arctic-indigenous-peoples-leading-way-ecological-restoration-climate-resilience-says-major-new-study/

Riebeek, Holli. "Paleoclimatology: The Ice Core Record" in NASA Earth Observatory, 19 December 2005. https://earthobservatory.nasa.gov/Features/Paleoclimatology_IceCores/

Riley, Alex. "The Women with a Controversial Plan to Save Corals." *BBC Earth*, 22 March 2016. http://www.bbc.com/earth/story/20160322-the-women-with-a-controversial-plan-to-save-corals

Robertson, Kirsti. "Plastiglomerate." *e-flux Journal* 78 (December 2016). http://www.e-flux.com/journal/78/82878/plastiglomerate/

Rose, Deborah Bird. "In the Shadow of All This Death." In *Animal Death*, edited by Jay Johnson and Fiona Probyn-Rapsey, 1–20. Sydney: Sydney University Press, 2013.

Rose, Deborah Bird. *Wild Dog Dreaming*. Charlottesville and London: University of Virginia Press, 2011.

Rose, Deborah Bird. "Judas Work: Four Modes of Sorrow." *Environmental Philosophy* 5 no.2 (2008): 51–66.

Rosenthal, Michael A. "Miracles, Wonder, and the State in Spinoza's Theological-Political Treatise." In *Cambridge Critical Guide to Spinoza's Theological-Political Treatise*, edited by Yitzhak Y. Melamed and Michael A. Rosenthal, 231–49. Cambridge: Cambridge University Press, 2010.

Rothwell, James. "Melbourne Inundated with Thousands of Love Letters Addressed to the City's Trees." *The Telegraph*, 15 July 2015. https://www.telegraph.co.uk/news/worldnews/australiaandthepacific/australia/11740957/Melbourne-inundated-with-thousands-of-love-letters-addressed-to-the-citys-trees.html

Roy, Eleanor Ainge. "New Zealand River Granted Same Legal Rights as Human Being." *The Guardian*, 16 March 2017. https://www.theguardian.com/world/2017/mar/16/new-zealand-river-granted-same-legal-rights-as-human-being

Royoux, Jean-Christophe, Marina Warner, and Germaine Greer. *Tacita Dean*. Contemporary Artists. London and New York: Phaidon Press Ltd, 2013.

Ruddiman, William. *Earth's Climate: Past and Future*. Third Edition. New York: Macmillan Learning, 2014.

Rudwick, Martin J. S. *Georges Cuvier, Fossil Bones, and Geological Catastrophes: New Translations and Interpretations of the Primary Texts*. Translated from 'Espèces des elephants' [1796]. Chicago and London: University of Chicago Press, 2008.

Said, Edward. *Representations of the Intellectual*. New York: Vintage, 1994.

SBS World News. "Asia Faces Climate Change Disaster: Report." 14 July 2017. https://www.sbs.com.au/news/asia-faces-climate-change-disaster-report

Schuppli, Susan. "Dirty Pictures." In *Living Earth: Field Notes from the Dark Ecology Project 2014–2016*, edited by Mirna Belina, 189–208. Amsterdam: Sonic Acts Press, 2016.

Schwartz, Stuart B. *Sea of Storms: A History of Hurricanes in the Greater Caribbean from Columbus to Katrina*. Princeton and Oxford: Princeton University Press, 2015.

Scranton, Roy. *Learning to Die in the Anthropocene: Reflections on the End of a Civilization*. San Francisco: City Lights Books, 2015.

Scranton, Roy. "Learning How to Die in the Anthropocene," *New York Times*, 10 November 2013. https://opinionator.blogs.nytimes.com/2013/11/10/learning-how-to-die-in-the-anthropocene/

Scripps Institution of Oceanography. "The Keeling Curve." https://scripps.ucsd.edu/programs/keelingcurve/

Searle, Adrian. "Age and Beauty." *Guardian UK*, 20 February 2001. https://www.theguardian.com/arts/critic/feature/0,,728587,00.html

Senior, Olive. "Hurricane Watch." *Kunapipi: Journal of Postcolonial Writing and Culture* 34, no. 2 (2012): 181.

Senior, Olive. *over the roofs of the world*. Toronto: Insomniac Press, 2005.

Senior, Olive. *Encyclopedia of Jamaican Heritage*. St. Andrews: Twin Ginep Publishers, 2003.

Senior, Olive. *Gardening in the Tropics*. Toronto: McClelland and Stewart, 1994.

Senior, Olive. *Talking of Trees*. Kingston: Calabash, 1985.

Sennett, Richard. *The Craftsman*. New Haven: Yale University Press, 2008.

Serres, Michel. "Revisiting the Natural Contract." *CTheory.net 1000 Days of Theory* (2006). https://journals.uvic.ca/index.php/ctheory/article/view/14482/5325

Shelley, Percy Bysshe. *Selected Poetry and Prose: Shelley*. New York: Signet, New American Library, 1966.

Shonogon, Sei. *The Pillow Book*. Translated by Meredith McKinney. London: Penguin, 2006.

Sirocco Kākāpō (@siroccokakapo). "BOOM! Guess who's back..." Facebook, 8 February 2018. https://www.facebook.com/siroccokakapo/

Sloterdijk, Peter. "Atmospheric Politics." In *Making Things Public: atmospheres of democracy*, edited by Bruno Latour and Peter Weibel, 944–951. Karlsruhe and Cambridge, MA: ZKM and The MIT Press, 2005.

Solnit, Rebecca. *A Field Guide to Getting Lost*. London: Penguin, 2006.

Spinoza, Benedict de. *Ethics*. Edited and translated by Edwin Curley. London: Penguin, 1996 (1677).

Spivak, Gayatri Chakravorty. "World Systems and the Creole." *Narrative* 14, no. 6, (January 2006): 102–12.

Spivak, Gayatri Chakravorty. *Death of a Discipline*. Columbia: Columbia University Press, 2005.

Stafford, Barbara Maria. "Revealing Technologies/Magical Domains." In *Devices of Wonder: From the World in a Box to Images on a Screen*, edited by Barbara Maria Stafford and Frances Terpak, 1–19. Los Angeles: Getty Research Institute, 2001.

Steffen, Will, Jacques Grinevald, Paul Crutzen, and John McNeill. "The Anthropocene: conceptual and historical perspectives." *Philosophical Transactions of the Royal Society A*, 369 (2011): 842–867. https://doi.org/10.1098/rsta.2010.0327.

Stengers, Isabelle. "Wondering About Materialism." In *The Speculative Turn: Continental Materialism and Realism*, edited by Levi Bryant, Nick Srnicek, and Graham Harman, 368–80. Melbourne, Australia: re.press, 2011.

Stengers, Isabelle. "Introductory Notes on an Ecology of Practices." *Cultural Studies Review* 11, no. 1 (2005): 183–196.

Stewart, Kathleen. "Atmospheric Attunements." *Environment and Planning D: Society and Space*, 29 (2011): 445–453.

Stewart, Kathleen. *Ordinary Affects*. Durham and London: Duke University Press, 2007.

Steyerl, Hito. "In Free Fall: A Thought Experiment on Vertical Perspective." *e-flux* 24 (April 2011).

Stiegler, Bernard. "Escaping the Anthropocene." In *The Crisis Conundrum: How to Reconcile Economy and Society*, edited by Mauro Magatti, 149–163. Cham: Palgrave Macmillan, 2017.

Stirling, Graham R., and Simon Mattsson. "Intercropping sugarcane with sunflower and mixtures of plant species: effects on the soil biological community." *Proceedings of the Australian Society of Sugar Cane Technologists* 40, (2018): 86–96.

Thomson, Amanda. "Making a Place: Art, Writing, and a More-than-Textual Approach." *The Geographical Review* 103, no. 2 (2013): 244–255.

Thompson, Nato. ed. *Living as Form: Socially Engaged Art from 1991–2011*. New York: Creative Time Books, 2012.

Thompson, Richard C. "Plastics, environment and health." In *Accumulation: The Material Politics of Plastics*, edited by Jennifer Gabrys, Gay Hawkins, and Mike Michael, 150–169. New York: Routledge, 2013.

Tredinnick, Mark. "Days in the Plateau." *Kunapipi: Journal of Postcolonial Writing and Culture* 29, no. 2 (2007): 135–141.

Tsing, Anna, Heather Swanson, Elaine Gan, and Nils Bubandt, eds. *Arts of Living on a Damaged Planet*. Minneapolis: University of Minnesota Press, 2017.

Tsing, Anna Lowenhaupt. *The Mushroom at the End of the World: On the Possibility of Life in Capitalist Ruins*. Princeton and Oxford: Princeton University Press, 2015.

Turner, Victor. *The Forest of Symbols: Aspects of Ndembu Ritual*. Ithaca and London: Cornell University Press, 1967

United Nations, UNESCO. "Botanical Garden (Orto Botanico) Padua" World Heritage List, December 1997. http://whc.unesco.org/en/list/824

Università Degli Studi Di Padova. "Botanical Garden." (2018). http://www.unipd.it/en/university/cultural-heritage-0/botanical-garden

US Department of Energy. "The Manhattan Project: an interactive history." *Office of History and Heritage Resources*, (2013). https://www.osti.gov/opennet/manhattan-project-history/

Van Schaik, Leon. "Spatial Intelligence." In *Kowloon Cultural District: An Investigation into Spatial Capabilities in Hong Kong*, edited by Esther Lorenz and Li Shiqiao, 248–254. Hong Kong: MCCM Creations, 2015.

Wainwright, Alfred. *Pictorial Guides to the Lakeland Fells: Being an Illustrated Account of a Study and Exploration of the Mountains in the English Lake District*. London: Frances Lincoln, 2008.

Waters, Colin N., Jan Zalasiewicz et al. "The Anthropocene is Functionally and Stratigraphically distinct from the Holocene." *Science* 351, no. 6269 (8 January 2016): 1–10. https://doi.org/10.1126/science.aad2622.

Watters, Aliza ed. *Taryn Simon: Paperwork and the Will of Capital*. Ostfildern and New York: Hatje Cantz, Gagosian, 2016.

Wesson, Sue. *Murni Dhungang Jirrar: Living in the Illawarra*. Sydney: Office of Environment and Heritage, 2009. http://www.environment.nsw.gov.au/resources/cultureheritage/illawarraAboriginalResourceUse.pdf

Whiston Spirn, Anne. "Helen and Newton Harrison: The Art of Inquiry, Manifestation, and Enactment." In *The Time of the Force Majeure: After 45 Years Counterforce is on the Horizon*, edited by Harrison Studio. 434–438. Munich: Prestel Verlag, 2016.

Whitehead, Alfred North. *The Concept of Nature*. Cambridge: Cambridge University Press, 1920.

Williams, David R. "Earth Fact Sheet." NASA Space Science Data Coordinated Archive. https://nssdc.gsfc.nasa.gov/planetary/factsheet/earthfact.html

Williams, Kim, Brogan Bunt, and Lucas Ihlein. *Walking Upstream: Waterways of the Illawarra,* exhibition, October 2017–February 2018, Wollongong Art Gallery, Wollongong, New South Wales, Australia.

Williams, Kim, Brogan Bunt, and Lucas Ihlein. *12 Creek* Walks. Wollongong: Leech Press, 2017.

Williams, Kim, Brogan Bunt, and Lucas Ihlein. *Walking Upstream: Waterways of the Illawarra* blog. http://walking-upstream.net/

Williams, Linda. "Affective Poetics and Public Access: The Critical Challenges of Environmental Art." *Australasian Journal of Ecocriticism and Cultural Ecology* 3 (2013-2014): 16–30.

Wilson, Alexander. "Pragmatics of Raw Art." In *Deleuze and the Schizoanalysis of Visual Art*, edited by Ian Buchanan. and Lorna Collins, 57–76. London and New York: Bloomsbury Publishing.

WISE. "Wide Infrared Survey Explorer." Posted 27 July 2011. https://web.archive.org/web/20180501051703/http://www.astro.ucla.edu/~wright/WISE/

Woinarski, John CZ, Andrew A Burbidge, and Peter L Harrison, "Ongoing unraveling of a continental fauna: Decline and extinction of Australian mammals since European settlement." *Proceedings of the National Academy of Sciences of the United States* 112, no. 15 (2015): 4531–4540. https://doi.org/10.1073/pnas.1417301112

Wong, Vanessa. "Amazon Knows Alexa Devices Are Laughing Spontaneously And It's 'Working To Fix It.'" *Buzzfeed*, 8 March 2018. https://web.archive.org/web/20180519060442/https://www.buzzfeed.com/venessawong/amazon-alexa-devices-are-laughing-creepy?utm_term=.ea9jjv3WkW#.rtnmmeKQNQ

Worland, Justin. "More than 700 North American Bee Species Are Headed Toward Extinction," *Time Science*, 2 March 2017. http://time.com/4688417/north-american-bee-population-extinction/

Wright, Judith. *Collected Poems*. Sydney: Angus and Robertson, 1994.

Yeats, W. B. *The Collected Poems of W. B. Yeats: A New Edition*. Edited by Richard J. Finneran. New York: Collier Books, 1989.

Zalasiewicz, Jan, Colin N. Waters, Colin P. Summerhayes, Alexander P. Wolfe, Anthony D. Barnosky, Alejandro Cearreta, Paul Crutzen et al. "The Working Group on the Anthropocene: Summary of evidence and interim recommendations." *Anthropocene* 19 (2017): 55–60. https://doi.org/10.1016/j.ancene.2017.09.001.

Notes on contributors

Susan Ballard is the co-director of the Centre for Critical Creative Practice, University of Wollongong. She writes on contemporary art and media with a particular concern for the diverse ways that artists negotiate the ecological and social transformations of the 21st century.

Louise Boscacci brings art into conversation with the feminist environmental humanities as a practitioner, scholar and lecturer. She is currently a postdoctoral researcher in the Centre for Critical Creative Practice at the University of Wollongong writing about species extinctions and futures in the more-than-human Anthropocene.

David Carlin co-directs RMIT University's non/fictionLab. His literary nonfiction is published widely; he has also written and directed work for theatre, film and radio.

Anne Collett is an Associate Professor in English Literatures at the University of Wollongong. She has published widely on postcolonial poetry and is the past editor of *Kunapipi: Journal of postcolonial writing* (1979-2012).

Eva Hampel focuses on environmental humanities, with extensive work and teaching history in environmental assessment and creative arts. Her PhD investigates art, nature, and liminality.

Lucas Ihlein is an artist and ARC DECRA Research Fellow at the University of Wollongong. His work explores the interactions of socially engaged art, collaboration and environmental projects.

Jo Law is an artist and researcher who investigates the transformative potential of art, science, and technology in response to our changing sociocultural and political environments.

Joshua Lobb teaches creative writing at the University of Wollongong. His stories appear in *Bridport Anthology, Best Australian Stories, Animal Studies,* and *Southerly.* His novel in twelve stories *The Flight of Birds* (2019) is published by Sydney University Press.

Jade Kennedy is a Yuin man from the Illawarra and South Coast of NSW and has been privileged with the intimate knowledges of his people's customs, culture and Country.

Catherine McKinnon is a novelist and playwright and University of Wollongong academic. Her most recent novel, *Storyland* (2017), was published by Harper Collins, and was shortlisted for the Miles Franklin Literary Award in 2018.

Teodor Mitew's research background is in actor network theory, philosophy of technology and Internet studies. His current projects range across the Internet of things, swarm content networks, memetic warfare, object oriented ontology, and smart textiles.

Jo Stirling is a designer and lecturer at the University of Wollongong. Her research and teaching focus on social impact design for environmental benefit.

Kim Williams is an artist and current PhD candidate at the University of Wollongong exploring the interactions of socially engaged art, collaboration and environmental projects.

www.ingramcontent.com/pod-product-compliance
Lightning Source LLC
Chambersburg PA
CBHW031604210526
45464CB00004B/1420